THE
UNEXPLAINED

THE UNEXPLAINED

Edited by

Lorrie Mack, Eric Harwood and Lesley Riley

Acknowledgements

Associated Press, Aerofilms, Aerospace Publishing, Agence France Press, Aldus Archive, D L Anderson/Bellingham Herald, Anglia TV, BBC, Clive Barda, Paul Begg, Bermuda Tourist Board, Birmingham Public Library, Borough of Brighton, B Bourroughs, Bridgeman Art Library, British Aerospace, British Library, British Tourist Authority, Brooke Bond Oxo Ltd, Richard Burgess, John Cain, Cambridge Evening News, Jean-Loup Charmet, Bruce Coleman, Colorific!, Contrad Research Library, W E Cox, Culver Pictures, Daily Telegraph Colour Library, René Dazy, Arnold Desser, Tim Dinsdale, Anne Dooley, Robert Estall, Mary Evans Picture Library, Reay Faiz, Fate Magazine, Joel Finler, M L Finton, Flying Saucer Review, Werner Forman Archive, Fortean Picture Library, Fort Worth Star Telegraph, Foto EFE, Foto Monsted, John Frost Historical Newspaper Service, Roy Fulton, Fred Gettings, Dennis Gifford, Glaister and Rentoul, Colin Godman, T Good, Maurice Grosse, Ground Saucer Watch, Elmer Gruber, Sonia Halliday, Robert Harding and Associates, J Hasted, Herbert, B Heuvelmans, Hans Hinz, Toby Hogarth, Michael Holford, M J Hooks, Stuart Howe, John Hughes, Robert Hunt Library, The Image Bank, Imperial War Museum, Julian Isaacs, Guy Jouhaud, Keystone Press Agency, A G Khan, M W Kingsland, Kobal Collection, Frank Lane, Cyrus Lee, Leicester Mercury, Liverpool Daily Post and Echo, Lisbon Academy of Science, London Express News and Features, Manchete, Mansell Collection, McDonnell Douglas, Meteorological Office/J H Golden, Jeannie Morison, Graham Morris, T Morrison, Musée de l'Homme, National Archives, National Council on Tourism/Lebanon, National Enquirer, National Portrait Gallery, Natural Science Photos, Peter Newark's Western Americana, Newsday, PSI Search, Parabond Productions, Peabody Museum, Photri, Picturepoint, Pix Features, Guy Lyon Playfair, Popperfoto, Press Association, Psychic News, A Puharich, S Puthoff/Stanford Research Institute, Neville Pyne, W C Reeves, Religious News, Rex Features, Roswell Daily Record, Royal Geographical Society, Scala, J Schuessler, Schwortz, Sheffield Newspapers, Ronald Sheridan, B Snellgrove, Sorrat, Spectrum, Sri Sathya Sai Baba Trust, Stadium Publishing Services, Roy Stemman, Sunday Times, Syndication International, Tate Gallery, D C Thomsen, John Topham Library, David Towersey, Transworld Features, Turners Photography, Tyne Tees TV, UPI, Victoria and Albert Museum, Washington Post, Zenka Woodward, World Government of the Age of Enlightenment, John Worsley, Yorkshire Post, ZEFA, Zdener Burian/Artia.

This edition first published exclusively
for Marks and Spencer plc in 1984 by
Orbis Publishing
20–22 Bedfordbury
London WC2

Printed in Italy

Contents

Introduction

The chances that you have had a psychic experience are very high indeed – although you may not have been aware of it at the time. How often, for instance, have you mysteriously lost some ordinary item that you were using, only to find it in another room, some time later, in a perfectly obvious place? Perhaps this is an example of spontaneous teleportation, the ability that material objects occasionally have of flitting from one place to another without, apparently, travelling through 'normal' space.

Almost everyone has had the image of an old friend or relative – someone who hasn't been seen for a long time – spring suddenly to mind, and very soon after received a letter or telephone call from that very person. Here, some kind of extra-sensory perception seems to be at work.

Everyday examples like this give us cause to suspect that there is more to the world we live in than the accepted truths in which conventional science deals. However baffling it may be, thousands of people during the First World War had visions of young men – soldiers or sailors, sons or brothers – within minutes of their death in combat. Something undoubtedly odd *is* lurking beneath the forbidding waters of Loch Ness. Fish *do* fall in shoals from empty skies. People *are* cured of their afflictions without the aid of medicine. Weird lights in the sky *do* stop cars dead in their tracks. The very oddity of these events makes them worth our attention, even though we may never be able to explain them. It certainly is not logical to say that because we can't explain them, they can't happen, or that the hundreds of people who report them must all be cranks.

One of the reasons why we can't explain such things, and also why many people find them difficult to take seriously, is simply that they happen so infrequently. Science has great difficulty investigating an event as utterly bizarre as a living human being bursting into flames for no apparent reason, because it doesn't happen that often – and by the time a scientist arrives on the scene there is little left but the ashes. Occurrences like this, or like the sighting of a flying saucer (never mind meeting with an alien) cannot be taken into the laboratory. Conventional science feels very uncomfortable when it can't reduce 'reality' to a set of numbers or an object that can be seen, felt and manipulated.

The learned doctors who were invited by Anton Mesmer, the father of modern hypnotism, to watch an amputation performed under hypnosis are a fine example of this. 'Ah,' they declare, 'the patient has simply *pretended* not to feel pain.' And that attitude still exists. A group of astronomers at a recent scientific congress were told that what appeared to be a UFO was at that moment in sight outside. Not a soul stirred himself to look.

Those with slightly less blinkered vision, however, can find plenty of hints and clues in their daily lives to indicate that an immaterial reality is at work. Coincidences, for example, are frequently so extraordinary as to seem more than mere accidents. They can also suggest that our universe has a sense of humour: why else should a truck laden with carrots collide with one full of olive oil except to make a huge carrot salad on the highway? Isn't it very odd that the letters of the Latin name (*Nessiteras rhombopteryx*) bestowed in all seriousness on the Loch Ness monster by Sir Peter Scott can be re-arranged to read 'Monster hoax by Sir Peter S'? What makes a man called Phang become a dentist? It is unlikely that we shall ever find the answers to such questions, but part of the fascination of unexplained phenomena is undoubtedly the tantalising nature of their inexplicability.

Nevertheless, even the academic world is at last preparing to take such things seriously. A Chair of Parapsychology has been founded at Edinburgh University, the result of a bequest made by the late Arthur Koestler – who among his many other writings produced a brilliant analysis of coincidences. Koestler cared deeply that the areas of our greatest ignorance should be explored, not cast aside out of laziness or prejudice. If, as a society, we can accomplish this, the benefits we shall reap will be immeasurable.

CHAPTER ONE

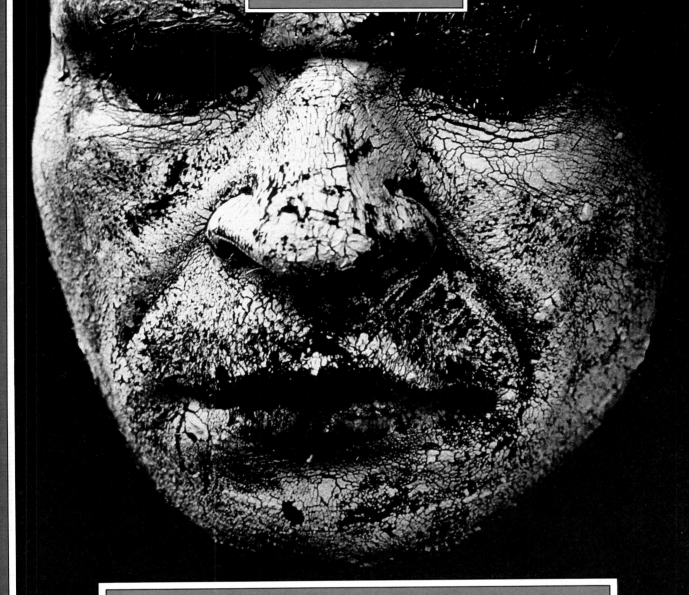

The Human Enigma

Spontaneous human combustion, Electric people,
Chinese puzzles, The file on twins, Connection
and coincidence

Right: the remains of Dr J. Irving Bentley, a retired physician of Coudersport, Pennsylvania. He was found on 5 December 1966 by gas-meter reader Don Gosnell who had noticed a 'light-blue smoke of unusual odor' in the air. There was more strange smoke in the bedroom, but no sign of Bentley. Gosnell peered into the bathroom and was faced with this sight. A large hole had burned through the floor, on the edge of which he saw 'a brown leg from the knee down, like that of a mannequin'

Spontaneous human combustion

People have long believed that in certain circumstances the human body can burst into flames of its own accord. Flames, furthermore, of such ferocity that within minutes the victim is reduced to a heap of carbonised ashes. This idea – some call it a superstition – has been around for centuries, smouldering in the belief in divine retribution. 'By the blast of God they perish,' says the book of Job, 'and by the breath of his nostrils are they consumed.'

There is an extensive history documenting the nature of spontaneous human combustion (SHC). But it is a history of scientific refusal to face up to this bizarre phenomenon. Why has it bemused scientists for so long and how does it wreak such terrifying destruction?

Perhaps SHC's most common characteristic is the sheer speed with which it strikes. Many victims were seen alive only a few moments before the fire struck from nowhere. An Italian surgeon called Battaglio reported the death of a priest, named Bertholi, in the town of Filetto, in 1789. Lodging with his brother-in-law, he had been left alone in his room reading a prayerbook. A few minutes later he screamed. People came running to find him on the floor surrounded by a pale flame, which receded as they approached.

Bertholi wore a sackcloth under his clothes, next to his skin, and it was immediately apparent that the outer clothes had burned away leaving the sackcloth intact. Under the sackcloth the skin on the man's trunk was in shreds.

Some investigators deduce that the fire develops very quickly because the victims are often discovered still sitting calmly, as though nothing had happened.

In one dramatic example in 1960 five charred bodies were found in a burned-out car near Pikeville, Kentucky. The coroner commented: 'They were sitting there as though they'd just gotten into the car. With all that heat it seems there'd be some sort of struggle to escape. But there hadn't been.'

The baffling aspect of SHC is the extreme intensity of heat involved. In normal circumstances the human body is very hard to set alight, especially if still alive, and people who die in fires usually sustain only partial or superficial damage to the body. Reduction to a pile of calcined ashes, experts agree, demands a fierce heat which needs to be externally fuelled and maintained for hours, and even so crematoria still have to grind up the bones that remain afterwards.

The disturbing circumstances surrounding the death of Mrs Mary Reeser in Florida on 1 July 1951 were investigated by Dr Wilton M. Krogman, a renowned forensic anthropologist from the University of Pennsylvania School of Medicine, who has researched into deaths caused by fire.

The ashes of the 67-year-old widow were mixed with the remains of the chair she had been sitting in at the time of her death. Damage to the surroundings was minimal. The overstuffed chair was burned down to its springs, there was a patch of soot on the ceiling above and a small circle of carpet was charred around the chair, but a pile of papers nearby was unscorched. Dr Wilton Krogman said he had watched bodies in a crematorium burn for over eight hours at 2000°F (1110°C) without any sign of the bones becoming ashes or powder; and that it takes a heat of about 3000°F (1650°C) to make bone melt. He said:

'I cannot conceive of such complete cremation without more burning of the apartment itself. In fact the apartment and everything in it should have been

consumed. Never have I seen a human skull shrunk by intense heat. The opposite has always been true; the skulls have been either abnormally swollen or have virtually exploded into hundreds of pieces . . . I regard it as the most amazing thing I have ever seen. As I review it, the short hairs on my neck bristle with vague fear. Were I living in the Middle Ages, I'd mutter something about black magic.'

Police considered every likely theory: suicide by petrol, ignition of methane gas in her body, murder by flame-thrower, magnesium, phosphorus and napalm substances . . . and even a 'ball of fire' which one anonymous letter-writer claimed to see. In the end the coroner accepted the theory that she had fallen asleep while smoking and set her clothes alight, although the case remains open.

But if the baffled Dr Krogman exemplifies the confusion of modern investigators, his reference to the Middle Ages is a reminder that human combustion has also bewildered our less scientific ancestors.

The phenomenon had, by the 18th and 19th

Above: workmen clear away the remains of the chair in which Mrs Mary Reeser was sitting when she suddenly combusted on 1 July 1951

Below: the Reverend Mr Adams who, while away from his parish in Stockcross, Newbury, England, spontaneously combusted in a hotel room in New York in 1876

Above: in chapter 32 of Bleak House, *Charles Dickens' characters William Guppy and Tony Weavle, discover that the evil Krook has been mysteriously burned to a few charred lumps and ashes – they conclude that it was a case of SHC*

Below: Charles Fort, who spent a lifetime collecting reports of SHC and other paranormal events. He thought SHC might be linked with demonology

centuries, become a widely known and often feared horror. Charles Dickens was one of many intelligent enquirers fascinated by the nightmare details and case histories of SHC. In fact, he probably based his description of Krook's death in his novel *Bleak House* (1852–3) upon the case of one Countess Baudi.

The death of the 62-year-old Countess Cornelia Baudi, near Verona, is perhaps one of the first reliable reports of SHC. According to a statement by a clergyman of Verona, dated 4 April 1731, the Countess had been put to bed after supper, and fell asleep after several hours' conversation with her maid. In the morning the maid returned to wake her and found a grisly scene. As the *Gentlemen's Magazine* reported: 'The floor of the chamber was thick-smear'd with a gluish moisture, not easily got off . . . and from the lower part of the window trickl'd down a greasy, loathsome, yellowish liquor with an unusual stink.'

Specks of soot hung in the air and covered all the surfaces in the room, and the smell had penetrated adjoining rooms. The bed was un-damaged, the sheets turned back, indicating the Countess had got out of bed.

Four feet [1.3 metres] from the bed was a heap of ashes, two legs untouch'd, stockings on, between which lay the head, the brains, half of the back-part of the skull and the whole chin burn'd to ashes, among which were found three fingers blacken'd. All the rest was ashes which

had this quality, that they left in the hand a greasy and stinking moisture.

Spontaneous human combustion received its severest criticism from the great pioneer chemist, Baron Justus von Liebig (1803–1873), who complained that no expert witnesses had seen it happen. As a scientist he saw the historical evidence as an unsupported record of the *belief* in SHC, rather than actual proof of spontaneous burning deaths.

Despite Liebig's assertion, however, there is plenty of evidence from both medical and police sources. Many of these bear witness to the ferocity of the phenomenon, as in the case investigated by Merille, a surgeon in Caen, recorded in Trotter's *Essay on drunkenness* (1804). On 3 June 1782, Merille was asked by 'the king's officers' in the city to report on the death of Mademoiselle Thaurs, a lady of over 60 who had been observed, that day, to have drunk three bottles of wine and one of brandy. Merille wrote:

The body lay with the crown of the head resting against one of the hand-irons . . . 18 inches [45 centimetres] from the fire, the remainder of the body was placed obliquely before the chimney, the whole being nothing but a mass of ashes. Even the most solid bones had lost their form and consistence. The right foot was found entire and scorched at its upper junction; the left was more burnt. The day was cold but there was nothing in the grate except two or three bits of wood about an inch in diameter, burnt in the middle. None of the furniture in the apartment was damaged. The chair on which she was sitting was found at the distance of a foot [30 centimetres] from her, and absolutely untouched.

Our documented knowledge of spontaneous human combustion is primarily due to the pioneering efforts of Charles Fort. In the first half of this century, Fort devoted his life to collecting accounts, newspaper reports and extracts from medical journals relating to strange phenomena, including SHC. However, frustratingly, few accounts mention SHC, because officially there is no such phenomenon, and coroners and their advisers have the un-enviable task of dealing with evidence that seems to contradict accepted physical laws and medical opinion. Inevitably, suppositions are made about knocked over heaters, flying sparks, careless smoking, and in the case of child victims, playing with matches. Faced with the alternative, SHC – a nightmare out of the Dark Ages – it is not surprising that they are accepted.

There are occasional exceptions, like the report in *Lloyds Weekly News* of 5 February 1905. A woman asleep by a fireplace woke to find herself in flames and later died. The honest coroner said he could not understand: the woman had gone to sleep facing the fire, so

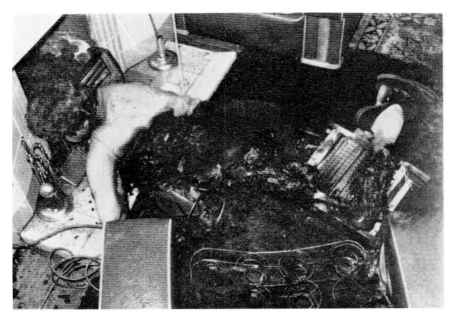

Above: an anonymous victim of SHC lies with her apparently unburnt head resting in a grate. An electric fire is also visible – but how did the body burn so thoroughly without setting fire to the rest of the room?

Right: the great chemist Baron Justus von Liebig. He rejected tales of SHC because of the lack of expert witnesses – and because his attempts to make flesh burn with the same intensity as SHC were, without exception, a dismal failure

any cinder that shot out from the grate would ignite the front of her clothes. Yet it was her back that bore the severe burns.

At worst, a story may be rejected out of fear or disbelief, as in the case of the elderly spinster, Wilhelmina Dewar, who combusted near midnight on 22 March 1908, in the Northumberland town of Whitley Bay.

Wilhelmina was found by her sister Margaret who, in a shocked state, managed to summon her neighbours. In the house they found the severely charred body of Wilhelmina in an upstairs bed. The bedclothes were unscorched and there was no sign of fire anywhere else in the house.

When Margaret told this story at the inquest, the coroner thought it preposterous and asked her to think again. Repeatedly she said she was telling the truth and could not change her story

– even after a policeman testified that Margaret was so drunk she couldn't have known what she was saying. As Fort points out, the policeman 'was not called upon to state how he distinguished between signs of excitement and terror and intoxication.' The coroner adjourned the inquest to give her more time to think. When it was reconvened a few days later it was obvious that a great deal of pressure had been placed upon poor Margaret.

Eventually she changed her story, saying she had found her sister burned, but alive, in another part of the house and had then carried her up to bed. The court accepted this unlikely scenario despite the lack of fire damage anywhere in the house.

But perhaps the mystery of human combustion has been sustained by the absence of witnesses to these terrifying events. Some SHC chroniclers have drawn attention to the lack of struggle or outcry by victims. 'In their grim submission,' Charles Fort wrote, 'it is almost as if they had been lulled by the wings of a vampire.' This lethargy cannot be due solely to drink and fumes. Combustion appears to be preceded by psychological inertia, which renders victims helpless and leaves survivors unable to explain what happened to them.

For example, the *Hull Daily Mail* of 6 January 1905 describes how an elderly woman, Elizabeth Clark, was found in the morning with fatal burns, while her bed, in the Trinity Almshouse, Hull, was unmarked by fire. There had been no outcry or sounds of struggle through the thin partitions. She was 'unable to give an articulate account' of her accident, and later died. Of course that could mean that the authorities – not for the first time – simply didn't believe her account.

In another bizarre case in 1885, a husband suffocated from the smoke of his wife's combusting body. Her ashes lay in a charred hole beside his unburnt corpse.

Fear of the truth

The weight of accumulated case histories is a reminder that spontaneous combustion cannot continue to be brushed aside by coroners, or simply disregarded by medical experts as a phenomenon too rare to warrant investigation. In fact, modern researchers reject the idea that SHC is as rare as some suggest.

There is a growing number of cases testified to by doctors and pathologists, and this number would probably increase if the fear of ridicule could be completely removed. Maxwell Cade and Delphine Davis, authors of the imaginative study of ball lightning *Taming of the thunderbolts* (1969), confessed they themselves would not have put much faith in the existence of SHC, 'if a doctor friend had not told us of a lecture which he attended at the Massachusetts Medico-Legal Society, where

Above: only the legs remain of Mrs E.M., a widow who died on 29 January 1958. Was she burnt by the fire in the grate, or did she combust of her own accord? The same question remains unanswered in the case of the anonymous victim pictured below right

several such cases were discussed. When we expressed cautious doubts, the doctor assured us that he had been called to a similar case himself as recently as the autumn of 1959.'

When Dr D. J. Gee, a lecturer in forensic medicine at Leeds University, delivered his well-known paper on 'A case of spontaneous combustion' he was surprised by the candid discussion that followed. He said of it:

Dr George Manning described his experience of several similar cases, and indicated that the phenomenon was certainly not as rare as might be supposed from the literature. This view was supported by Dr David Price, who said that he met with this phenomenon approximately once in every four years.

The medical profession has always been embarrassed by deaths that appear to have been caused by SHC. The refusal to believe in the phenomenon is not the result of a deliberate conspiracy to suppress the evidence, however. Rather there has been a turning away, a wish not to think about such an outrage of accepted medical and scientific knowledge.

If SHC is mentioned at all, it is only to be dismissed as a belief mistakenly held by the uninformed, or as a superstition lingering from less enlightened times. J. L. Casper, for example, in his *Handbook of the practice of forensic medicine*, complained: 'It is sad to think that in an earnest scientific work, in this year of grace 1861, we must still treat of the fable of "spontaneous combustion".' And opinion today is hardly less compromising. Dr Gavin Thurston, the coroner for Inner West London, has said that 'no such phenomenon as spontaneous combustion exists, or has ever occurred'.

At the same time, those scientists and doctors who have examined the effects closely, acknowledge that there have been cases of

Above: bodies that are cremated – like the one on this far Eastern funeral pyre – are never burnt to the same degree as victims of SHC. It takes very high temperatures sustained over long periods of time to reduce a body to boneless ashes

Below: London coroner Dr Gavin Thurston, who despite extensive evidence, has firmly stated that SHC does not exist and has never occurred

death by burning that are genuinely inexplicable.

More recently, coroners have tended to adopt the suggestions of Dr Gee as set forth in his 1965 article in *Medicine, science and the law*. He found that small quantities of body fat could be set alight, but that the burning could be sustained only by placing the sample in a draught. Despite the fact that this resulted in slow smouldering rather than the spectacular blaze of SHC, coroners have favoured Dr Gee's rational explanation rather than accept the unexplained human combustion alternative.

The search for a solution for SHC began almost two centuries ago. The 19th-century investigators evolved a partly religious, partly medical explanation for the phenomenon. A typical combustion victim was thought to be a drinker and smoker, most likely an elderly, solitary, bulky woman of sedentary habits. A drink-sodden body was thought to be highly inflammable and the sudden ignition was considered divinely inspired as a punishment for drunkenness.

However, Baron Justus von Liebig, sceptical of SHC though he was, utterly discredited the notion that there was any connection between the phenomenon and drinking. Liebig showed conclusively that alcohol-saturated flesh will burn only until the alcohol is used up; and fatty tissue behaves in the same way – when it can be set alight.

But can we, in the 20th century, offer any real explanations for SHC? Enquirers of the 19th century can be forgiven for thinking only in terms of conventional fire. But since the admirable Liebig's day the physical and medical sciences have made enormous progress. Today we know of many forms of death that can penetrate a man's body silently and invisibly. Military research into 'radiation weapons' has supplemented nuclear radiation with beamed ultrasound, x-ray lasers, microwave projectors and other horrors, all of which can cook a man inside his clothes.

A strange unnatural fire

Today there are several theories that might account for spontaneous human combustion; while none is conclusive, some do appear more credible than others.

One of the least likely is the 'psychic suicide' theory, which suggests that SHC might be self-induced by depressed or resentful people. Their reserves of physical and psychical energy may suddenly be released in a fatal, destructive, explosion.

This explanation, however, offers no proof and would account for only some SHC cases, as would the hypothesis that postulates organic or mechanical malfunctions of normal bodily processes, which may lead to accumulations of explosive compounds within the body. More speculation has concerned the build-up of

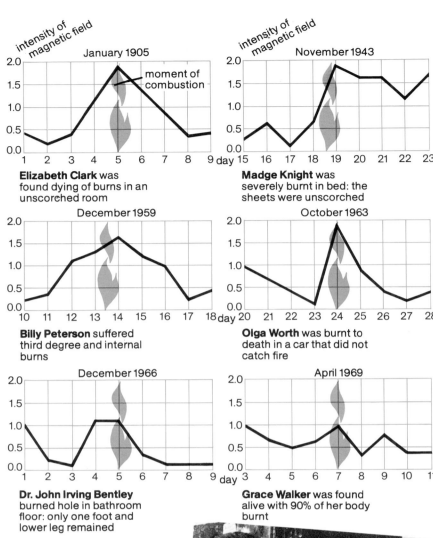

January 1905

moment of combustion

Elizabeth Clark was found dying of burns in an unscorched room

December 1959

Billy Peterson suffered third degree and internal burns

December 1966

Dr. John Irving Bentley burned hole in bathroom floor: only one foot and lower leg remained

November 1943

Madge Knight was severely burnt in bed: the sheets were unscorched

October 1963

Olga Worth was burnt to death in a car that did not catch fire

April 1969

Grace Walker was found alive with 90% of her body burnt

Above: the force of the Earth's magnetism is surprisingly uneven. It is unequally distributed around the globe and fluctuates in intensity (measured in gausses). These six charts show the curious relationship between a high reading on the geomagnetic scale and the incidence of SHC

Right: the charred remains of a slim lady, aged 85, who was in good health when she was consumed by flames in November 1963. Photographic evidence of SHC incidents are very rare

phosphagens in muscle tissue, particularly the vitamin B10, vital to normal energy supplies. A technical paper in *Applied Trophology* (December 1957) included this relevant paragraph:

> Phosphagen is a compound like nitro-glycerine, of endothermic formation [that is, absorbs heat]. It is no doubt so highly

developed in certain sedentary persons as to make their bodies actually combustible, subject to ignition, burning like wet gun-powder under some circumstances.

This may explain the readiness of some bodies to blaze, but we still have no clues as to how they are ignited.

Equally unlikely is the proposition that SHC is the result of people who have caught fire themselves after their clothes have been set alight. This is disproved by numerous cases in which only the flesh of victims was burned while their clothes remained unscorched.

Another somewhat unsatisfactory thesis is the 'corrosive liquid' theory, and it likewise attempts to explain *away* certain cases of death by fire. Nevertheless this was the reason suggested for the death of Madge Knight. At about 3.30 a.m. on 19 November 1943 she was asleep alone in the spare room of her house in Aldingbourne, Sussex. She awoke feeling as if she were on fire. Her screams brought her husband and others sharing the house.

Madge was naked under the bedclothes, but she was in agony because extensive burning had removed most of the skin from her back. A doctor administered morphine, and, be-mused, called in a Harley Street specialist. The specialist later told the coroner that he thought the burns must have been caused by a corrosive liquid because there was no sign of fire on the sheets or anywhere else in the room, and no smell of burning. Madge was re-peatedly questioned but could not, or would not, say what had happened before she died in hospital in Chichester, on 6 December.

The lack of any sign of fire in many cases has led some researchers to theorise about substances that can burn without flame. In Madge Knight's case, no trace of any corrosive chemical could be found, nor any possible container for it. The notion that Madge hid the evidence before crawling into bed is absurd.

Perhaps the most fruitful clue to the nature of the phenomenon came in 1975, with Livingston Gearhart's article in the Fortean journal *Pursuit*. He had discovered that a significant number of SHC cases took place on or near a peak in the geomagnetic flux. The strength of the Earth's magnetic field rises and falls quite dramatically in relation to solar activity. Global averages of the daily figures are gathered for astronomers and geophysicists, and these show a distinct correlation between the incidence of SHC and high geomagnetic readings. This seems to indicate that SHC may be the result of a very complex chain of events, in which there is an interaction between certain astronomical conditions and the state of an individual's body. These in turn form the preconditions for the 'ball lightning' theory.

Ball lightning has been offered as one possible culprit for Mrs Reeser's demise. And hers is not the only case. According to an article in *Fate* (April 1961) by the Reverend

Winogene Savage, a friend's brother awoke one morning to his wife's screams. Rushing to their living room he found her on the floor, ablaze, with a strange fireball hovering over her blackened form. With the help of neighbours and several buckets of water the flames were put out; but the lady later died. Witnesses noted that although the wife's clothes had been burnt off, there was no scorching on the rug where she had collapsed, and no other sign of fire damage in the room.

Maxwell Cade and Delphine Davis include this account in *Taming of the thunderbolts*, and note its similarity to the records of spontaneous human combustion. They review the theories of several physicists who suggest that the huge energies of ball lightning could, in certain circumstances, manifest short radio waves of the kind used in microwave ovens. And they speculate:

> If this theory is correct . . . it is possible for victims to be burned to death, not merely within their clothes, but even within their skin, either by the proximity of a lightning ball or by having a ball form within their body, or just by the action of the intense radio-frequency field which, in the absence of their body, would have formed a lightning ball at that place.

As it is a natural phenomenon, and because ball lightning is notoriously capricious, it is the best candidate so far for the cause of SHC cases, whether ancient or modern. It would also account for the victims being fried from the inside out. Micro-wave diathermy can heat different materials at different rates, and this may explain the curious phenomenon of selective burning that is associated with SHC.

Not one of these theories can, by itself, account for the bizarre varieties of human combustion on record. It is conceivable that we have almost all the pieces of the SHC puzzle, but that medical science has yet to fit them together. Perhaps science fails because the mystery of what makes human bonfires is a mixture of physical and earthly forces combined with human psychological phenomena. We await a science that can analyse and interpret both together.

Below: could SHC be caused by ball lightning like this photographed in Castleford, Yorkshire, at 2 a.m. in August 1961? The woman who owned the house pictured remembers hearing a loud explosion at the time

Left: ball lightning was seen near St Petersburg, Russia, on 30 July 1888. If such an intensely hot ball of fire came into contact with a person could it cause the damage associated with SHC?

Electric people

Spontaneous human combustion may be the most destructive unexplained phenomenon, but there are other manifestations that, although somewhat less deadly, are nonetheless bizarre, such as people whose bodies glow or who can retain massive amounts of electricity.

In one case a blue glow emanated from the breasts of an ill woman as she lay asleep. It happened regularly for several weeks, and each time the luminescence lasted for several seconds. No one could explain it.

The woman was Anna Monaro, an asthma sufferer who lived in Italy. When she started to glow during an attack in 1934, she became a news sensation for a time as the 'luminous woman of Pirano'. The blue light was recorded on film and was also witnessed by many doctors. One psychiatrist said that it was caused by 'electrical and magnetic organisms in the woman's body developed in eminent degree', which did little to clarify the matter. Another doctor speculated that she had an abnormally high level of sulphides in her blood because of her weak condition and also her fasting, inspired by religious zeal. These sulphides, he said, were stimulated into luminescence by a natural process of ultra-violet radiation. Even if this were true, it did not explain why the glow came only from the breasts and only while the woman slept.

Data on glowing humans is found in medical literature, religious writings and folklore. Many toxicology textbooks discuss 'luminous wounds', and in their encyclopedic collection of *Anomalies and curiosities of medicine* (1897), Dr George Gould and Dr Walter Pyle described a case of breast cancer that produced a light from the sore strong enough to illuminate the hands of a watch several feet away.

But the only case of a glowing human who was otherwise healthy comes from a letter to the *English Mechanic* of 24 September 1869:

An American lady, on going to bed, found that a light was issuing from the upper side of the fourth toe on her right foot. Rubbing increased the phosphorescent glow and it spread up her foot. Fumes were also given off, making the room disagreeable; and both light and fumes continued when the foot was held in a basin of water. Even washing with soap could not dim the toe. It lasted for three quarters of an hour before fading away, and was witnessed by her husband.

When it comes to luminescent animals, such as the glow worm and firefly, the scientific explanation is that they light up as the result of chemical reactions within the body involving oxygen, luciferase, luciferin and adenosine triphosphate (ATP). But this kind of chemical reaction would not explain why humans glow, and the mystery remains.

There is similar puzzlement about people with unusual electric or magnetic abilities. Such people can become like 'human spark plugs' or magnets, disturbing electrical machines, shocking others with their touch, or attracting objects to their bodies. 'Electric people' – perhaps inevitably – also attract publicity.

For example, the *Daily Mirror* of 23 March 1967 told the story of Brian Clements, known to his friends as 'Flash Gordon'. Clements was so highly charged that he had to discharge his voltage into metal furniture before he touched anyone. The previous week the *Sunday Express* of 19 March 1967 reported the miserable life of Mrs Grace Charlesworth, who had been tormented by electric shocks in her house for two years after having lived there uneventfully for 40 years.

She said: 'Sometimes they have swung me round bodily and in the night my head has started to shake as though I was using a pneumatic drill. One day sparks ran up the walls.'

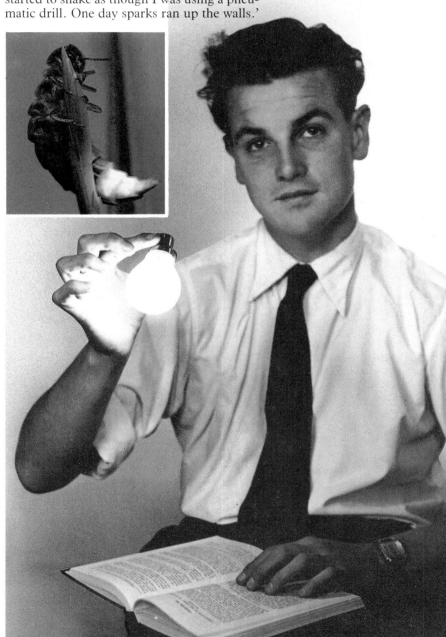

Below: Brian Williams of Cardiff made the news in 1952 as a human so full of electricity that he could light a lamp simply by rubbing it with his hand

Inset: the common European glow worm has a relatively bright light in its tail. Scientists know how the glow worm lights up – it is as a result of a chemical reaction – but they do not know why

Above: the electric eel – really a fish – can readily store and use electricity. It is capable of delivering a shock of up to 500 volts

Below: her hair standing on end, a science teacher demonstrates the phenomenon of static electricity to her students. The Van der Graaf generator she touches is producing 500,000 volts; but she is standing on a deep pad of insulation, which cuts the current so drastically that no damage is done

Curiously, it was only Mrs Charlesworth who was affected; her husband was aware only of an occasional humming noise.

Not surprisingly, many instances of 'electric people' have been noticed or recorded by doctors. In January 1869, the doctor who delivered a baby in St Urbain, France, said the infant shocked all who touched him, and luminous rays emanated from his fingers.

Other 19th-century cases are even more spectacular. Vincent Gaddis mentions three in his book *Mysterious fires and lights* (1967). One occurred in 1889 and concerned Frank McKinstry, of Joplin, Missouri, USA. He was plagued in a peculiar way: his charge was so strong in the early morning that he had to keep moving. If he stopped even for a second, he became fixed to the ground and had to wait until a helpful passer-by would pull one of his legs free. There would be a small faint flash and the grip would be broken – until the next time he stood still.

Both humans and animals have nervous systems that generate electricity – electric eels can, in fact, discharge 500 volts through their tails – but the peculiarity of 'electric people' is that they seem able to store and discharge powerful electric currents. Often, this ability appears dependent on their state of health.

Disease may play a part – not in itself, but in its alterations of the metabolism and other physiological functions. An astonishing report was made in 1920 by Dr Julius Ransom, chief physician at a state prison in New York, after 34 inmates developed botulinus poisoning. During convalesence, one of them screwed up a piece of paper and tried to throw it away, but the paper stuck fast to his hand. Investigation showed that the man was carrying a high static charge, and so were all of his fellow sufferers. They could deflect compass needles and make a suspended steel tape sway by moving their hands towards and away from it. The phenomena ceased when the men recovered.

There is also evidence that atmospheric and geomagnetic conditions may play a part in the strange phenomenon of 'electric people'. Consider the case of 'a lady of great respectability', reported in the *American Journal of Science* (1838) by her physician Dr Willard Hosford. She was aged 30, of a nervous temperament and sedentary habits, and the wife of a prominent man in Orford, New Hampshire. For two years she had suffered from acute rheumatism and an unknown ailment called 'unseated neuralgia'.

The electrical phenomena began on the evening of 25 January 1837 when she was feeling strange. She happened to pass her hand over her brother's face and, as she did so, vivid sparks shot from her fingers, to the astonishment of both. When she stood on a thick carpet, the sparks could be seen and heard discharging into objects near her hands – they were brilliant and shocking, felt by the woman and anyone she touched. The conditions favourable to bringing on the phenomena included hot weather with temperatures of about 80°F (20°C). Then the sparks would be about 1½ inches (4 centimetres) long, coming at the rate of four a minute. After six weeks the electric charges ceased, as did all her infirmities.

The atmospheric aspect was raised by Dr Hosford when he observed that 'a crimson aurora of uncommon splendour' was lighting the heavens and exciting scientific interest at the time of the Orford woman's strange attack. Her charges began on the same evening as this heavenly display of electricity, and Dr Hosford felt it was no mere coincidence. One is strongly reminded of the theory, put forward by Livingston Gearhart, that relates instances of spontaneous human combustion to moments of change in the intensity of the Earth's magnetic field.

Between 1979 and 1981, a spate of newspaper stories publicised the strange telepathic and paranormal abilities of many Chinese children. Some of the most convincing youngsters were then trained by *ch'i* masters. The newspapers told of children who were supposed to be able to 'read' not only with their ears but with the tops of their heads, their armpits, pigtails, buttocks, feet and so on. Many of the children were said to have more than one such paranormal faculty. A 25-year-old woman was found who, it was claimed, could read simultaneously and without confusion with five parts of her body, and a particularly outstanding young girl of nine was said to be able to read perfectly efficiently with 10 parts of her body.

Chinese historians found similar reports in classic works written over 2000 years ago. The

Above: the cover of the Chinese journal Nature *of April 1980 showing some of the children said to be able to 'see' with their ears, fingers and even armpits. This trend in psychic abilities began in 1979, when 12-year-old Tang Yu (bottom right) stumbled against a bystander and found he could read the name on a cigarette packet in the man's jacket pocket with his ear. Chinese scientists are treating such claims very seriously*

Above right: Zhen Xiao-hui and her mother at their Canton home. This little girl has shown remarkable powers, especially reading with her fingertips

Chinese puzzles

The powerful forces found within 'electric people' have been harnessed for centuries in the ancient civilisation of China. In fact, China has a collection of weird and wonderful people who exhibit paranormal phenomena, and rare details about them were released in a three-year period of liberal government that ended in 1981.

For instance, Chinese *ch'i* masters (*ch'i* meaning, literally, 'breath', 'inner power', or non-muscular energy) are said to have extraordinary powers because of their ability to control the energy that flows along the acupuncture lines in the body – a force that is developed by the practitioners of the 'internal school' of martial arts. They can root themselves to the ground and resist all efforts to push them over, repulsing attacks by means of an invisible force, transmitting a surge of energy resembling electricity or magnetism.

Shanghai scientific journal *Nature* argued the validity of such phenomena in a series of 10 articles in 1979. For the rest of that year ESP became a major topic of conversation, not only in tea house gossip but also within the country's leading scientific research establishments.

In an effort to determine the validity of these claims, scientists and doctors performed hundreds of tests on these gifted children. The most elaborate were organised in Shanghai by *Nature* from 4 to 10 February 1980. There were 14 subjects, aged between 9 and 25. They were tested before 10 audiences, totalling more than 2000 scientists, doctors, teachers and journalists.

The test subjects were seated in the centre of the hall. Behind each of them stood a monitor to minimise the possibility of trickery. Members of the audience left the hall, wrote words or pictures on sheets of paper, folded the papers, placed them in heavy paper bags or plastic boxes and then returned to the hall where they presented them to the children, who examined them using their own particular

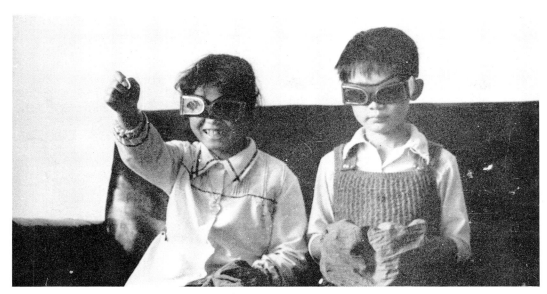

Left: Tu Ping and Tu An, a young sister and brother, taking part in an eyeless sight experiment. Here Tu Ping gleefully describes the target object – five seconds after the experiment began

Below: Lai Shi-Lung, a Chinese professor engaged in research into extraordinary human body functions, and Cyrus Lee (right), a Chinese-American psychologist who has helped to make such research known in the West

Bottom: a group of psychic children who demonstrated their bizarre talents to American parapsychologist Dr H. E. Puthoff. He reported this experience to an SPR conference in 1982

methods. The expressions of the children differed widely: some closed their eyes, some bowed their heads, others smiled or looked shy.

Little Jiang Yan was the star of the test on 6 February. Her performance almost brought the house down, according to the report in the Hong Kong newspaper *Ta Kung Pao* (31 July 1980). Her clear Peking accent rang from the loudspeakers: 'Mine is a cluster of yellow bananas painted on a green background!' She had 'read' this picture with the tip of her finger, with which she was allowed to feel about in a cloth sleeve. The six children tested on that day were given three papers each to 'read'; the results were 17 correct out of 18.

Much attention was focused on two young Peking sisters, Wang Qiang and Wang Bin. Not only could they read with their ears and armpits, but if one sister placed a message under her armpit, the other could read it telepathically.

In addition to being tested before large audiences, the 14 youngsters were also examined by a team of 30 experts and scholars in various fields. Some had been sceptics before the tests, but changed their minds afterwards. Among the converted was Wu Xueyu, director of the eye, ear, nose and throat hospital of the Shanghai No 1 Medical College. 'I surrender,' said the 70-year-old doctor. 'There is no arguing with facts.'

The Chinese-American physicist Dr Chih Kung Jen was among a team of specialists who conducted tests on 12 psychic children in the autumn of 1980. The children achieved a 98 per cent accuracy in 'reading' concealed messages with parts of their bodies. When holding the wrapped paper, he said, 'the children told us they experienced both a warmth and a tingling sensation in their hands – like pinpricks – and that the sensation travelled along the nerve lines of their bodies to their heads.'

Professor Wang Chu, deputy director of the department of radio engineering at Peking University, reported on the descriptions given by 40 children he had studied. At first, the children say, the image appears in their minds as a disordered jumble of dots and lines, which gradually rearrange themselves until the picture becomes clear. According to Wang's study, the faster this process takes place the more likely the child is to get the correct answer. The process speeds up as the child becomes more experienced in the use of the special sense, and is also influenced by the state of the child's health.

When the sisters Wang Qiang and Wang Bin returned to Peking after the Shanghai tests, the Traditional Chinese Medicine Institute arranged for them to be trained by *ch'i* masters. As a result of their *ch'i* training, the armpit-reading sisters increased their already remarkable powers. During tests they were able to indicate the location of scars on the body of a fully clothed person and successfully describe the shape of a pendant hidden under the clothing of another.

The file on twins

Of the hundred million or so twins in the world, about a third are *monozygotic*. This means that the babies have come from a single fertilised egg, which then divides into two in the womb. Such twins have identical sets of genes and are alike in every physical detail. Yet there are also many strange psychological bonds between twins, which puzzle scientific investigators.

Since 1953, Professor Luigi Gedda of the Gregor Mendel Institute in Rome has studied more than 15,000 pairs of twins, and has elaborated a 'clock of life' hypothesis to account for the extraordinary correspondences in the lives of twins, which he describes in his book *Chronogenetics* (1978).

There seems to be a whole range of major and minor manifestations of the mental bonds that link twins, from fairly commonplace telepathy – such as a simultaneous impulse to contact each other – to the actual transmission of pain and even physical wounds. Beyond these mental bonds are the even more astonishing cases of 'carbon-copy' accidents, which stubbornly defy rational or scientific explanation.

It was 4.35 on a summer Saturday afternoon in 1948 when Alice Lambe, a 20-year-old typist, suddenly felt an enormous jolt in the left side of her body, followed by a sharp stabbing pain and a feeling of shock. She had been reading at her home in Springfield, Illinois, USA, as the impact of this unseen blow had knocked her off her chair. Before passing out she shouted to her father: 'Something's happened to Dianne!'

Dianne was her identical twin who had spent the day in St Louis, 70 miles (110 kilometres) away. At 4.35 p.m. the train on which she was returning was derailed and Dianne was thrown right across the carriage,

landing on her left side. The next thing she knew was waking up in hospital. She had suffered two fractured ribs and severe concussion. She was off work for three weeks – but then so was Alice, whose continual complaints of stabbing pain eventually led to her being x-rayed. It turned out that she had fractured the same two ribs in the same place as her sister.

On 21 July 1975 Nettie Porter was involved in a car crash in Roseville, California. At the same time her twin sister Nita Hust, at work in a hospital 400 miles (640 kilometres) away, felt severe pains down her left leg, rolled up her trousers and was amazed to see bruises working their way up the left side of her body. The matron at the hospital bore witness to the spontaneous development of her marks, which corresponded to Nettie's injuries.

Sometimes the transference of injury can be

Above: 300 sets of identical twins take part in The Frost Programme *on 17 January 1968 in London. At first glance each pair seems identical, but closer inspection reveals slight differences – enough, in most cases, to tell them apart*

Below left: twins Maureen Smith and Yvonne Gale gave birth to sons within 23 minutes of each other in Kingston Hospital, Surrey, on 15 January 1975. Does Professor Gedda's 'clock of life' account for such startling correspondences?

Above: English twins Bridget Harrison of Leicester and Dorothy Lowe from Burnley, Lancashire, who took part in Professor Bouchard's twin study. Aged 36 when they met for the first time, it almost seemed as if the same person had been living in two places at once, so strong were the similarities between them

Right: identical twins come in all shapes and sizes, from these appealing babies in their seats to the unwieldy 24-year-olds who posed with them at the greatest ever 'get together' of twins at Barvaux, Belgium, in 1966

fatal. Mrs Joyce Crominski wrote to the Australian magazine *Truth* about her identical twin sisters Helen and Peg. At 11.15 one evening Helen awoke, white-faced and screaming, with a terrible pain in her chest. Her parents sent for an ambulance but she died on the way to hospital – as did Peg, who had been in a car accident at exactly the same time as Helen awoke. The steering wheel had penetrated her chest.

Dizygotic – or non-identical – twins also experience pain transference, even though genetically they are no more alike than ordinary brothers and sisters. Martha Burke of California, USA, suffered from burning pains in her chest and stomach as her non-identical twin was burned to death in the Canary Island aeroplane crash of 1977, which claimed 582 lives.

Twins frequently give birth together. Jacky and Geraldine (née Herz) had babies within days of each other on 12 occasions. Many other twins have managed this feat at least once, often with greater synchronisation. In June 1970 Vera and Anita, twin daughters of Otto Heise of Einbeck, West Germany, who were

quite unlike each other in looks, character and ways of life, were both taken to the same clinic and delivered of babies at the same moment.

Death, too, can strike at the same time. Twins John and Arthur Mowforth, aged 66, were seized with chest pains on the same evening, 22 May 1975; they were rushed to hospitals in Bristol and Windsor respectively, and died of heart attacks in the evening. Twins Ida Torrey and Freda Palmer were born in Geronimo, Texas, in 1905. They died on the very same day in 1979, 350 miles (560 kilometres) apart.

Another, perhaps even more frequent event, is twins thinking of each other at the same time. Dr David Lykken of the University of Minnesota notes that when Nettie or Nita concentrates on her twin, the other soon telephones. This telepathic link is widely known but difficult to test by controlled experiment. Results are never quite conclusive. Thus we see from an undated clipping from the *Journal* of the American Association for the Advancement of Science that Doctors Duane and Behrendt wired up a pair of identical twins in separate rooms to record their brain waves, and found that a stimulus administered to the brain of one twin was simultaneously received by the other. Yet of 16 other pairs of twins later tested by the doctors only one pair responded similarly.

Twin telepathy is sometimes strikingly demonstrated by examination results. Twins Nancy and Ruth Schneider were born in Virginia, USA, in 1927. Sitting for college entrance exams in opposite corners of the room, they chose the same essay subject and wrote 'word for word' the same story, according to one of the invigilators, Dr Sara Roody.

Some identical twins can behave so similarly that to a casual observer they seem to share one identity, one personality. Sometimes these copy-cat tendencies can become a bizarre and sinister condition. One of the most striking examples of this phenomenon became known in 1980 when the 38-year-old Chaplin twins, Greta and Freda, were brought before magistrates in York, England, charged with behaving in a manner likely to cause a breach of the peace.

They had, it was asserted, been harassing Mr Ken Iveson, once a neighbour of theirs, for 15 years: following him about, waiting for him outside the glassworks where he was employed as a lorry driver, shouting abuse at him and even hitting him with their handbags. This extraordinary fixation, however, was not the reason that psychiatrists, social workers and journalists were so fascinated by the case – for the twins spoke in what appeared to be *precise synchronisation*, especially when excited or under stress; careful listening, however, reveals that the words of one come out a split second later than those of the other.

21

Below: the bizarre Chaplin twins, Freda and Greta, wear identical coats, but as one came with green buttons and the other with grey, they cut two off each so both coats had two green and two grey buttons. When given two separate pairs of gloves, they simply took one from each pair. A gift of two different bars of soap caused them real anguish until they cut the bars in half and shared them. When Greta got a prescription for her bronchitis, Freda demanded the same medicine. The twins eat in unison as well, slowly raising forks and spoons together, finishing up one item of food before starting on the next

The twins fixation with Ken Iveson (right) became intolerable: they would lie in wait for him and shout abuse or hit him – this, it seemed, was their way of showing affection

They exhibit other signs that seem to indicate that they are effectively one person. They are so alike in the way they think, speak, move and dress that children, believing them to be witches, have thrown stones at them in the street and adults have spat in their faces.

They also exhibit 'mirror-imaging', which is characteristically found in monozygotic twins. In typical cases one twin is right-handed, the other left-handed; the whorls of the hair grow clockwise in one and anti-clockwise in the other; the left thumbprint of one almost matches the right thumbprint of the other, or similar wrinkles appear on opposite ears. Photographs of twins are most similar if one negative is flipped to produce a reversed image.

The Chaplins dress in mirror image of each other, although a casual observer would say they dress identically, and eccentrically, in their long skirts, clashing colours and head-scarves. When Greta wears a bracelet on her left wrist, Freda wears one on her right, and if one breaks a shoelace, the other pulls a lace out of her opposite shoe.

In a highly significant comment the twins said: 'We're so close that we're really one person. We know exactly what each other is thinking because we're just one brain.'

A closer examination of their history shows that their extraordinary togetherness was actively fostered by their parents, especially by their mother, who dressed them identically and allowed them no friends. They were not mentally abnormal and attended a secondary school near their York home. Teachers and fellow pupils remember them as neat, clean and quiet – and although among the slowest students they could read and write fairly well.

The deputy headmaster of the school has no doubts about what turned them into the disturbed adults they are today: 'It was clear that they had a doting mother who never allowed them any separate identity. . . . The other kids just saw them as a bit quaint. I don't think they were acutely isolated then or maladjusted.' They had not, at that point, begun to speak simultaneously.

Left: 'Snap aduk, Cabenga, chase die-dipana' – at this mysterious command from one of the Kennedy twins, Grace and Virginia, they both began to play with their doll's house. Born in Columbia, Georgia, USA in 1979, the girls were believed to be mentally handicapped until it was discovered that they had developed a language of their own, complete with extensive vocabulary and syntax. 'Poto' and 'Cabenga', as they called themselves, were investigated at the Children's Hospital in San Diego, California

Clearly their mother's attitude towards them had triggered off a pattern of abnormal behaviour, perhaps aided by their biological affinity. Both parents seem to have been uncommunicative and friendless and Mrs Chaplin is said to be obsessively houseproud. This emphasis on cleanliness may explain why the twins' only apparent pleasure is bathing together, grooming each other, washing each other's long hair. They are said to use an average of 14 bars of soap and three large bottles of shampoo each week.

The unfortunate Ken Iveson had grown up next door to the Chaplins; he married when the twins were two years old, but continued to live at his parents' home with his wife and children. Iveson would pass the time of day with the girls, who, isolated from the outside world, obviously took this as some kind of romantic encouragement. They rapidly became a nuisance and eventually, after 15 years, Iveson could take no more of it. Their case came to court.

The twins' parents had, it transpired, forced them to leave home. When asked about this, Freda and Greta reply as one: 'Something must have happened. Yes yes yes. Something strange. Must have happened.' They now live in a hostel for the mentally handicapped.

Perhaps the Chaplins' peculiarity of speech is just one aspect of the way twins communicate with one another. Better known is *ideoglossia*, the phenomenon in which two individuals, most often twin children, develop between them a unique and private language complete with highly original vocabulary and syntax.

It is, however, commonly confused with a sub-category, *twin speech* – a private collection of distorted words and idioms used, it is estimated, by 40 per cent of all twins because they feel isolated, or secretive, or both. Most twins tend to give it up at the age of three, although

twin Robert A. Nelson wrote to the *New York Times* in 1932 that 'It is a matter of record in my family that when my brother and I first started to talk, and until we were well past six, we conversed with each other in a strange tongue of our own.' The only other person who could understand their particular speech was their brother, who was eight years older.

In contrast to twins brought up to be alike, there are many examples of incredible coincidences between identical twins who have been separated at birth without knowing it. A study of these – there are some 80 documented cases – can help scientists discover how much human character and intelligence is determined by genetic inheritance and how much by environment, education and upbringing.

The case of the 'Jim twins' , for instance, has so many bizarre details that it makes one wonder whether something more than coincidence lies behind it.

Below: Dr David Lykken and his colleague Dr Thomas J. Bouchard of the University of Minnesota, USA. Their extensive investigation of identical twins suggests that many possess a strong telepathic link

Above: twins Oscar Stohr and Jack Yufe, reunited in 1979. Their story was particularly ironic: Oscar had been reared as a Nazi – Jack as a Jew

Far right: Denise and Wendy Styles of Brading, Isle of Wight. In December 1973 the twins both fell and broke a leg within minutes of each other. Denise broke her right leg, Wendy her left: is this a case of 'mirror-imaging'?

Below: the 'Jim twins' – with Jim Lewis's adoptive mother. Separated at birth and reared by different families in Ohio, USA, they were reunited in 1979

In August 1939 in Piqua, Ohio, USA, five-week-old identical twin boys were adopted by different families. One set of adoptive parents, Jess and Lucille Lewis, lived in Lima, while Ernest and Sarah Springer lived in Dayton 80 miles (130 kilometres) away. Both couples were told that the other twin had died; but Mrs Lewis learned the truth by accident six years later when she returned to probate court to complete adoption procedures. When she said that she had called the child James Edward, the court official said: 'You can't do that. They named the other little boy James.' The secret was out. But James he remained.

James Springer grew up believing his twin was dead, while James Lewis had no idea where his twin was, and hesitated for many years before tracing him painstakingly through the bureaucratic processes of the adoption courts. They were 39 when they finally met in February 1979. The high level of

synchronicity between them was quite astonishing.

Both grew up with adopted brothers called Larry; at school both liked maths and hated spelling; and as boys both owned dogs called Troy. Both had married women called Linda, divorced and then married 'Bettys'. Their first sons were named, respectively, James Alan and James Allan. Both families had taken their holidays for years at the same small beach in St Petersburg, Florida – driving there in Chevrolets. Both men had worked as attendants at filling stations, for the same hamburger chain, and part-time as deputy sheriffs. They had both taken up carpentry and technical drawing as hobbies. They were compulsive nail-biters; shared the same sleeping problems, smoking and drinking habits, and used the same slang words. Each is 6 feet (1.8 metres) tall and weighs 180 pounds (80 kilograms). After they met, their families noted similarities in speech patterns, mannerisms and posture.

At the age of 18, both the Jim twins started having tension headaches, which always began in the afternoon then turned into migraines. (They later used almost identical words to describe the pain.) Both stopped having them at the same age, then they started again for a time before stopping finally. It had never been thought that such a complicated migraine pattern could be 'programmed' by heredity. Moreover, both men have had confirmed or suspected heart attacks, had developed haemorrhoids, and both put on 10 pounds (4.5 kilograms) at the same time, then lost it again.

News of the Jim twins prompted psychologist Thomas Bouchard of the University of

Above: the McWhirter twins, Norris and Ross, creators of The Guinness book of records. *They were both sub-lieutenants in the Royal Navy during the Second World War; Norris being detailed to a minesweeper in Singapore, Ross to one in the Mediterranean. The vessels made their separate ways to Valletta, Malta, where they collided*

Minnesota, USA, to instigate a much more detailed study of separated twins than had previously been attempted. As a result of publicity, more than 30 cases of identical twins, separated in the first few months of their lives and not reunited until adulthood, have come to light, and each pair has been intensively studied for a week at Minnesota.

In 1979, one set, Mrs Bridget Harrison of Leicester and Mrs Dorothy Lowe of Burnley, Lancashire, discovered they were twins. They had been apart since their birth in Lancashire in 1943. They had both married within a year of each other. One had called her son Richard Andrew, and the other caled hers Andrew Richard. Bridget's daughter is Catherine Louise, Dorothy's daughter is Karen Louise (and even then she was only called Karen to please a relative – Dorothy had really wanted to call her Katherine). Both had studied piano to the same grade, then stopped playing altogether after taking examinations at the same level. Both had had meningitis. Both collect soft toys, have cats called Tiger and wore almost identical wedding dresses. They leave their bedroom doors ajar; they wear the same perfume. They both kept a diary for just one

year – 1960 – and the diaries they bought were the same make and design. The entries they made matched, day for day.

When Bouchard picked them up at Minneapolis airport in December 1979 he was astonished to see that both were wearing seven rings on one hand, and, on the other, a bracelet and a watch. The Minneapolis study showed striking similarities between them in all areas, including their IQS, although, interestingly, the twin who had been raised in the more modest household did slightly better.

Bouchard and his team deny an hereditarian bias themselves, being more interested in environmental influences and individual differences, but admit that the scores on many tests were incredibly close. The only striking exception was of twins, one of whom was a fisherman in Florida, the other a CIA electronics expert. The fisherman was raised by an uneducated manual labourer, his twin by a highly educated man. Although both were great raconteurs, the difference in their IQS was considerable – about 20 points. It seems that the differences in background have to be very drastic before affecting IQS significantly.

But the most striking case of highly-synchronised, separated twins must be that of Oscar Stohr and Jack Yufe. They were born in Trinidad in 1933 and separated shortly afterwards when their parents quarrelled. Oscar was taken to Germany by his mother, where he became an ardent Nazi. With profound irony, Jack was reared in Trinidad by his father, a Jewish merchant.

In 1979, Jack read about the Jim twins and wrote to Bouchard suggesting that the scientists arrange a meeting between Oscar and himself to study them. When they met at the airport, they were both wearing wire-rimmed, rectangular spectacles and blue shirts with epaulettes, and both had moustaches.

The study revealed they had identical habits. They have the same gait and way of sitting, and they speak with the same rhythms, even though Oscar speaks only German and Jack only English. Nazi and Jew were brothers.

But if these similarities seem beyond coincidence, consider the following events.

In January 1974 twins Frank and Jack Clatworthy, from Somerset, England, were in adjoining hospital beds after being injured within an hour of each other in separate accidents 3 miles (5 kilometres) apart on the same road, returning from the same party.

Similarly, twins George and Stephen Youngblood went off on motorbikes in October 1980, in opposite directions, to joy-ride along the backroads of Missouri, USA. They met in a head-on collision.

Most of these incidents could be dismissed as the results of blind chance. Coincidences in general have the curious quality of seeming to be tremendously important, yet the nature of their significance remains elusive.

25

Left: the assassination of King Umberto 1 of Italy by the anarchist Bresci on 29 July 1900. Many important events in his life – and even his death – were astonishingly closely paralleled by the life of another Umberto – a restaurant proprietor in a small town in northern Italy

Connection and coincidence

Coincidence has puzzled and fascinated philosophers, mathematicians and scientists for more than 2000 years. It is something that all of us have experienced at some time or another, yet few of us understand. Many of the more startling cases seem to defy all attempts at explanation. Consider the example of King Umberto I of Italy.

On the evening of 28 July 1900, King Umberto dined with his aide in a restaurant in Monza, where he was due to attend an athletics meeting the next day. With astonishment, he noticed that the proprietor looked exactly like him and, speaking to him, he discovered that there were other similarities.

The restaurateur was also called Umberto; like the King, he had been born in Turin – and

on the same day; and he had married a girl called Margherita on the day the King married his Queen Margherita. He had opened his restaurant on the day that Umberto I was crowned King of Italy.

The King was intrigued, and invited his double to attend the athletics meeting with him. But the next day at the stadium the King's aide informed him that the restaurateur had died that morning in a mysterious shooting accident. And even as the King expressed his regret, he himself was shot dead by an anarchist in the crowd.

Throughout historical speculation into coincidence, the same questions emerge: do coincidences have a hidden meaning for us, and what unknown force, if any, do they represent? Only in this century have any real answers been suggested, answers that strike at the very roots of established science and prompt the question: are there powers in the Universe of which we are still only dimly aware?

Early cosmologists believed that the world was held together by a kind of principle of

Above: the German philosopher Arthur Schopenhauer (1788–1860) who believed that coincidences were a reflection of the 'wonderful pre-established harmony' of the Universe

Above: Dr Paul Kammerer who, in 1919, published the first systematic study of coincidence

Far right: the celebrated oboist Leon Goossens. In 1952, he lost a pocket diary while crossing a field. Over a year later, he was walking across the field when he suddenly came across the diary. He picked it up – and found that the cover had been stiffened using a square of newspaper carrying a gossip column item (inset) about his own marriage, 19 years before

Below: Wolfgang Pauli (1900–1958), the Nobel prize-winning physicist who, together with the eminent psychologist C. G. Jung, introduced the concept of synchronicity *to help explain the occurrence of coincidences*

hair turning grey. Bull-necked, and looks like a bull-fighter retired and running slightly to flesh.

OBOIST LEON GOOSSENS is getting married a second time, at the age of thirty-six. His first wife was recently married in the United States to nephew of novelist Mary Roberts Rinehart. He is considered finest oboe-player in the world. Also plays part of sporty gent. in spare time : yachtin', shootin', golf.

IS easily shocked, however. Drinks little. Has inverted

wholeness. Hippocrates, known as the father of medicine, who lived at some time between 460 and 375 BC, believed the Universe was joined together by 'hidden affinities' and wrote: 'There is one common flow, one common breathing, all things are in sympathy.' According to this theory, coincidence could be explained by 'sympathetic' elements seeking each other out.

The Renaissance philosopher Pico della Mirandola wrote in 1557: 'Firstly, there is a unity in things whereby each thing is at one with itself. Secondly, there is the unity whereby one creature is united with the others and all parts of the world constitute one world.'

This belief has continued, in a barely altered form, in much more modern times. The philosopher Arthur Schopenhauer (1788–1860) defined coincidence as 'the simultaneous occurrence of causally unconnected events.' He went on to suggest that simultaneous events ran in parallel lines and 'the selfsame event, although a link in totally different chains, nevertheless falls into place in both, so that the fate of one individual invariably fits the fate of another, and each is the hero of his own drama while simultaneously figuring in a drama foreign to him. This is something that surpasses our powers of comprehension and can only be conceived as possible by the virtue of the most wonderful pre-established harmony. Everyone must participate in it. Thus everything is interrelated and mutually attuned.'

The first person to study the laws of coincidence scientifically was Dr Paul Kammerer, Director of the Institute of Experimental Biology in Vienna. From the age of 20, he started to keep a 'logbook' of coincidences. Many were essentially trivial: people's names that kept cropping up in separate conversations, successive concert or cloakroom tickets with the same number, a phrase in a book that kept recurring in real life.

For hours, Kammerer sat on park benches recording the people who wandered past, noting their sex, age, dress, whether they carried walking sticks or umbrellas. After making the necessary allowances for things like rush-hour, weather and time of year, he found the results broke down into 'clusters of numbers' of a kind familiar to statisticians, gamblers, insurance companies and opinion pollsters.

Kammerer called the phenomenon 'seriality', and in 1919 he published his conclusions in a book called *Das Gesetz der Serie* (The law of seriality). Coincidences, he claimed, came in series – or 'a recurrence or clustering in time or space whereby the individual numbers in the sequence are not connected by the same active cause.'

Coincidence, suggested Kammerer, was merely the tip of an iceberg in a larger cosmic principle that mankind, as yet, hardly recognises. Like gravity, it is a mystery; but unlike gravity, it acts selectively to bring together in space and time things that possess some affinity. 'We thus arrive,' he concluded, 'at the image of a world mosaic or cosmic kaleidoscope, which, in spite of constant shufflings and rearrangements, also takes care of bringing like and like together.'

The great leap forward happened 50 years later, when two of Europe's most brilliant minds collaborated to produce the most searching book on the powers of coincidence – one that was to provoke both controversy and attack from rival theorists.

The two men were Wolfgang Pauli – whose daringly conceived exclusion principle earned him the Nobel Prize for Physics – and the Swiss psychologist-philosopher, Professor Carl Gustav Jung. Their treatise bore the unexciting title: *Synchronicity, an acausal connecting principle.* Described by one American reviewer as 'the paranormal equivalent of a nuclear explosion', it used the term 'synchronicity' to extend Kammerer's theory of seriality.

Interpreters of the Pauli-Jung theory have concluded that telepathy, precognition and coincidences themselves are all manifestations of a single mysterious force at work in the Universe that is trying to impose its own kind of discipline on the utter confusion of human life.

Not surprisingly, sceptics reject these theories. They explain coincidence in terms of the laws of probability: if something *can* happen then, however small the probability of the event, you should not be too surprised if it eventually *does* happen. A classic example is that a monkey at a typewriter, pressing the keys at random, will eventually – 'as time tends to infinity', as the mathematicians say – type out the entire works of Shakespeare. As the science writer Martin Gardner puts it,

The promising Hollywood actor James Dean (left) was killed in a tragic motoring accident in September 1955. Afterwards when the wreck (above left) was towed to a garage, the engine slipped and fell onto a mechanic, breaking both his legs. The engine was bought by a doctor who put it into a racing car and was killed shortly afterwards. In the same race another driver was killed in a car with the drive-shaft from Dean's car. Dean's car was later repaired – and a fire broke out at the garage. It was displayed in Sacramento, and fell off its mount, breaking a teenager's hip. Then, in Oregon, the truck on which the car was mounted slipped and crashed into a shop-front. Finally, in 1959, it broke into 11 pieces while resting on stationary steel supports

'Trillions of events, large and trivial, happen to billions of human beings every day. Therefore, it is inevitable that surprising things occur now and again.'

Modern research, however, now divides coincidences into two categories: trivial and significant. Trivial coincidences are minor similarities like spinning coins, runs of numbers and amazing hands of cards. Researchers are more concerned with the 'significant' coincidences, those that shuffle together people, events, space and time. They have identified recognisable types, such as the literary coincidence, warning coincidence, it's-a-small-world coincidence and conjuring coincidence

(incidents that are like a psychic sleight-of-hand).

There are classic examples in each category, but the quintessential literary coincidence happened just before the Allied invasion of Europe in 1944.

Every aspect of the huge campaign – to drive out the Nazis and end the Second World War – was top secret and referred to only by code-words. The operation itself was known as OVERLORD. The naval spearhead was disguised by the name NEPTUNE. The two French beaches where the landing was to take place were coded UTAH and OMAHA. And the artificial harbours to be used to supply the troops at the beach-head were known as MULBERRY.

Incredibly, in the 33 days before D-Day, 6 June, each of these secret words appeared as the answer to a clue in the London *Daily*

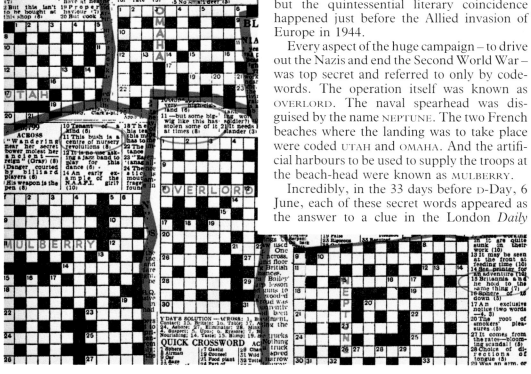

Far left: by an amazing coincidence, many of the key code words used in the Allied invasion of Europe in 1944 – OVERLORD, NEPTUNE, MULBERRY, UTAH, OMAHA – appeared as solutions to Daily Telegraph crossword clues in the weeks before D-Day. Security men quickly checked the Telegraph offices – but found no Nazi spy, only schoolmaster Leonard Dawe, who had been compiling the crossword for 20 years

Telegraph crossword. The key word OVERLORD appeared only four days before the landing.

Security men immediately descended on the Fleet Street offices of the *Telegraph*, expecting to bag a Nazi spy. Instead, they found schoolmaster Leonard Dawe, who had been harmlessly compiling the paper's crossword for 20 years. Dawe was flabbergasted, and took a long time to convince them that he had been totally ignorant of the significance of the words.

For an extraordinary conjuring coincidence, however, one can do no better than listen to the curious, and strangely inconsequential, experience of Mrs Eileen Bithell, of Portsmouth, Hampshire.

'For more than 20 years, a framed sign saying Closed on Wednesdays hung in the window of my parents' grocery shop. A few days before my brother's wedding, the sign was taken down to be altered. When we removed it from the frame, we discovered to our surprise that the sign had been painted on the back of a photograph. There was an even bigger surprise. The picture showed my brother's bride-to-be as a small girl, in the arms of his future father-in-law.

'Nobody knows how this particular photograph came to be used as the shop sign. For none of the people were known to my family at the time the sign was put up. Yet now, 20 years later, our two families were to be joined in marriage.'

Warning coincidences often have an extraordinarily long reach, which is why many are ignored or go unrecognised. That was certainly the case with three ships, the *Titan*, the *Titanic* and the *Titanian*. In 1898, the American writer Morgan Robertson published a novel about a giant liner, the *Titan*, which sank one freezing April night in the Atlantic after hitting an iceberg on her maiden voyage.

Fourteen years later – in one of the world's

Coincidence linked the Titanian *(above) with the famous disaster liner* Titanic. *Both hit icebergs in the same waters; but the* Titanian *survived, though somewhat dented (inset)*

Below: Charles Coghlan, whose dead body travelled more than 3500 miles (5600 kilometres) by sea before being cast up on the shore of his home town

worst sea disasters – the *Titanic* sank on a freezing April night in the Atlantic after hitting an iceberg on *her* maiden voyage.

The coincidences did not end there. The ships, both fact and fiction, were around the same tonnage and both disasters occurred in the same stretch of the ocean. Both liners were regarded as 'unsinkable', and neither carried sufficient lifeboats.

With the extraordinary story of the *Titanian*, the *Titan-Titanic* coincidences begin to defy human belief. On watch one night in April 1935 – during the *Titanian*'s coal-run from the Tyne to Canada – crewman William Reeves began to feel a strong sense of foreboding. By the time the *Titanian* reached the spot where the two other ships had gone down, the feeling was overpowering. Could Reeves stop the ship merely because of a premonition? One thing – a *further* coincidence – made the decision for him. He had been born on the day of the *Titanic* disaster. 'Danger ahead!' he bellowed to the bridge. The words were barely out of his mouth when an iceberg loomed out of the darkness. The ship avoided it just in time.

If coincidence can reach so easily across time and space in its quest for 'order out of chaos', it is not surprising that it can stretch beyond the grave, too, as in this bizarre case of a 'small world' coincidence.

While on a tour of Texas in 1899, the Canadian actor Charles Francis Coghlan was taken ill in Galveston and died. It was too far to return his remains to his home on Prince Edward Island, in the Gulf of St Lawrence – more than 3500 miles (5600 kilometres) away by the sea-route – and he was buried in a lead coffin inside a granite vault. His bones had rested less than a year when the great hurricane of September 1900 hit Galveston Island, flooding the cemetery. The vault was shattered and Coghlan's coffin floated out into the Gulf of Mexico. Slowly, it drifted along the Florida

Above: a contemporary engraving of Mary Ashford whose body was found on 27 May 1817 in a flooded sandpit close to Erdington. 157 years later to the day Barbara Forrest (far right) was murdered near Erdington. Both girls had spent the evening dancing – Mary Ashford at the Tyburn House Inn (below) – and the man charged with the murder in each case was called Thornton. They were both eventually acquitted

coastline and into the Atlantic, where the Gulf Stream picked it up and carried it northwards.

Eight years passed. Then, one day in October 1908, some fishermen on Prince Edward Island spotted a long, weather-scarred box floating near the shore. Coghlan's body had come home. With respect mingled with awe, his fellow islanders buried the actor in the nearby church where he had been christened as a baby.

Some theories suggest that coincidences – especially those transcending time periods – may be the result of astrological conditions. Perhaps the influence of stars and planets is part of that force – identified by many coincidence researchers – that may be imposing some kind of order upon the chaotic Universe.

The strange case of the 'identical' Erdington murders apparently offers some evidence to support this theory. Two girls of the same age (and, according to some sources, the same birth dates) were the victims of murders committed on the same day of the year – but with a time difference of 157 years. The identical factors in the two cases are so striking and so numerous that it could be argued that some kind of astrological influence must have governed the actions of those who committed the crimes.

On 27 May 1817, 20-year-old Mary Ashford was found dead, apparently murdered, at Erdington, then only a village, 5 miles (8 kilometres) outside Birmingham. On 27 May 1974, Barbara Forrest, aged 20, was strangled and left in long grass near the children's home in Erdington at which she was a nurse.

That in itself is perhaps a remarkable coincidence, but no more. It is when one examines each case in detail that the identical factors begin to proliferate. Both in 1817 and 1974 Whit Monday was on 26 May. Barbara Forrest and Mary Ashford had both been raped before being murdered and their bodies were found within 400 yards (360 metres) of one another,

death taking place at approximately the same time of day. It would appear (though there must be some doubt about this in the case of Mary Ashford) that there were attempts by the killers to hide the respective bodies.

But the coincidences do not end there. Both girls had visited a friend early in the evening of the Whit Monday to change into a new dress and then go on to a dance. After each murder a man was arrested – and in each instance his name was Thornton. To round off this narrative of astonishing parallels, both men were charged with murder but were acquitted.

It was when the police were checking through archives after Barbara Forrest's death that they came across full reports of the murder of 1817 – and noted these similarities with amazement.

Coincidences still tease us. When two separate happenings are suddenly and inexplicably brought together we find it difficult, in our excitement, to think of the numerous events that have *failed* to converge in this coincidental way. Hence, we see coincidence in isolation and exaggerate its significance.

But although there is no agreement on a definite answer to the question of what lies behind coincidences, it is undeniable that sceptics and believers alike find coincidences inescapably fascinating. For all coincidences make one wonder, and the more idiosyncratic examples never fail to fire the imagination.

CHAPTER TWO

The Power of the Mind

ESP, Hypnosis,
The healing touch, Psychic surgery,
Mind over matter, Levitation,
Fireproof people

The sixth sense

The human mind has powers of understanding that are beyond the five senses: this is a fact, but one that nonetheless is still shrouded in mystery. Thousands of people have had experiences in which information reaches them in a way that bypasses their 'normal' senses. During the past 50 years investigators have used the term *extra-sensory perception* (ESP) to describe the phenomenon, and hundreds of experiments have been conducted around the world in an attempt to confirm its existence scientifically and understand how it works.

What is clear from this research, and from a study of spontaneous cases, is that ESP is not an isolated phenomenon. For example, one day in 1946 14-year-old Stanley Krippner (now a noted psychical researcher) decided that he wanted a set of encyclopedias very badly. His parents could not afford to buy him one and, while thinking of ways of raising the money himself, his thoughts turned to his rich Uncle Max. How could he best approach him for funds?

Suddenly the teenager sat bolt upright in bed as a horrible thought flooded his mind: 'Uncle Max can't help me because he's dead.' At that moment the telephone rang: it was Krippner's cousin giving the news that Uncle Max had been rushed to hospital and had died.

There are three 'psychic' ways, all classified as types of ESP, in which Krippner might have found out about his uncle's unexpected death:

Telepathy It is possible that the teenager's mind 'tuned in' to his cousin's mind and read his thoughts just as he was about to telephone with the bad news.

Clairvoyance It is just as likely that young Krippner had an awareness of his uncle's death – he sensed it had happened – without having any mind-to-mind communication.

Precognition Yet another possibility is that his knowledge came not from past or present events but from the future. Somehow he jumped fractionally ahead in time and knew what his mother was about to learn from the telephone call.

Telepathy – the ability of one person to 'look into' the mind of another – was one of the first subjects to be studied by the early psychical researchers a century ago. Typical of the spontaneous cases considered was the experience of an English clergyman in 1883.

Canon Warburton sat in an armchair in his

Below: an experiment in psychokinesis conducted by Dr J. B. Rhine. Together with his wife Louisa, Dr Rhine began the first major scientific investigation into all forms of extra-sensory perception in 1927

Above: Sir Oliver Lodge who, at the turn of the century, carried out many experiments into ESP

a note explaining that he had gone to a dance in the West End and would be back at about 1 a.m.

Recovering from the experience, Canon Warburton dozed off again for half an hour until his brother came in and woke him up. 'I have just had as narrow an escape of breaking my neck as I ever had in my life!' he exclaimed. 'Coming out of the ballroom, I caught my foot, and tumbled full length down the stairs.'

By the early part of this century many groups of researchers were involved in imaginative telepathy tests. In the 1920s Rene Warcollier conducted group telepathy experiments between France and the United States, many of which produced very impressive results. But not all early research is acceptable by today's strict scientific standards. The famous physicist Professor Oliver Lodge (later Sir Oliver Lodge) carried out tests with two girls who claimed to be able to read each other's minds. He found their demonstrations convincing and published them in 1909 in his book *The survival of man*. But since the girls were allowed to hold hands while 'sending' their telepathic images of playing cards, the possibility that they were using a code cannot be eliminated. This suspicion is reinforced by Lodge's statistics, which show that when the girls were not touching, results fell nearly to chance levels.

It was to give the subject respectability in the eyes of science that Dr J. B. Rhine and his wife Louisa began to research telepathy in the laboratory in the late 1920s.

The Rhines' method of researching ESP was to give their subjects guessing tasks. They used a pack of 25 cards, which was divided into five sets of five cards, each set carrying a different symbol: star, circle, cross, wavy lines, rectangle. These cards, called Zener

brother's flat and began to doze. Suddenly, he woke up with a start exclaiming, 'By Jove! He's down!' The canon had just had a vivid dream in which he had seen his brother come out of a drawing-room on to a brightly illuminated landing, catch his foot on the edge of the top stair and fall headlong down the stairs, just managing to save himself from serious injury by using his hands and elbows. The house in the dream was not one he recognised. All the canon knew, having just arrived in London from Oxford, was that his brother had left him

Below: a set of Zener cards used to test ESP *in individual subjects. Each of the five symbols is designed to make a distinct impression on the memory*

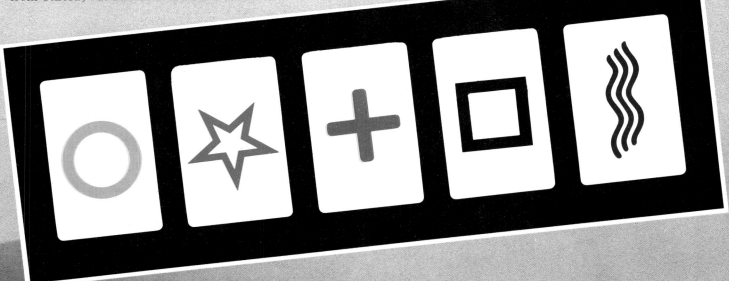

cards, were shuffled, then looked at one at a time by the sender, or agent. In another part of the university the receiver, or subject, would point to the symbol he thought the agent was looking at. According to the laws of chance, a subject would get 5 out of 25 right if only guesswork were involved. Occasionally, luck might enable him to guess more than five correctly, but on other occasions he would do less well so that, in an extended series of tests, the results would even out. If, on the other hand, the subject had ESP abilities, the results should be above average. And that is precisely what Rhine found.

Rhine's work continued for many years, but with more and more researchers carrying out their own research programmes into various aspects of ESP, telepathy was soon overshadowed by subjects such as clairvoyance and precognition.

The definition of clairvoyance is 'extra-sensory knowledge about material objects or events which is not obtained from another person's mind' – in other words, not simple telepathy. It can take many different forms, ranging from a vague awareness of a distant event to a vision in which scenes unfold vividly before the eyes of the clairvoyant.

For ordinary people, clairvoyance is most likely to occur in stressful situations or when people or places connected with them are in danger. A well authenticated instance concerns the 18th-century Swedish scientist and seer Emanuel Swedenborg, investigated and recorded by the distinguished German philosopher Immanuel Kant. On one occasion Swedenborg arrived in Gothenburg from England at around 4 p.m. on a Saturday. Soon he became restless and disturbed and left his friends to go for a walk outside.

On his return, he described a vision he had

Late in 1978 Los Angeles police called in a local psychic, Joan (below), to help solve the case of a small boy's disappearance. The psychic said the boy was dead and described the man she thought was the murderer. When shown a sketch (below left) based on her description, the victim's parents recognised one 'Butch' Memro (left). Memro was arrested and confessed to the crime

SOUTH GATE
OCT 27, 78
F.G Ponce

Emanuel Swedenborg (1688–1772), the Swedish scientist, philosopher and theologian who was well known during his lifetime as a clairvoyant

had of a fire which, he said, had broken out just three doors away from his home, 300 miles (480 kilometres) away. A fierce blaze was raging, he said, and he continued to be disturbed until 8 p.m. when he announced that the fire had been extinguished. News of this clairvoyant vision spread rapidly through the city and Swedenborg was asked to give a first-hand account to the Governor of Gothenburg. It was not until a royal messenger arrived in Gothenburg on the following Monday that the events of Swedenborg's vision were confirmed.

There are so many outstanding cases of clairvoyance on record that it is not surprising to find possessors of these abilities being consulted in particularly baffling crime cases. For example, late in 1978 Los Angeles police called in a local psychic – known only as Joan – to help solve the case of a small boy's mysterious disappearance. The psychic told the police that the boy was dead and, on the basis of her description, a police artist was able to make a sketch of the murderer. The victim's parents immediately recognised the face in the picture as a man called 'Butch' Memro, who was quickly arrested and confessed to the crime.

One of the most remarkable psychic sleuths is Peter Hurkos, a psychometrist – someone who divines details about a person through contact with, or proximity to, something belonging to that person. And Gerard Croiset, who died on 20 July 1980, was a clairvoyant whose reputation as a finder of missing children remains without parallel.

The Yorkshire Ripper investigation between 1975 and 1980 attracted hordes of psychics who honestly believed they had vital information about the killer's identity. Reviewing these claims in the light of what is now known about Peter Sutcliffe, the Ripper, it can be seen that few of these people came anywhere near the truth. One exception, however, was Mrs Nella Jones.

Mrs Jones said the killer's name was Peter, that he lived in a large house, No 6 in the street, on an elevated site in Bradford, Yorkshire. 'Peter', she said, was a lorry driver, and his cab bore the name of the company he worked for; the name began with the letter C. She said that 'Peter' had been a tearaway in his youth, and added that he had committed other crimes. In an interview in early November 1980 she told journalist Shirley Davenport that the next murder by the Ripper would be on 17 November.

Peter Sutcliffe lived with his wife Sonia in a large house on an elevated site; the address was No 6, Garden Lane, Heaton, Bradford. He worked as a lorry driver for a haulage company named Clarks. He had been a tearaway in his youth and had been charged with a number of offences. On 17 November he killed Leeds student Jacqueline Hill.

The gift of precognition – the ability to see into the future – has attracted much attention from researchers into paranormal phenomena, and attempts to record and monitor predictions are now in operation in both Britain and the United States.

Sometimes a number of people have dreadful forebodings of the same event. Many of them have no direct connection with the tragedy they foresee, but some, like Eryl Mai Jones, become its victims. On 20 October 1966, this nine-year-old Welsh girl told her mother she had dreamed that when she had gone to school it was not there. 'Something black had come down all over it,' she said. Next day she went to school in Aberfan – and half a million tons of coal waste slithered down onto the mining village, killing Eryl and 139 others – most of them children.

After the disaster, many people claimed to have had premonitions about it. They were investigated by a London psychiatrist, Dr John Barker, who narrowed them down to 60 he felt were genuine. He was so impressed by the evidence for premonitions of the tragedy

Of the many psychics who believed they held the key to the identity of the Yorkshire Ripper, Nella Jones (right) was the only one to give a really accurate description. In an interview given in early November 1980, Mrs Jones stated that the Ripper was called Peter, that he worked as a lorry driver for a firm whose name began with the letter C, and that he would kill his next victim on 17 November. The Ripper (right) is called Peter Sutcliffe; he worked as a lorry driver for a firm named Clarks (above), and he claimed his final victim, Leeds student Jacqueline Hill, on 17 November

that he helped set up the British Premonitions Bureau, in the hope that it could be used to give early warning of similar disasters and enable lives to be saved.

When Dr Barker analysed the Aberfan premonitions he noticed that there was a gradual build-up during the week before the Welsh tip buried the school, reaching a peak on the night before the tragedy. Two Californian premonition bureaux – one at Monterey, south of San Francisco, the other at Berkeley – are now sifting through predictions from members of the public in the hope of detecting a similar pattern. An earthquake is expected on the San Andreas fault in the near future and it is hoped it will be possible to predict it by monitoring

Above: the terrible events of 21 October 1966, when the entire Welsh mining village of Aberfan was obliterated by coal waste, were foreseen by many people. Among them was nine-year-old Eryl Mai Jones (inset), who became one of the victims

premonitions so that a mass evacuation can be made before the event.

Sceptics often point out that information about premonitions is published only after the event, and that the vast majority of such predictions are discarded when they are found to be wrong. This may be true in many cases, but there are exceptions.

A Scottish newspaper, the *Dundee Courier & Advertiser*, carried a story on 6 December 1978, headlined 'Prophet didn't have a ticket'. It told of the appearance of Edward Pearson, 43, at Perth Sheriff Court, charged with travelling on the train from Inverness to Perth on 4 December without paying the proper fare.

Pearson – described as 'an unemployed Welsh prophet' – was said to have been on his way to see the Minister of the Environment to warn him about an earthquake that would hit Glasgow in the near future. The *Courier*'s readers doubtless found it very amusing. But they were not so amused by the earthquake that shook them in their beds three weeks later, causing damage to buildings in Glasgow and other parts of Scotland. Earthquakes in Britain are rare. Prophets who predict them are even rarer.

Another successful seer is Jeane Dixon, who

predicted the assassinations of President John F. Kennedy, his brother Robert Kennedy, and civil rights leader Martin Luther King. Her premonition of the American president's murder came 11 years before the event and before he had even become president.

A devout woman, she had gone to St Matthew's Cathedral in Washington one morning in 1952 to pray, and was standing before a statue of the Virgin Mary when she had a vision of the White House. The numerals 1 – 9 – 6 – 0 appeared above it against a dark cloud. A young, blue-eyed man stood at the door. A voice told her that a Democrat, who would be inaugurated as president in 1960, would be assassinated while in office.

She predicted his brother's death in 1968 – in an even more startling way – while addressing a convention at the Ambassador Hotel, Los Angeles. She invited questions from the floor and one woman asked if Robert Kennedy would become president. Suddenly, Jeane Dixon saw a black curtain fall between her and the audience, and she told the questioner: 'No, he will not. He will never be president of the United States because of a tragedy right here in this hotel.'

A week later Robert Kennedy was gunned down in the Ambassador Hotel.

But even Jeane Dixon doesn't get all her predictions right. In fact, even the best seers claim no more than a 70 per cent success rate, and sceptics argue that it appears so high only because their predictions are vague.

Sceptics, of course, will argue that it is impossible to look into the future. Many of them feel that, until the existence of premonition is proved in the laboratory, it cannot be taken seriously. But, although it may not be

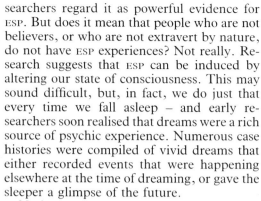

searchers regard it as powerful evidence for ESP. But does it mean that people who are not believers, or who are not extravert by nature, do not have ESP experiences? Not really. Research suggests that ESP can be induced by altering our state of consciousness. This may sound difficult, but, in fact, we do just that every time we fall asleep – and early researchers soon realised that dreams were a rich source of psychic experience. Numerous case histories were compiled of vivid dreams that either recorded events that were happening elsewhere at the time of dreaming, or gave the sleeper a glimpse of the future.

Modern parapsychologists use a technique that induces a state of altered consciousness easily at any time of day or night. The subject is asked to rest on a mattress. His eyes are then covered with half ping-pong balls onto which a soft coloured light is shone and his ears are covered with headphones into which 'white noise' (a gentle hissing sound) is fed. In this state of sensory deprivation the subject's mind has no visual or auditory distractions to occupy it and is, at least theoretically, more open to receiving telepathic signals from an agent some distance away, who is concentrating on a

easy to look ahead at will, there remain on record some extraordinary stories of premonition that are difficult to explain according to the laws of conventional science.

Perhaps the most exciting aspect of more than a century of psychical research is that it suggests that ESP is a gift most of us possess. Some of the most fascinating studies have examined personality in relation to psychic abilities: what kind of person is most likely to experience ESP? One of the first researchers to delve into the subject was Dr Gertrude Schmeidler.

In thousands of clairvoyance tests in the late 1940s and early 1950s, Dr Schmeidler, of the City University of New York, asked each person before he was tested whether he believed ESP was possible under the conditions of the experiment. The purpose was to see whether those who believed ESP was possible scored more highly than those who did not. And, indeed, Dr Schmeidler's score sheets showed such a difference: the believers scored consistently slightly above chance, whereas the scores of the non-believers were slightly below.

Another link between ESP and personality was discovered by Dr Betty Humphrey of the Duke Parapsychology Laboratory. Before testing individuals for ESP she gave them a blank sheet of paper and asked them to draw anything they liked. Bold pictures that filled most of the sheet indicated the person was an 'expansive' type; small, timid or conventional drawings showed that the person was a 'compressive'. Analysis of their ESP results showed that the expansives scored more highly than the compressives.

This work has continued into the 1980s, with different researchers using slightly different methods to gauge their subjects' personalities. The current trend is to divide people into extraverts (expansives) and introverts (compressives) using a detailed questionnaire.

The reasons for this link between extra-sensory abilities and personality are still subject to a great deal of conjecture, but many re-

Above: the funeral of President John F. Kennedy. The American seer Jeane Dixon predicted the assassinations of the President, his brother Robert Kennedy (left, below) and civil rights leader Martin Luther King

Below: Dr Carl Sargent of the University of Cambridge conducts a Ganzfeld experiment. In the Ganzfeld state, the subject is deprived of normal sensory stimulation which, parapsychologists have found, makes him or her receptive to ESP. While the subject speaks her mental impressions into a microphone, Dr Sargent writes them down (right)

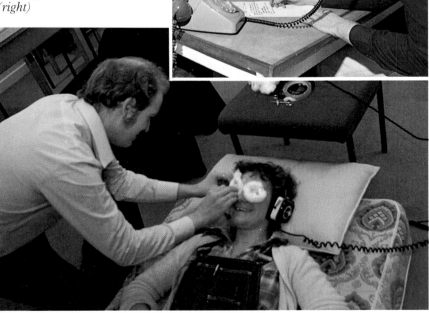

In tests at Cambridge, a young computer expert, Hugh Ashton, produced some remarkable ESP results while in a Ganzfeld state. He perfectly described this picture (left) of firemen seen from the back – 'people but not faces' – except for one of them, who Ashton said looked as if the photographer had said 'Oi', and only he turned round. After the session, four pictures were brought into the room. They were duplicates of the pictures contained in the target envelope, of which only one had been selected for the experiment. Hugh Ashton was asked to identify the one he thought had been chosen for the test and he was able to do so instantly. In another session, a subject was even able to name the picture that was being 'sent' by telepathy: William Blake's The ancient of days *(left)*

picture chosen at random. This technique induces a *Ganzfeld state* in the subject, and Dr Carl Sargent of Cambridge University is one of the researchers who has had outstanding results with it, with average scores of 17 per cent above chance expectancy. One of his top-scoring subjects is a young computer expert, Hugh Ashton. In one session he described seeing buildings in a corner, adding:

> Keep thinking of firemen and fire station . . . Firemen definitely seen, black and white. People but not faces. I think one man at bottom in foreground: facing . . . Young face, as if photographer says, 'Oi' and only he turned round.

The description contained much more detail. At the end of the session the agent brought into the room four pictures, and Hugh Ashton instantly identified the one he thought had been used for the experiment.

Although researchers cannot yet produce telepathy, clairvoyance and precognition to order in their laboratories, their investigations show that ESP *is* a very real phenomenon. The latest research even holds out the hope that we may all, one day, be able to use our psychic powers at will.

Hypnosis

Most people still think of hypnotists as slightly shady characters practising a highly dubious craft. If our imaginations do not conjure up the image of a power-mad Victorian doctor forcing his will on the unsuspecting, we think instead of the modern, smooth-talking stage hypnotist who exercises his talents by making fools of his night-club audiences. But today hypnotism – while still a mystery – is gathering a new respectability by serving some remarkable practical functions in crime-detection, medicine and psychology.

There is not, as yet, any clear explanation of the nature of hypnotism. Hypnosis is generally defined as a trance, that is, an altered state of consciousness. The extent of the alteration depends upon the individual. In any group, some of the volunteers will remember everything that has been done while others may recall nothing. But they will all have come under the hypnotist's influence.

What this means is that each of them has shed some of the controls, or thrown off some of the inhibitions, that training and habit normally impose on us. If somebody said to any of them, in ordinary conversation, 'You are a watchdog and you hear a burglar', it would raise only a laugh. On stage, the hypnotised subject gets down on hands and knees and barks. The hypnotist is he-who-must-be-obeyed; commands from other people are ignored unless he has given instructions that they should be obeyed, too.

Even more impressively, the accomplished hypnotist can give commands that will be obeyed after the subjects have come out of their trances. If he gives them a 'post-hypnotic suggestion' that they should stand up and shout 'hip-hip-hooray' whenever the orchestra plays a certain tune, they will do so, without knowing why.

Watching people behave in this way appears to demonstrate the hypnotist's powers. But this is an illusion. The powers really lie in the hypnotised subjects. And these powers are far greater and potentially far more valuable than is generally realised, in spite of numerous demonstrations of a more serious nature of just what can be achieved under hypnosis.

In one form or another, hypnotism has been used throughout history. It has been exploited by tribal witch doctors and by priests in the temples of ancient Greece. But we owe the form in which it is practised today to Franz

Hypnosis appears to switch off some part of our minds that ordinarily monitors our behaviour, instructing us what to do in any given set of circumstances without thought on our part. We hand this control system over to the hypnotist, much as an airline pilot may hand over the controls of his aircraft to somebody on the ground, who guides it in by radar with the help of an automatic pilot.

Top: unscrupulous stage hypnotists can give their profession a bad name. This French entertainer made a girl from the audience undress, apparently under hypnosis, during each show. But the same girl was used every night!

Above: an early 19th-century illustration of a French street mesmerist

Left: a 19th-century cartoon showing J. M. Charcot, a pioneering hypnotherapist, as an evil mind-manipulator. The sinister image of the hypnotist has persisted for years, being dispelled only when the media began reporting the success of hypnotherapy

Mesmer and his disciples. Two hundred years ago, they realised that subjects in the trance state could be made to obey every command. But more important, in the course of their experiments they made two discoveries of great potential significance.

For a start, they found that if they told a subject 'You will feel no pain', he could be struck, pricked and even burned without so much as a yelp. The Mesmerists proceeded to demonstrate that pain-free surgical operations could be performed under hypnosis – and this was before the invention of anaesthetic drugs.

The medical profession refused to accept the evidence. When distinguished surgeons were invited to watch the amputation of a leg under hypnosis, they insisted the man was only pretending to feel no pain! Hypnosis, they argued, was occult; it could not work.

The second discovery was that some hypnotised subjects enjoyed talents they did not know they had in their ordinary lives. One might draw well under hypnosis; another sing melodiously. A few appeared to become clairvoyant, describing places or events that they could not have seen. This, too, was dismissed as occultism.

The extravagance of Mesmeric theory and

Above: a dramatic moment in the history of medicine: Charcot demonstrates the ease with which a hysterical patient can be hypnotised, at the Salpêtrière Hospital in 1855. However, it has since been conclusively proved that almost anyone can be hypnotised

its claims, together with the undertones of occultism that went with them, aroused intense opposition; and throughout the 19th century, serious investigators into hypnosis, and the few medical men bold enough to experiment with its use, met the kind of hostility once reserved for witches.

In the 1840s a hard-headed Scot, James Braid, did his best to convert sceptics by presenting a new explanation of somnambulism, which he termed *hypnosis*. He could induce the trance, he showed, without recourse to animal magnetism (the term then used for hypnotism), or indeed any psychic or psychological force, if he held some bright object just above a subject's eyeline. This, he insisted, showed that the trance was a *physiological* reaction.

This still left much unaccounted for, however; and Braid had to resort to some rather desperate rationalisations to keep accusations of 'occultism' at bay. When, for example, he found subjects who could describe the shape of an object held some distance behind their backs, he was forced to argue that their additional sensitivity in the trance state enabled them to *feel* the object – even when not touching it – much as they could feel heat. This was too much for orthodox scientists; and although Braid's new term for the trance state caught on, hypnotism continued to be experimented with only by a handful of researchers, who were still seeking a way to surmount the establishment's objections.

The Society for Psychical Research, which was founded in Britain in 1882, set up a committee to investigate hypnosis that continued to exist until a few years ago. Its findings, however, were not easily communicated to the general public and the phenomena it showed to be genuine were remarkable enough to

maintain hypnotism's occult reputation, in spite of the society's careful, objective and scholarly approach.

In the 1880s and 1890s, serious hypnotists were plagued by amateurs who would entrance psychic subjects into hysterical states, bringing criticism from scientific quarters that hypnosis could be applied only to superstitious hysterics.

At Nancy, France, Professor Hippolyte Bernheim had been experimenting with the use of hypnosis to treat patients at the local hospital, and he was able to show that whatever else the patients who entered the induced trance state might be, they certainly were not hysterics. They were ordinary people, suffering from a range of everyday symptoms that hypnosis could often banish.

But the potential value of hypnosis continued to be ignored and only gradually, in the first half of this century, has opinion been changing. At first it was superficial. The British public's idea of a hypnotist came to be of a 'smoothie' playing the music hall circuit, but such entertainment was stopped by law because of fears about what might happen to hypnotised members of the audience if they were not brought out of their trances. However, in the second half of the 20th century, hypnotism has begun to attract more serious attention, for a variety of reasons.

A great deal of interest in the subject was aroused in 1976 by the BBC-TV programme on the Bloxham tapes, presented by Magnus Magnusson. It had long been accepted that hypnotised subjects could be regressed to, say, their fifth birthday – and that in their trance state they could remember details of their life that they had long forgotten. But the hypnotist, Arnall Bloxham, had found that he could regress some subjects to what appeared to be past lives; and sometimes their accounts were historically accurate.

The best-known demonstration that such a memory could be accurate came in the case of Jane Evans, who when regressed became Rebecca, a 12th-century Jewess who had lived in York. Her description of the Jewish massacre there, besides sounding terrifyingly real, contained a description of a church with a crypt. The church was identified from her description; disappointingly it had no crypt. Or so it was thought; but some months later a workman undertaking repairs found a crypt, answering exactly to her description.

More lives than one? (published in 1976) by Jeffrey Iverson, the producer of the television programme, set out the evidence from the Bloxham tapes; and further confirmation of the power of regression to turn up information about the past is given in Peter Moss's *Encounters with the past* (1979), featuring the work in this field of hypnotherapist Joe Keeton. The evidence is not yet clear-cut. It is comparatively rare to find cases where what is

Hypnotherapist Joe Keeton (top) has conducted more than 8000 regressions. One of his subjects, Ann Dowling (above), went back over 100 years and became Sarah Williams, who lived in Liverpool in the 1850s. Among the many bizarre but accurate facts recalled by Mrs Dowling was the visit to the city of Swedish singer Jenny Lind (below)

described can be checked and found entirely accurate; when this does happen, sceptics are apt to say that the regressed subject must have found the right books and read all about it in advance. But there are now so many reasonably convincing case histories that such scepticism is becoming hard to sustain.

There are two main theories about regression. One is that it is evidence that people have lived previous lives. Many of those regressed not only assume another personality, but they can describe details from the past that often prove to be so historically accurate that it seems they lived through the experiences described. An example of this is shown by one of Joe Keeton's subjects, Ann Dowling, an ordinary housewife who, during over 60 hours of regression, became Sarah Williams, an orphan living a life of utter squalor in a Liverpool slum in the first half of the 19th century.

When asked what was happening in Liverpool in 1850, Ann Dowling mentioned the visit of a foreign singer whose name had 'summat to do wi' a bird'. Research showed that Jenny Lind, the 'Swedish Nightingale', sang for two nights in Liverpool's Philharmonic Hall in 1850.

The second theory, however, suggests that when people are regressed their subconscious mind creates a persona and living action – much like a dream – that perhaps draws from the knowledge, reading and experience of the person. The personality might also be moulded by the approach, questions and suggestions of the hypnotist. There are many cases of regression containing historical inaccuracies or glaring factual errors. For instance, one person was regressed to the early 1830s and when asked who ruled England replied 'Queen Victoria', although four more years of William IV's reign had still to run.

The method employed in hypnotic regression is simple. After hypnotising the subject, the operator takes him back step by step to the beginning of his present life, then into the womb, and then instructs him to go back and back until he comes to some experience that he can describe. This is sometimes an 'existence' in the intermission between death ending a former life and birth beginning the present, sometimes experience of the former life itself, the period and circumstances of which the hypnotist can elicit by careful questioning.

The process is not merely used for interest's sake or to prove reincarnation – it can be therapeutic. Neuroses and other psychological disorders may be caused by traumas, the existence of which has been caused by shocks or other experiences in childhood or youth apparently too horrible for the conscious mind to face. To cure the neurosis, the trauma must be discovered and faced by the patient, and hypnosis is one technique able to dig it out.

In fact, there is a long established tradition of medical hypnosis called hypnotherapy. The story of hypnotherapy is perhaps the most disturbing, as well as one of the saddest, in the history of medicine. It has offered the human race what is potentially an immensely valuable therapeutic weapon that has never been properly exploited – and is still neglected, in spite of the evidence in its favour.

Many famous hypnotists used the method as an anaesthetic throughout the 19th century; but despite several medical investigations, hypnotism was still ignored. Doctors such as Bernheim, professor of medicine at Nancy, used hypnotherapy to great effect.

A committee appointed by the British Medical Association went to Nancy and returned in

1892 to report that Bernheim's methods worked. Hypnotherapy, they could confirm, would be an asset in Britain. Their verdict was ignored. By the turn of the century hypnotherapy had faded out of the picture. It was not repudiated, the French psychiatrist Pierre Janet was later to recall; it simply fell into disuse.

Why? Unquestionably the main reason was that in this period the theory established itself that physical, 'organic' diseases could be treated successfully only by physical means – drugs or surgery. Hynotherapy might be all right for people suffering from neuroses or hysteria, but not for people suffering from coughs and colds, let alone from more serious disorders. So although a few individual doctors continued to use it, along with dentists who found it useful when patients reacted badly to 'jabs', little was heard of hypnotherapy for half a century.

The first reminder of just how unwise the British medical profession was to ignore hypnotherapy came in the *British Medical Journal* in 1952: a report on the case of a boy suffering from congenital ichthyosis – a condition that caused a warty layer, which gave off a foul odour, to cover most of his body. After all the standard forms of treatment had failed, he had been taken to the hospital at East Grinstead in Surrey, where remarkable feats of plastic surgery had been achieved during the Second World War, to see if skin from parts of his body that were unaffected could be grafted to replace the affected areas; but that was equally ineffective.

One of the doctors at the hospital suggested that, as a last resort, they should try hypnotism. The boy was put into a trance and told that the condition of his left arm would clear (they decided to proceed in this way so that if the warty layer disappeared only from his arm, it would be related to the suggestion, and could not be dismissed as coincidence). After a few days the scaly layer on the arm softened, and fell off, showing that the skin underneath was normal in texture. And in time the condition later disappeared altogether.

Not merely was the 'rhino boy' – as press reports called him – healed; he was able to return to live the full social life that his appearance (and repulsive smell) had denied him.

It would be gratifying to be able to record that this case caused a change of heart in the medical establishment. It has made no perceptible difference. The fact is that most doctors have for so long been conditioned to assume that organic diseases can be treated only by organic methods that they cannot think in any other terms.

So what does hypnotherapy positively achieve?

There are many different answers to this question; but for simplicity, hypnotherapy can be divided into two main categories. It can be used simply as a means of getting rid of un-

wanted symptoms, in particular pain. In this capacity it is on a par with chemical analgesics such as aspirin and, although rapport has to be established first between therapist and patient, which takes time (and not all patients are susceptible), there are no adverse side effects, and no prescription charges.

Most hypnotherapists, however, regard their work as a branch of psychotherapy and they use hypnosis as an aid to the treatment of, among other conditions, burns, migraine, asthma and impotence

In the last 10 years dramatic research into a form of hypnosis called biofeedback has proved especially fruitful. These investigations have shown how individuals can control many bodily functions – heartbeat, blood pressure, gastric secretions – by auto-suggestion: self-hypnosis.

In fact, auto-suggestion can do much more. Individuals like the American Jack Schwartz

Above: Dr A. A. Liébeault (standing left), one of the most influential hypnotherapists, seen with staff and patients at his clinic in Nancy, France, in 1900

Below: a group consents to take part in an extremely effective cure for insomnia: they were plunged into a hypnotically induced sleep by Jacquy Nuguet for a record 10 days in Nice, France, in 1976

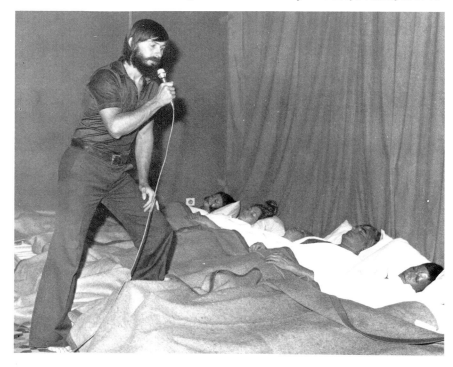

have demonstrated how they can control bleeding, staunching the blood flow as if by turning off a tap. Much the simplest way to remove warts and other skin blemishes is by suggestion under hypnosis. It can also be a help in curing allergies and in stopping smoking (though good hypnotherapists emphasise that they can only help those who want to help themselves).

The distinguished Australian psychiatrist Ainslie Meares and Americans Carl and Stephanie Simonton have shown how hypnosis and auto-hypnosis can be used to help terminal cancer patients, not merely by enabling them to control pain, but also by giving them a welcome distraction from their worries. In some cases this has prolonged survival; in a few, x-rays have revealed actual regression of tumours. No false hopes are raised of miracle cures, as has so often happened with other forms of cancer treatment. Patients are told that it is how they react to their own voyages of discovery in altered states of consciousness that counts. Some experts, however, have suggested that the power of auto-suggestion can account for many well-attested 'miracles' of healing, which sceptics have always tended to dismiss as superstitious fairy tales.

Outside the medical field, too, the possibilities of hypnosis are just beginning to be appreciated, particularly by sportsmen. Laboratory trials had shown for years that hypnotised subjects could do better at mental and physical tasks than in their normal state of consciousness, before it began to dawn on sportsmen that they might take advantage of the opportunity. In *The master key to success at golf* the British professional S. L. King, one of the most respected teachers of the game, described an experiment in which a journalist was given a hypnotic session in which it was impressed upon him that after a lesson from King, he would go out and play golf the way King showed him; and he did, playing perfect golf. Unknown to him, however, while he was deep in his trance he had also been told he would

play four of the last nine holes the way he would normally. Again, he did so, making a monumental mess of them.

Since then, many sportsmen have taken to having sessions with a hypnotist in which they are given post-hypnotic suggestion: that is, they are told they will come out of their trance but, in a sense, go back into it when they are involved in whatever game it is they play. The English fast bowler, Bob Willis, has been one beneficiary – though his later cricket career suggests that the benefit cannot be indefinitely extended. Others have been Roslaine Few, the champion high-jumper of the early 1970s; and Arthur Ashe, the American tennis champion.

Another intriguing development is the use of hypnosis for police work. This was originally tried out in California, as a way of getting more – or more precise – information from witnesses of crimes or accidents. It was found that a witness who had no recollection of an important car registration number might, when regressed to the time and place of the incident, be able to provide the number.

Police reluctance to use so 'suspect' a method as hypnotism has delayed its widespread use; but periodically it has been used with striking success, as in the case of an Israeli girl who had been mugged and raped. She had no conscious recollection of her attacker; but under hypnosis she was able to provide sufficiently accurate details for the police to be able to identify him.

It is open to speculation how well Western society will harness the power of hypnosis, and although the nature of it remains unexplained, it is clear from the research that altered states of consciousness can provide fascinating insights into the human mind as well as enabling us to heal our own minds and bodies.

Far left: a French caricature of 'le magnetisme' dated 1826. Hypnosis was widely regarded as a charlatan's trick or the sort of parlour game bored people might play after dinner

Bottom: a student of the biofeedback technique monitors his physiological state before attempting to change it deliberately

Hypnosis and crime

The value of hypnosis in police work has never been widely recognised, and in the United States in the late 1970s a bizarre case brought the use of the technique in crime detection seriously into question.

In five months from September 1977, the so-called 'Hillside Strangler' claimed the lives of 10 young women in Los Angeles: all were raped and strangled; some were subjected to torture. The murders stopped, suddenly, in February 1978, leaving the police with no clues.

In 1979, a 27-year-old security guard named Kenneth Bianchi was arrested in connection with the murder of two young women in Washington state, near the Canadian border. Bianchi denied any involvement with the crime, and the police could make little of a case against him. However, investigation revealed that in 1977 he had lived in Los Angeles, near two of the Strangler's victims.

In the face of relentless questioning Bianchi insisted that he had had no part in any of the crimes. Psychologists and psychiatrists, called in to assess his state of mind, eventually tried hypnosis. And, astonishingly, a separate personality emerged: a violent man called Steve who confessed to many of the murders.

Bianchi was diagnosed insane: 'a clear-cut multiple personality', said one professor of psychiatry, Dr John Watkins. The police, however, disagreed. 'Kenneth Bianchi is as cold a killer as I have met,' said Sergeant Dudley Varney of the Los Angeles Police Department; 'the psychological defence is a bunch of hooey.'

Such totally differing opinions were hard to reconcile, until the involvement of Dr Martin Orne, professor of psychiatry and psychology at the University of Pennsylvania. For he was able to show that Kenneth Bianchi had been lying, that he had merely *pretended* to be hypnotised. When Bianchi was in his waking state, Orne nonchalantly mentioned to him that genuine multiple personality cases usually displayed at least three different personas. When Bianchi was next hypnotised, a third personality suddenly appeared. Later, using video-tape, Orne convincingly showed that Bianchi's behaviour under hypnosis was calculated and contrived. Police further discovered that he owned many books on multiple person-

ality. But how were the experts so easily fooled? As Dr Orne himself put it:

Being a therapist is rather different from being merely a diagnostician. A therapist, of course, diagnoses. But usually there isn't much riding on it – it is simply the adoption of a strategy for treatment.

A second point is that, in therapy the patient is virtually always co-operative – he is sick and in need of help and he knows it. And this means that psychiatrists who are therapists have no experience of lying.

The point in the case of the Hillside Strangler was that he was clever and had a considerable vested interest in being diagnosed insane – it would absolve him of responsibility; it would be his way of beating the system. It was, I think, an unusual situation – and inevitably there was a certain . . . gullibility.

Above: defence lawyer Dean Brett with a bizarre two-faced skull made by Bianchi when he was at school. Is this an early manifestation of his disturbance?

Below: listening to the evidence at his trial, the prisoner is near to tears

The healing touch

The growing recognition that the power of the mind is such that it can influence, even control, the functions of the body is one of the most important developments in the history of healing.

Yet primitive, tribal communities have always realised that if 'mind' includes the emotions then miracles can happen – through 'mind' power alone. A standard method of tribal healing is to put the sick person into a trance, which frequently culminates in convulsions. In this uninhibited state the subject can release his repressed feelings and tensions – 'let out the unclean spirits'. In most cases, it seems to work.

In fact, Christ's own method of healing relied to a certain extent on the same 'shock-release' principle, although judging by the Gospel accounts he had no need to induce trances. His approach was simple, even blunt. 'Take up thy bed and walk' – spoken with what one must assume was considerable authority – shocked the victims of paralysis so profoundly that their 'useless' limbs were literally galvanised into action. Sick people were shown in the most immediate way that they could, after all, exercise control over their bodies. All they needed was a powerful enough stimulus.

Frequently the exhortation to rise from their sick beds was prefixed by the phrase 'thy sins are forgiven thee', an enormously potent reinforcement in the 'shock' healing method. Exorcism also followed this pattern (and still does), as did 'stroking', the secular version of the Church's 'laying on of hands'. Whereas Christians assume that there is a divine force, manifested through the Holy Spirit, that can restore health by casting out unclean spirits, believers in 'stroking' relied on a belief that it was some kind of magnetic 'fluid' that worked the miracle.

The Roman Catholic tradition of healing is undoubtedly the greatest repository of claims for divine healing in the modern world, and healings that have apparently taken place within that tradition have given their title to those claimed in many others. Thus, the oddest and most unlikely healings are given the general title of 'miracles'.

Many of the followers of Sathya Sai Baba, the Indian mystic who is widely respected in both the West and East, regard him as being a manifestation of God in this age. But even if we ignore such extreme claims, Sai Baba has impressed those who have witnessed his 'miracles'.

His most spectacular healings have been two cases where he is said to have brought the dead back to life; of the two, the most widely

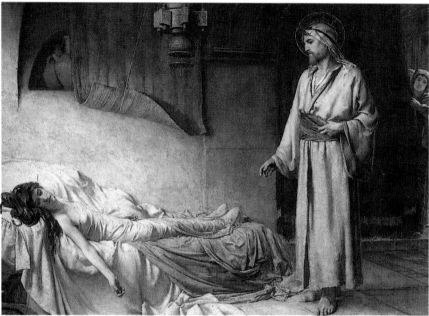

reported was his raising of V. Radhakrishna, aged 60, at an ashram at Puttaparti. There was no question in this case that the man was dead, for he had already begun to decompose when Sai Baba raised him to life, three days after being pronounced dead by doctors.

This is as direct an example of a miracle cure as one can expect to find; it is either true or not. If it is false then many people have been duped. But Sai Baba's record of producing other miraculous phenomena – such as 'apporting' hot food or 'sacred ash' – makes even raising from the dead more credible. Yet, as with many of Christ's miracles, there seems to be an obvious question left unanswered – if Sai Baba was able to revive the man from the dead, why did he permit him to die in the first place? What possible benefit could three days of widowhood have for the man's wife? Does it become more of a self-promoting trick than a miracle in this context? The glib theological answers – that God's purpose is subtle but sure and that miracles make us 'glorify the Lord' – do not seem to help much.

Certainly more straightforward and much

The healing miracles of Jesus were the most common manifestation of what Christians believe to be his divine power, as the son of God

Top: Christ heals the paralytic at Capernaum with the words 'Take up thy bed and walk' – a blunt command that, some say, activated the man's own powers of healing

Above: the raising of Jairus's daughter. Christ's miracle cures were usually accompanied by thought-provoking statements; in this case, 'the maid is not dead, but sleepeth' has been taken to mean that the girl was in a coma, but could also indicate that Christ did not see death as irreversible

simpler in their motivation were the miraculous cures associated with Linda Martel, a hydrocephalic child who spent her short life in Guernsey, dying aged five in 1961. At the time of her death the media were full of stories about her supposed cures, but gradually her name has faded into comparative obscurity, being remembered only by her family and – presumably – by those whom she cured.

During her few years Linda, who also suffered from spina bifida and whose legs were paralysed, showed herself to be very advanced intellectually, and often her most perceptive remarks were deeply religious; she would, for example, speak of '*my* Jesus Christ' with a conviction that seemed to smack of experience, yet her family was not particularly religious, and unlikely to have inculcated such an attitude in her. And, like other leading healers, she seemed to have had some power of diagnosis, as well as that of healing; but such a small child is highly unlikely to have learned the skill of diagnosis in the conventional way, as might an adult. Her healing was occasionally direct, but more often affected by the sufferer touching an item of clothing that

Right: the 'miracle healer', five-year-old Linda Martel, being treated by faith healer Harry Edwards. Although she died in 1961, she is still credited with healing powers – as are her clothes and even her grave

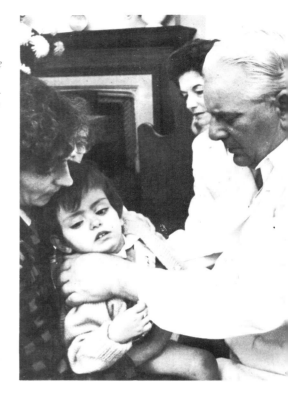

Below: Hindu healer and mystic Sai Baba, whose miracles are so incredible they invite disbelief. The witnesses who have come forward to testify to his astonishing powers often have impeccable credentials and include government officials, scientists and religious leaders

Linda had worn. Such healings are reported to have occurred both before and after her death, and the illnesses and problems cured are said to have included a spinal injury, haemorrhoids, eczema, warts, cartilage trouble, and cancer of the throat. And a multitude of such cures were claimed in the years following her death.

In the case of Linda Martel, one must conclude either that those who claimed to have been cured with her direct or indirect help were deceived or deceiving – or that the cures were genuine. Healing by the power of the mind – by faith – no doubt accounted for a great many of the claims: cures were even attributed to her grave. But if the claims regarding the curing of spinal injuries or cancer are genuine, then we must start considering what 'miracle' means in this context. Could such a small and helpless child have the power to heal of herself, and to impart that power in some way to the clothes she wore, or was some external power working through her, so that those who associated themselves with her simple and naïve faith in Christ could benefit from his legendary healing powers? It is not an easy case to assess, but at least we do not have the suggestion of self-promotion that springs to mind in the cases connected with Sai Baba.

There is something compelling about some of the claims made for Linda Martel, despite the lack of verifiable evidence. And there may have been genuine miracles in a few of these cases. Yet there is an American case, of some fame, in which there is both photographic evidence and abundant personal testimony that, though it fits the definition 'miracle', and undoubtedly concerns cures of a kind, many still find absurd and unacceptable. This case

Left: an artist's impression of one of the 18 visions experienced by Bernadette Soubirous at Lourdes in 1858. The identity of the figure was by no means certain until the local priest told the peasant girl that she must have seen the Virgin Mary

concerns the healing ministry of Willard Fuller, a former Baptist minister with a marked evangelistic style.

Initially, he healed all kinds of ailments, but one day a man whose ulcer he had cured came to him and said: 'Preacher, I have one cavity in a tooth back here. I believe that if God can heal an ulcer, He can fix this cavity for me. Will you lay hands on me and pray for me for the meeting of my dental needs?' Fuller did so, and the tooth was, apparently, 'miraculously' filled. To quote the American healer and writer Bryce Bond in *Alpha* magazine:

Those who have seen a filling gradually form describe it as a small bright spot which becomes larger until it fills the whole cavity, like the speeded-up picture of a rose blooming. Porcelain fillings are common occurrences and are of particular interest because they form fast enough for witnesses to watch the growth, but slow enough to give many people a chance to witness at first-hand what is happening. . . . Today, conservatively, there are some 25,000 people in America who have evidence of this 'miracle in the mouth'.

Further, the minister of a church where Fuller appeared in 1967 reported: 'Right before our eyes, teeth have been filled with gold, silver and porcelain – not just one night but every night. Over 200 people have experienced this miracle in two weeks. Last night one man received seven silver and two gold fillings. This is done in such a way that there can be no doubt.'

To most people the very mention of miracle cures brings to mind the shrine at Lourdes in France, scene of some of the most famous healing miracles of the 19th and 20th centuries.

Lourdes was an obscure village until 11 February 1958, when an uneducated peasant girl, Bernadette Soubirous, saw a vision of a young woman, who quickly became known as the Virgin Mary. There were 18 visions altogether: during the ninth, the apparition ordered Bernadette to scrabble in the muddy earth, where she found a spring. It is the water of this spring – and the belief that the Virgin herself caused it to flow – that attracts the hordes of pilgrims to Lourdes, and creates their fervent belief in the healing power of the shrine.

Of the many thousands of alleged cures at Lourdes, the Roman Catholic Church recognises only the few that its rigorous medical tests allow as genuine. Since 1858 only 65 cures have been recognised as being miraculous in origin.

Below: psychic dentist Willard Fuller shines his torch into a patient's mouth to examine his new 'miracle' fillings. One of Fuller's most amazing stories concerns a woman who had no teeth of her own but whose false ones were loose. Immediately after Fuller's treatment, her plate felt better, but several days later it was so tight it did not fit at all. It soon became clear that the woman was cutting a whole new set of teeth, which were fully formed after only 17 days

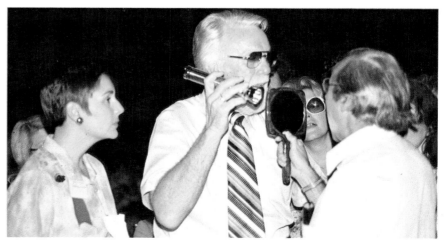

If one assumes that a true 'miracle cure' is brought about by the direct, conscious intervention of some non-human power, it is, of course, impossible to prove which cures are miraculous and which are not. Some cures are so spectacular and so sudden that even in this sophisticated age the only source would seem to be divine.

The only alternative explanation is that the human capacity for self-healing is infinitely more effective than we have imagined – and that faith, whether it causes visions or is the result of them, is the trigger that releases this astonishing power within us. Many healers recognise this, whatever they claim as the source of their healing powers.

For example, the gifted psychic Matthew Manning, who has now turned his powers to healing, considers that a genuine will to improve on the part of the patient, or an attitude of unquestioning belief, as with children, is

Above: Matthew Manning concentrates on influencing the enzyme monoamine oxidase which, if inefficient, can cause migraine – in an experiment at Birkbeck College, London. Professor John Hasted, who supervised the experiment, is convinced that Manning effectively altered the structure of the enzyme – although this is still contested by other scientists. Manning is said also to have partially destroyed cancer cells in similar experiments in the USA

Left: in an Anglia television programme, The Healers *(January 1982), Manning worked with two patients. One showed no improvement, but the other, a woman with an agonising hip-joint infection, was completely freed from her pain, and remained so even though her doctor had admitted nothing more could be done for her*

likely to encourage the healing process.

Manning's career in healing began in 1977 with a lengthy series of tests carried out in the United States. Dr William Braud, who supervised some of the tests, announced in the *Journal* of the Society for Psychical Research (December 1979) that 'Matthew Manning was able to exert significant psychokinetic influences upon a variety of biological systems.' In other words, it had been demonstrated under controlled conditions that mind can influence *living* matter to a significant degree.

A very important feature of Manning's laboratory experiments was that the more interested he was in the individual test, the better the results were likely to be. This was most evident when he attempted potentially the most important task of all – the destruction of cancer cells.

Working with Dr John Kmetz, of the Science Unlimited Research Foundation in San Antonio, Manning was apparently able to do this, either by laying his hands on the flask containing the cells or at a distance with no physical contact at all. In 30 experiments he achieved positive results 27 times, once increasing the cell death rate compared to the control sample by a staggering 1200 per cent.

Manning now has an enormous international practice in three continents, and reckons that he has managed to bring relief, partial or total, to about three quarters of the several thousand people who have gone to him. What exactly does he do?

Healing, he insists, does not come from him, but through him. 'I am merely a channel,' he says, though he believes that he makes himself a better channel by using what he sees as the healer's most powerful tool – visualisation. The successful healer, he says, must not only want to help somebody and believe he can, but actually learn to *expect* results by 'seeing' what he wants happening. The more vivid the visualisation, the better the cure.

Manning has frequently tackled cases considered incurable by orthodox doctors. In Switzerland, he brought immediate benefit to a six-year-old autistic child, Simon Acherman, and completely cured Claude Fontana, aged eight, of a malfunctioning bladder. There is also evidence indicating that he brought about the total disappearance of a malignant stomach tumour for patient Heinz Suter, and a noticeable improvement in the condition of a French victim of multiple sclerosis.

The healer John Cain also seems to have the ability to effect cures when all else has failed.

Mary Price, from Neath in South Wales, suffered from osteo-arthritis, a bowel disorder, stomach ulcers and a respiratory problem. In August 1979 she underwent a week of treatment by Cain – and afterwards allegedly no longer needed to take pain killers or use her wheelchair.

One feature of Cain's treatment is that during it his patients go into an altered state of consciousness. In very few cases, however, is there a complete blackout; people generally experience instead a deep relaxation and other sensations such as floating or a dream-like detachment, remaining aware of what is happening to them throughout. Depending on the nature of their problem, they may find themselves moving their limbs in ways they cannot control or simply enjoying a profound sense of peace that they have never felt before.

Those who move while in the altered state of consciousness have found themselves doing things that are impossible for them during full consciousness. Valerie Wooding, one of Cain's patients who suffers from multiple sclerosis, says she has 'frequently exercised in ways which I never considered within my capabilities – yoga, ballet, judo, even head stands. . . . I am fully conscious of what my body is doing – almost as if I am observing it – but I am also aware of the reasons for it.'

She is convinced that these exercises have a beneficial effect and are a vital part of the healing she is receiving through Cain. They ensure that muscles that would otherwise atrophy receive exercise and so regain their strength. There are non-physical benefits, too. Valerie Wooding says, 'it also increases my optimism, giving me confidence in my own physical ability, knowing that my body can allow, and survive, such apparently extreme exertion.'

As well as being able to induce an altered state of consciousness in his patients himself, Cain found that the same effect could be produced by his photograph alone. This has happened even with people who have no idea of the picture's unusual properties, as the publisher of two books about Cain can verify. A visitor from another publishing house promptly slumped back in his chair in a state of deep relaxation after looking at Cain's picture. The

Above: one of John Cain's public healing sessions. To cope with the large numbers of patients, Cain uses a team of helpers – many of whom he has healed – to whom he can transfer his abilities

Below: Cain heals a child. He has been known to cure cancer and multiple sclerosis

photograph is just one way in which Cain can reach people beyond his physical presence. Dealing personally with all the requests for help became increasingly difficult, but Cain found another solution to the problem.

Up to a hundred people have been known to visit his home each day, while several hundred attend the public sessions. While he usually gives personal attention to everyone present, there is a limit to the amount of time he can spend with each person. So, both at his home and at the public demonstrations, he uses a band of selected helpers, most of whom are ex-patients, to act as proxy healers. 'All I need do is give my consent for healing to work through others and it will happen,' says Cain. 'But they've got to get their egos out of the way.' For his part, one of his helpers says, 'I link up mentally with John. That's the only way I can explain it.'

Explanations for what Cain does have been sought by a number of researchers, but so far they have drawn a blank. Cain himself says that he doesn't know really how it works, only that it does. He believes he is helped by 'spirit guides', but prefers not to be dogmatic. Clearly, what Cain is doing affects the consciousness of his patients at a profound level and triggers off therapeutic processes that other forms of treatment have failed to reach. That, as far as his patients are concerned, is enough.

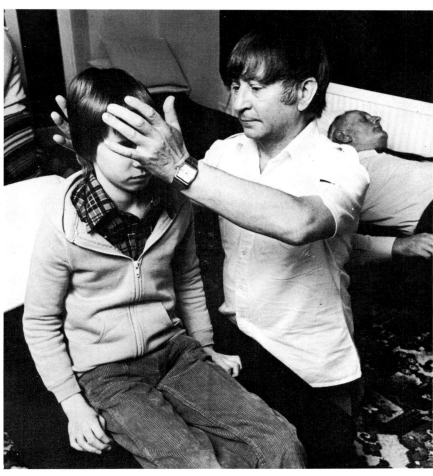

Of all forms of healing, that which has become known as psychic surgery is perhaps the most extraordinary. Since the 1950s there have been many reports of events, allegedly witnessed by scores of observers and undergone by thousands of willing patients, of bare-handed surgery – dramatic and incontrovertible evidence, it has seemed to many people, that the impossible occurs under the scrutiny of experienced investigators and scientists. There is, remarkably, nothing furtive about the practice: it can be seen taking place in broad daylight. Here at last, many people were convinced, was the real thing, a paranormal effect that was not only genuine, but could be produced to order in any circumstances.

Despite these extravagant claims, however, psychic surgery is now regarded by many people as no more than a shabby deception – or, more kindly, if patronisingly, as the product of primitive and superstitious cultures. Its history seems to have followed a now familiar pattern: it looked good at first, but its credibility was whittled away by the criticism that was levelled at it until it seemed there was nothing left to believe.

And yet there is, perhaps, another way of looking at the phenomenon. Like many debunking exercises, the ostensibly impartial efforts to get to the bottom of the whole business of psychic surgery leave a great deal of awkward evidence out of the picture – just as, of course, some of those who made excessive claims for the validity of the phenomenon have also been guilty of ignoring the facts that did not fit their case.

Psychic surgery, reported in testimonies and on film, seemed impressive. Investigators assured Western scientists that uneducated, medically ignorant men and women daily performed miraculous cures by carrying out what, for all the world, looked like real operations, using their bare hands and sometimes a pair of scissors or a kitchen knife. Despite the thoroughly unhygienic conditions, there was no evidence of infection or damaging after effects.

Great interest was aroused by the Brazilian José Pedro de Freitas, better known by his

nickname, Arigo (yokel). Until his death in 1971, he carried out thousands of crude operations using a rusty knife and other equally unsuitable implements that, nonetheless, brought about spectacular results. Later, under the threat of legal action, he restricted himself to diagnosis and prescriptions written after a mere glance at the patient, again with amazing results.

However, it is the more numerous healers of the Philippines who have attracted the greatest attention. They carry out what appear to be real operations using only their hands to open bodies and pull out diseased tissue and offending matter. It was in the mid 1960s that the interest of Western investigators was first stimulated by tales of their extraordinary performances. But after a while controversy centred on the Filipinos. What they were doing, the critics argued, was not carrying out operations at all. They were simply conning patients and onlookers into accepting a cleverly staged deception as real.

The evidence started to stack up heavily against the psychic surgeons. The cries of fraud grew louder as teams of investigators began to return, not with the glowing accounts of miraculous recoveries of the early days, but with evidence of shabby deceit and exploitation.

In the early 1970s, debunking articles appeared in the German press and on television. In Britain in 1975, Granada Television screened its own damning investigative programmes on psychic surgery, and these were followed in 1979 by the BBC *Nationwide*

Below: Michel Carayon, a Frenchman who learned psychic surgery in the Philippines, carries out an operation at his Paris clinic, leaving no trace of a scar (far right). He does not claim that the matter he 'removes' from patients (below, far right) originates inside their bodies – but his success rate is allegedly high

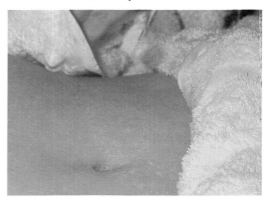

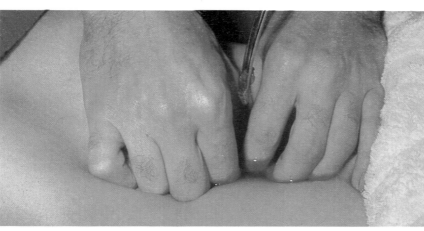

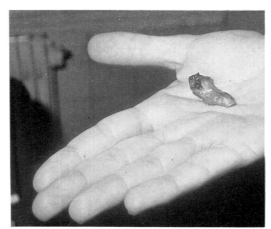

programme's exposé of the Elizaldes, a husband-and-wife team who visited the UK to treat people. Yet again, what had looked like a promising, repeatable demonstration of paranormal powers in action was subjected to the same kind of demolition as many other claims made in the past.

But can the case really be said to be closed? Some are convinced that there is nothing more to be said about psychic surgery. It is simply a case of gullible observers being taken in by impressive but, in the end, identifiable sleight of hand. Is this really all there is to it?

The biologist, writer and researcher Lyall Watson was one of several investigators who went to the Philippines to discover what psychic surgery was all about. During three separate visits occupying eight months in all, he witnessed over one thousand operations performed by 22 different healers. He was impressed, and remained so despite the controversy that had already begun to detract from the credibility of earlier accounts of the Filipinos' powers.

Watson went as a scientist to carry out an unbiased investigation of the healers, and *The Romeo error* (1976) gives an account of what he found. There is a blow-by-blow account of a typical operation lasting about five minutes that, as far as Watson is concerned, was a genuine demonstration of psychic surgery.

The subject of the operation was a middle-aged woman who complained of a nagging pain in the stomach. She was asked to lie down on a wooden table, fully dressed; her abdomen

was bared and her skirt covered with a towel. Like a true sceptic, Watson examined the towel for anything that might be concealed within it: 'I find it innocent, if none too clean.' The healer, dressed in cotton trousers and a short-sleeved shirt, entered and showed Watson he was concealing nothing in the folds of his clothes.

The healer said a prayer. Watson handed him some cotton wool and a bowl that he had himself filled with water from an ordinary tap,

Below: Andrija Puharich, investigator of the paranormal, undergoing ear surgery at the hands of Mexican healer Pachita. It seemed to him that the knife was plunged into his ear canal and probably penetrated the eardrum; the pain was intense, yet he was able to tolerate it

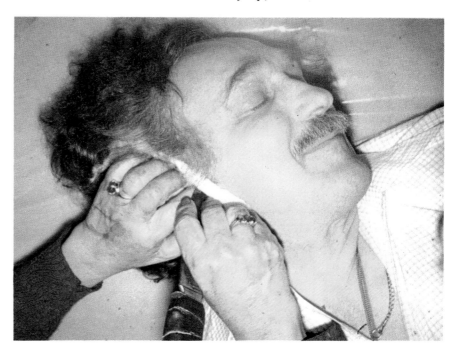

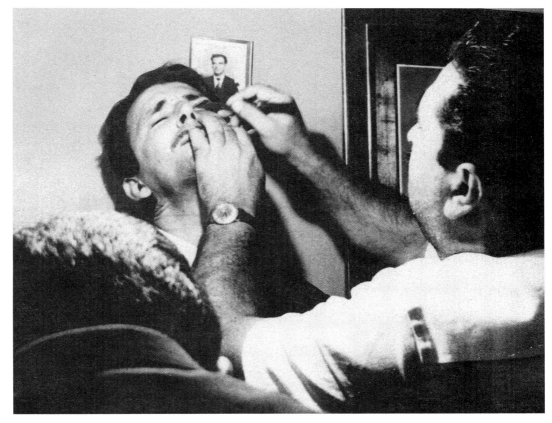

Right: José Arigo performs a delicate eye operation in his back parlour. Although it is the medium who goes into a trance, the patient feels no pain – nor, it seems, any fear, despite the unhygienic surroundings, primitive lighting and the complete lack of anaesthetics

British journalist Anne Dooley undergoing psychic surgery by the Brazilian Lourival de Freitas. Dooley travelled to Brazil in 1966 for an operation to improve a chronic lung condition

Above: Lourival makes a razor incision for the planned lung operation

Right: the healer shows the patient the clot he has removed

and the healer used them to cleanse the woman's abdomen:

> He is now working just to the right of her navel, and suddenly there is a red colour. It could be blood. At first it is watery, mixing with the moisture on her skin, but now it darkens and gurgles quite strongly up between his fingers. . . . I can see what looks like connective tissue, thin, almost transparent, obviously elastic, red and bloody.

The healer appeared to push his hands deep into the patient's body. Pressing hard, he spread the fingers of his right hand, and a large ball, apparently of the patient's flesh, began to grow between the first and second fingers. When, in a matter of seconds, it had reached the size of a tennis ball, an assistant reached over with a pair of forceps and lifted the lump clear of the patient's abdomen. He snipped away at the thread of tissue still connecting the cyst to the patient's body until it came clear,

and dropped it into Watson's hand. Watson commented, 'It is warm and when I press it, only a little blood oozes out. It seems to be hard inside.'

After the healer had finished his work and the remainder of the blood had been wiped off the patient's stomach, there was, astonishingly, no visible wound. 'I rub my hand over her skin,' says Watson. 'It is hot, but there is nothing on it, not a mark of any kind.' The woman got up slowly and walked away.

Lyall Watson's conclusion is that there is something behind the claims, although he does not pretend to have fathomed the secrets of psychic surgery.

The visit to the UK in 1978 of the Elizaldes, a husband-and-wife team practising psychic surgery, roused considerable interest because it appeared to offer scientists an opportunity to study the phenomenon closely at first hand. Perhaps, at last, they would be able to find a definitive answer to the many questions that the reports of psychic surgery had raised.

David and Helen Elizalde's visit was sponsored by the Spiritualists' National Union (SNU). Although they live in Australia, David Elizalde is Filipino by birth and his wife is English of Cypriot parentage. They claim to be able to penetrate the human body with their hands, in the same way as the native Filipino psychic surgeons, leaving the patient's body unblemished and free from scars. After the visit there were several testimonies to the effectiveness of their work, including reports of cures and improvements.

In 1979 they returned to give treatment to the sick at the SNU's headquarters at Stansted Hall, Essex. The operations were carried out in conditions screened from public gaze. Was this precaution simply designed to make for better operating conditions? Or was it designed to keep out the prying eyes of critical observers? Suspicions that this might have been so were strengthened by the forthright and scathing condemnation made by BBC-TV's *Nationwide* programme in May 1979.

The *Nationwide* evidence was made up of several elements: a film of the Elizaldes at work, and a critical commentary on it by the arch-sceptic and conjurer James Randi, interviews with patients and forensic reports on some of the blood and other substances produced during the operations.

While the *Nationwide* film looked impressive at first sight, Randi was able to point out, in a frame-by-frame analysis, that what was going on was almost certainly faked. He pointed to a number of sequences that, he maintained, were standard sleight-of-hand tricks. The surgeons did not have their fingers buried deeply inside their patients, but simply folded them, pressing down on the flesh with their knuckles. This is all very well – but where does the blood and gore come from? It was obvious to Randi. He showed how they could have been 'palmed' during the operation by the non-operating partner, who was ostensibly there simply to pass swabs and lend assistance to the other. Randi claimed that at one stage David Elizalde held his hand 'exactly as a conjurer would if he had concealed something in his hand'. He was able to give a fair imitation of a bare-hand operation incorporating the ploys he had noted on the film.

The case for fraud was reinforced by forensic tests carried out on samples of blood retrieved from an operation on Gordon Higginson, then president of the SNU. Unknown to the psychic surgeons, members of the *Nationwide* team were present incognito, and assisted during the operation. One of them held the bowl into which bloodstained cotton wool and blood clots were dropped. Analysis at a forensic laboratory showed that it was pig's blood. Blood-spattered clothing belonging to Higginson and another patient was also tested, and the same finding was made. Confronted by the evidence, Higginson simply refused to accept the report. 'I think that this is just put up. I think they [the forensic experts] are telling an untruth. I know that it is genuine.' Helen Elizalde had another line. 'Well, I think it is very strange, although I have heard that the structure of the blood does change.'

Despite the allegations of fraud, however, there were still a number of people who came forward to vouch for the benefit that they received. But if we accept this evidence for the moment, does it mean that psychic surgery may still be a reality? Perhaps.

Doctors know the value of suggestion. A persuasive bedside manner has always been suspected to be a powerful force in promoting improvement in the condition of patients. Formal confirmation by medical science of the placebo effect – the fact that, with enough faith in their doctors, patients will improve markedly even if they are administered sugar pills instead of real drugs – showed that there was definitely something in this belief. Confidence in the treatment and an expectation of results can be enough for physical changes to occur. Could the performance of a sham operation, with impressive blood-and-gore props, have the same effect? It seems quite possible that it could. In this case, the psychic surgeon would be manipulating the patient's propensity to believe in the authenticity of the psychic operation to bring about improvements. Of course, the psychic surgeon would have to protest the authenticity of his operation for the mind cure to work.

Alfred Stelter, a German researcher who made his own on-the-spot study of various psychic surgeons, thoroughly investigated the contradictory evidence that has been advanced to support and demolish the claims for their authenticity. His book *Psi-healing* contains many examples of failures or partial successes of psychic surgery, along with remarkable cures. There are also several telling case studies of attempts to investigate psychic surgery in which the evidence has been loaded in the final report to fit the conclusion that the authors want to reach. Like Lyall Watson, Stelter concludes that psychic surgeons do sometimes work 'miracles'. In his view, further research into psychic surgery will 'lead to a new spiritual and scientific territory tending to revolutionise our whole picture of man'.

Stelter's is a challenging conclusion that clashes with the more brutal findings of investigations such as *Nationwide*'s of the Elizaldes. It is certainly far more difficult to grasp than the bold accusation that the psychic surgeons were no more than liars and frauds who set out to exploit the sick in an unscrupulously heartless way. There is no simple answer that resolves all the facts and, despite the desire for neatly packaged, definitive solutions to mysteries such as this one, perhaps there never can be.

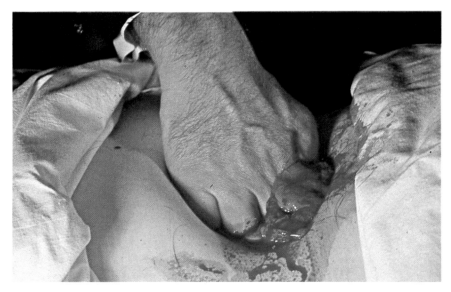

The attitude of the Christian Church to psychic surgery is ambivalent. In Brazil, where it seems that much psychic surgery is practised successfully, the Catholic Church is sceptical. Father Quevedo, the Jesuit director of the University of Parapsychology in São Paolo, has produced these photographs, with the aid of a model (left and below), to show how easy it is to fake pictures of psychic surgery

Mind over matter

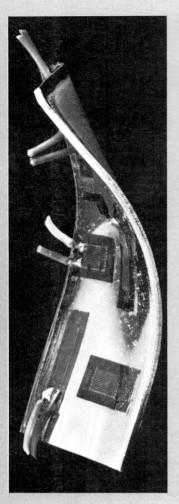

One of the most common and widely researched forms of mind power is psychokinesis (PK) – the ability of the mind to transform, affect or move physical matter. In recent years, PK has been studied by many serious, objective scientists, and the great advantage of investigating psychokinesis is that because the phenomenon produces a physical result scientific experimentation can control, measure and observe it in action. One of the most controversial and well-publicised forms of PK is metal bending.

Accounts of inexplicable contortions of metal objects date back at least to the 18th century, when pins were found twisted into 'a vast variety of fantastic figures' during a poltergeist case, while in 1879 victims of an American case reported that spoons 'suddenly twisted out of shape' in their hands. But it was not until 1972, with the arrival of Uri Geller on the international scene, that paranormal or psychokinetic metal bending (PKMB) became a field of study in its own right.

Over the next four years Geller took part in supervised experiments in 17 different laboratories. Dr George Owen of the New Horizons Research Foundation in Toronto pronounced his abilities as 'paranormal and totally genuine', while Eldon Byrd of the US Navy research centre in Maryland stated that Geller had bent metal under observation 'in a way that cannot be duplicated'. Five professional magicians testified that, despite allegations to the contrary by their colleague James Randi, whatever Geller was doing, it was not conventional stage magic.

After Geller's first television appearance in Britain in 1973, an epidemic of PKMB broke out in homes over the whole country, especially affecting young children and teenagers. For some it was a new game soon forgotten (as annoyed parents ran out of usable cutlery), while other children were encouraged to work at it. In 1974, 18-year-old Matthew Manning, then coming to the end of his period as a poltergeist victim, put on a spectacular display of PKMB in front of 21 scientists, including Nobel Laureate Professor Brian Josephson, and enabled psychiatrist Dr Joel Whitton to identify a hitherto unknown brainwave pattern linked to paranormal activity.

But the first scientist to commit himself to a thorough and long-term enquiry into PKMB was Professor J. B. Hasted, head of the physics department of Birkbeck College, London, who carried out a series of tests with several young subjects, both in his laboratory and in the children's homes. Although in the course of his investigations he introduced more rigidly conventional methodology, he soon realised that successful PKMB depends on many other, more subtle factors: for example, the psychological atmosphere in the laboratory was crucial, the state of mind of both subject and experimenter being a decisive factor. Metal benders, he discovered, had to be treated as

Top left: a metal bar fitted with strain gauges and then bent paranormally in Professor Hasted's London laboratory. A chart recorder was also attached to the metal and, to eliminate the possibility of trickery, the subjects were not allowed to touch the bar. It still bent, showing stress signals unlike those produced when attempts were made to bend it manually

Left: paperclips dropped into this glass ball were – under laboratory conditions – paranormally 'scrunched' into a fantastic shape by one of Professor Hasted's metal bending subjects

colleagues rather than as guinea-pigs. In an article he co-authored in *Nature* (10 April 1975), he declared that 'psychokinetic phenomena cannot in general be produced unless all who participate are in a relaxed state.' PKMB was, he assumed, a function of the unconscious mind, and too much conscious effort would upset the process, as would an atmosphere of tension, scepticism or hostility. The PKMB researcher should, he argued, adopt the attitude of a physiotherapist encouraging a patient to regain the use of a damaged limb, rather than telling him it could not be done.

The possibility of trickery had to be eliminated, and to this end Hasted devised experiments in which the metal object was attached to a strain gauge and a chart recorder. And (most important) the subject was not allowed to touch the metal at all. Three of his young colleagues were soon able to produce stress signals on the chart paper under these conditions, signals quite unlike those produced when metal is bent by normal physical force.

Next, Hasted set his subjects a series of 'impossible' tasks, such as the 'scrunching' together of straightened paperclips inside a glass sphere and the bending of alloy strips that snap rather than bend under normal stresses. Again, the young subjects responded to these challenges, producing a number of remarkable scrunches, while one managed to deform four strips of 'unbendable' alloy merely by leaving them, untouched, in his coat pocket for five minutes. By December 1976, Hasted was able to state categorically, in the *Journal* of the Society for Psychical Research (SPR): 'I therefore report my belief that I have been able to validate the metal-bending phenomenon on a number of occasions by visual witnessing,

chart-recording, "impossible" tasks and the bending of brittle metals.'

The following year, in the same journal, he described a series of 13 tests held with 17-year-old Nicholas Williams, the highlight of which was the chart recording of simultaneous strain signals from three different keys hanging from wires, and even from two metal objects 10 yards (9 metres) apart on different floors of the building. Eventually, Hasted was able to add some sequences of videotape to his evidence, in which metal objects can be seen bending without being touched. The PKMB phenomenon had, it seemed, been well and truly validated.

It had also been repeated in several other countries, under the supervision of qualified

Above: Uri Geller with David Dimbleby, experimenting with a key. There was a huge response to Geller's appearance on BBC-TV's David Dimbleby Talk-in *on the evening of 23 November 1973*

Below: Professor John Hasted checking equipment in his laboratory

Bottom left: Mark Shelley, aged 7, bent a spoon and fork after seeing Uri Geller on television in October 1973

researchers. At the Péchiney Laboratory in France, metallurgists Professor Charles Crussard and Dr Jean Bouvaist published a detailed report on the abilities of Jean Pierre Girard, the most thoroughly studied of all metal benders. They found that he could induce both anomalous hardening and softening in metal in a manner impossible to explain in terms of conventional metallurgy.

Girard, who was born in 1942, developed numerous psychic abilities shortly after being struck by lightning as a child. He made his début as a metal bender in 1975, in response to a radio appeal from Dr William Wolkowski for people with psi abilities to come forward. He successfully distorted a number of metal samples, including a steel spring, sealed inside

glass tubes under Wolkowski's supervision. In one of his most dramatic demonstrations of PKMB, he bent a 3-inch (8-centimetre) screw inside a plastic tube held by Swedish physicist Dr Georg Wikman in about 15 seconds, with-

out touching either the screw or the tube.

In West Germany, Professor Hans Bender of the University of Freiburg studied Girard with the co-operation of William Cox – well-known parapsychologist and magician – and a cameraman, and became one of the first to record PKMB on film. Girard produced more than 10 distinct bends under close scrutiny, but in fairly informal conditions. (Two French magicians, Ranky and André Sanlaville, have testified that his effects are not produced by

Left: Uri Geller bending a key with his mind, as he did so often publicly with household objects like this spoon (right). His frequent broadcasts brought metal bending into many homes. George Porter (far left) bent these objects by PK while listening to Geller on the Jimmy Young Show *on* BBC *radio in 1974*

conventional sleight of hand.) By 1977, Girard had demonstrated his abilities in front of at least 16 scientists.

As the evidence from laboratories all over the world mounted up, support came from theoretical physicists who found that not only was 'action at a distance' permitted according to the laws of quantum physics, but it could actually be predicted. At a conference on 'Frontiers of Physics' held in Iceland in 1977 it became clear, amid talk of 'collapsing wave

Above: while in a trance, SORRAT *member Joseph Mangini touches a metal table gently, causing it to rise*

Below: Dr J. T. Richards (in the striped shirt) and other members of SORRAT *make a light metal table levitate*

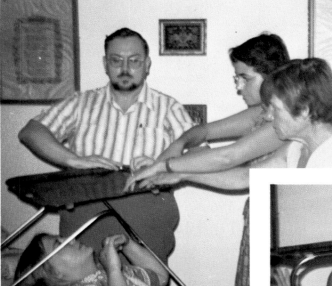

functions', 'intrinsic time symmetry' and 'additivity of partial amplitudes', that the human mind had been willingly accepted as a potential influence on physical processes. PKMB had become almost respectable.

The phenomenon has also come to the attention of psychiatrists, and in a lengthy study of young metal benders and their families, Dr Robert Cantor found that most youngsters had other paranormal abilities, from telepathy and clairvoyance to healing. Some of them had

also seen tiny lights moving around them, and heard high-pitched whistles. Others reported experiencing headaches while concentrating on bending metal (as did some of their investigators), plus tingling sensations in the arms and face. Cantor also found that PKMB seemed to have no harmful effects, and actually served to increase the children's self-confidence.

Belinda H. was only six when she responded to Uri Geller's invitation to bend metal during the transmission of BBC-TV's *Blue Peter* programme. She deformed a spoon through 40° in less than a minute, and later bent an 'unbendable' crystal in the presence of Professor Hasted. However, Belinda was more interested in healing. When she was only three years old she had spontaneously tried to cure her ailing grandmother, and on three other occasions she satisfied both her parents that she had been able to relieve severe pain by placing her hands on the affected parts of their bodies.

PKMB has repeatedly been demonstrated to be a fact, and scientists have begun to respond to the challenge it offers. A solution to the age-old mystery of how our minds interact with matter is much nearer than it was when Uri Geller came to public attention in 1972. Jean Pierre Girard feels that PKMB is an evolutionary mechanism necessary for Man's survival that science cannot afford to overlook. From the apparently useless ability to bend spoons there may develop enormously far-reaching effects on the world.

In fact, scientific tests designed to discover more about psychokinesis have been on the increase in America and Britain during the last two decades. One of the most sustained projects began in Rolla, Missouri, USA, in October 1961 with the formation of the Society for Research into Rapport and Telekinesis

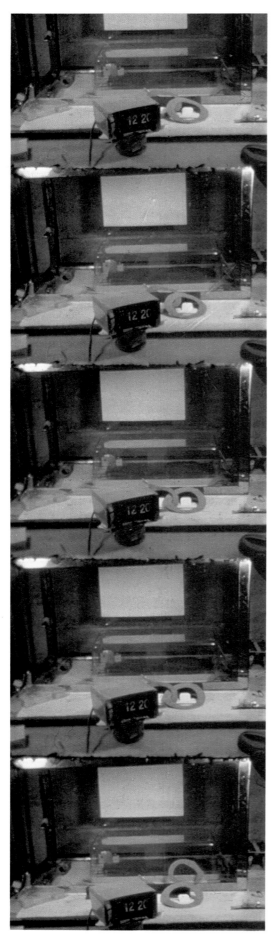

(SORRAT). This group is probably the USA's most successful producer of long-term, large-scale PK (called 'macro-PK' by parapsychologists).

SORRAT was founded by John G. Neihardt, professor of English literature at the University of Missouri at Columbia. A powerful, charismatic personality and a man of wide interests, he had been fascinated by the paranormal for many years. He was intrigued by the way those people with strong spiritualist beliefs or with a mystical background seemed to attract PK. Neihardt himself was a close friend of the Sioux Indian holy man Black Elk, and as a result was made an honorary member of the Oglala Sioux tribe.

This kind of belief may have helped the SORRAT group achieve their remarkable evidence of macro-PK; certainly some of its members were known to possess outstanding psychic gifts. The group, meeting every Friday night at Professor Neihardt's home, Skyrim Farm, Missouri, grew very close over the 16 years they were together. Originally there were 30 members, but the 'regulars' consisted of 15 to 20 of the more strongly motivated.

The techniques used by SORRAT to induce psychokinetic events were similar to those used by many Spiritualist development circles. Essentially they simply sat around in a group in a carefree and light-hearted manner while waiting for PK to occur. One member of the group, Mr Joseph Mangini, developed the ability to go into a trance – and then PK phenomena were often particularly strong. After meetings had continued for only two months it was found that areas of seemingly paranormal coldness would develop around small target objects laid out on a table top. Thermometers placed near these objects registered a drop of up to 5° in the normal room temperature. And a few months later paranormal rapping began.

The group's PK effects became so strong that by late 1965 a small oak table was successfully levitated. Encouraged, they then actually levitated a much more massive table weighing 82 pounds (37 kilograms). Then switching to a light metal tray as their PK target, they managed to levitate it without even touching it.

The SORRAT scrapbooks, kept by Dr J. T. Richards, the group's archivist and photographer, contain many photographs of a host of other objects being affected by psychokinetic forces.

Next, the group decided to develop a fraud-proof device inside which PK could take place, therefore providing stronger evidence of the phenomenon. A locked box of some sort seemed the obvious answer – in other words a miniature PK laboratory, or minilab.

The prototype minilab, constructed by Professor Neihardt, was a huge glass container, but effects in it were very rare and limited. Experienced parapsychologist

Above: the locked and sealed minilab in the basement of Dr J. T. Richards's home in Rolla, Missouri. A die has moved – apparently of its own volition – leaving a white trail where it has ploughed through a layer of coffee grounds on the floor of the minilab, exposing the white wood beneath. An unidentified white object has also levitated above the raised tin in the centre

Left: consecutive frames from one of the Rolla 'home movies' showing the paranormal linking of two seamless leather rings outside the minilab

Below: W. E. Cox with some metal objects that bent while secured in the minilab. The aluminium bar was bent 11 degrees. The round white object is what remained of a plastic thermometer after it melted while in the minilab. The spoon bent after being sealed in the minilab by a locksmith – who swore that the lock remained secure

Above: this sealed bottle acted as a kind of minilab. Various objects were placed in it: pipecleaners, a pencil stub, a piece of paper and a safety pin. Acted upon by PK the pipecleaners became the 'man' who wrote 'freedom, love, faith' on the paper with the pencil stub

William Cox adapted the idea, making smaller versions out of shallow wooden boxes, which were later called coffee boxes because in the experiments a layer of dried coffee grounds would usually be spread on the box floor. The joints of each box and the seal on its glass lid were constructed in such a way that the box could not be opened without disturbing the special markers that had been incorporated into the joints when they were made.

For the experiments, a variety of objects would be placed in the box, and a layer of coffee grounds would be spread on the box floor. Then the agency would be set a specific task. For example, one task consisted of moving one of a pair of dice through the coffee grounds, while leaving the other where it was. The task was specifically devised to prevent the effects being achieved simply by the box tilting – deliberately or accidentally – which would have made both dice move. This particular test was often successful, sometimes providing the added bonus of the moving die leaving a broken trail, as if it had hopped across the coffee grounds. The only conclusion was that the die had actually levitated from place to place.

The SORRAT group's outstanding success in inducing psychokinesis led William Cox to install a further minilab at their headquarters in 1977. This consisted of a perspex box of

about one cubic foot (0.03 cubic metres) volume, which was secured to a stout wooden base by steel strips and two padlocks. Cox put various 'toys' inside it for the PK agency to play with. Several minor PK effects happened while the box was at Skyrim Farm, the most outstanding of which was the apparently paranormal arrival of pieces of old Indian beaded leather inside the securely locked and sealed perspex minilab.

The minilab was then transferred to the home of Dr J. T. Richards in Rolla, Missouri, On one particularly dramatic occasion the minilab contained clean paper, a pencil, dried peas dyed white and blue, a small glass, leather rings firmly attached to a point inside the box, a set of six spools strung on a wire with twisted ends, and miscellaneous other small objects.

Several friends of Dr Richards who were interested in psychic matters had met at his house and gathered around the minilab, which was on a coffee table in the sitting room. They turned out the light and waited. Suddenly they heard noises from inside the box; PK activity was taking place. Cox was telephoned and he arrived at the house in time to hear what he construed as the dried peas jumping about inside the minilab. Then there was silence and the light was turned on again. On investigation, the group discovered that the locks were still secure, but some surprising changes had taken place inside the box. One of the six spools was missing and the ring of wire on which they had been strung had had its ends re-twisted differently. Thirty blue peas had apparently jumped into the glass, two straight pipecleaners were now twisted into linked rings and the leather rings had been dislodged.

Shortly before this, Cox set up ciné camera facilities so that any PK inside the second and third minilabs could be filmed while it was happening. Target objects for PK action were linked to special switches so that whenever an object moved the switch was triggered. The switches were wired to a timing device that in turn automatically switched on two lights and triggered a ciné camera to shoot a 30-second sequence of film showing whatever was happening inside the locked minilab.

The first filmed events were obtained in May 1979 and showed a levitating pen. Shortly afterwards further sequences were filmed of this pen engaged in 'direct writing' inside the locked and sealed minilab. Among the words written the name 'John King' was prominent, while on 4 July 1979 a pen was filmed writing the words 'Glorious Fourth' on some paper outside of, and in front of, the minilab. As with much of the direct writing, the motion of the pen was extraordinarily rapid – Cox estimates a writing speed of more than double his own. A slower example of PK from this early period is that of an aluminium film canister 'walking' inside the locked minilab. It can be seen slowly edging its way across the width of the tank,

stumbling a little over a minor obstruction near the middle.

It was in May 1979 that Cox unexpectedly obtained hard evidence of teleportation connected with the minilab. On the floor of the basement he found a green felt-tipped pen that he knew he had safely locked inside the minilab the night before.

Sceptics have felt, not surprisingly, that these experiments offer the tempting possibility of fraud. But if one wanted to assume that the minilab PK events were fraudulent, two questions would have to be asked: who is

Bottom: the first British minilab, designed and built by Julian Isaacs at Aston University, Birmingham

Above: the second British minilab, designed mainly to detect metal bending

Top left: 'Peter', who was first to test a minilab in Britain, seen with some of the metal he has bent

doing the cheating – and how? Given Cox's background of more than 30 years' PK research and a few years' successful work with minilabs it seems most unlikely that he would have failed to detect any fraud perpetrated by others in the group. Cox's record also speaks powerfully against his being in collusion with others.

Shifting their ground, sceptics might point out that the objects inside the minilabs could be manipulated with fine threads or by film animation, but judging by the evidence of all film shot it becomes obvious that the activity in the minilabs was too complex and coordinated to be produced in these ways.

The amazing PK effects produced in the first American minilabs were the result of 16 years' regular meetings of the SORRAT group, but when the British minilab programme began in 1980 it was hoped to obtain PK almost immediately. The idea was to use subjects who had already experienced PK in their lives *before* taking part in the experiment.

Parapsychologist Julian Isaacs based the programme on an assumption that seems, at first sight, startling to say the least. This was that at least some people were experiencing teleportation (the paranormal disappearance and reappearance of objects) sporadically and spontaneously in their everyday lives. This form of 'domestic PK' (paranormal happenings in the home) often goes unnoticed or is discounted because it is 'impossible'. Even gifted psychics usually tend to ignore odd disappearances or reappearances as 'silly' and meaningless because there is no rational explanation for them. It is only if events become overwhelming (such as in poltergeist cases) or if the person experiencing them is familiar with the concept of teleportation that the phenomenon tends to be acknowledged. And for the less psychic the chances of recognising it are even slimmer.

After seeing the SORRAT film and discussing

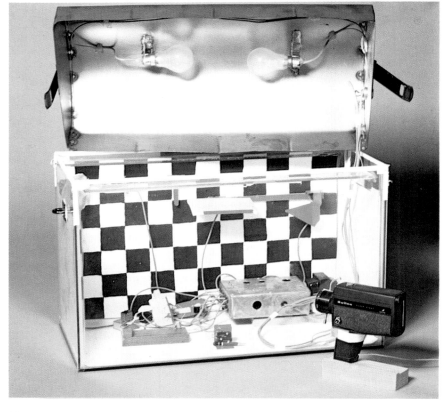

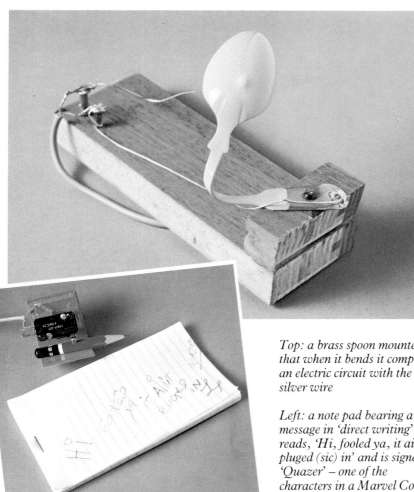

record is kept of which items are in the box and their position. The boxes and their contents are inspected every few days. The objects may move around inside the boxes or may even teleport from one box to the other.

By mid 1980 the first British minilab was in the home of 'Peter', a former poltergeist focus, in the Midlands. His exuberant and spontaneous PK had started after he discovered his very powerful metal bending ability. Besides this, Peter had apparently generated a large number of telekinetic and teleportation events. He achieved a limited success with his minilab. Although by late 1981 his powers had declined, he did generate some authentically paranormal metal bending inside the minilab, the tank itself was seen shaking and moving from place to place and in one incident a calculator was teleported round the living room.

So now that we have these case histories and experimental data are we any nearer to an understanding of what causes psychokinesis to happen? Although there are no straight answers the experimenters suggest that Spiritualists, or any others to whom the idea appeals, make contact with any spirits they believe will help and ask them to assist the minilab programme by causing PK. Requests for specific PK effects can be written down and the messages left near the target objects as they were at Rolla, along with pens, pencils and paper for any 'direct writing' replies. But if the idea of 'spirits' is too implausible appeals can be made in the same way to one's own subconscious, for it is generally accepted by parapsychologists that the subconscious often acts separately from the conscious mind. But if the subconscious is invoked it must be addressed as if it were a separate entity, for it will act only if kept dissociated from one's consciousness.

The PK phenomenon is yet another reminder of the hidden powers of the mind; perhaps it is a more visible version of our everyday desire to have our wishes fulfilled. Faith, as the saying goes, can move mountains. Psychokinesis is perhaps just one small example that proves the phrase, while reminding us of the mysterious forces that appear to lie deep within all of us.

Top: a brass spoon mounted so that when it bends it completes an electric circuit with the silver wire

Left: a note pad bearing a message in 'direct writing'. It reads, 'Hi, fooled ya, it ain't pluged (sic) in' and is signed 'Quazer' – one of the characters in a Marvel Comic read by Peter, who produced the minilab PK. The message refers to the fact that the minilab that had been installed in Peter's home was set up, but not plugged in, nor was the lid secured

Bottom: two yellow-painted aluminium strips, mounted in a U shape so that when bent by PK they press down a microswitch that activates a camera

the events filmed with William Cox and Dr J. T. Richards, Isaacs set out to achieve similar effects – but much faster – by choosing his subjects carefully. The British minilab programme began, therefore, with a series of three lectures given to a selected audience in the English Midlands in May 1980. It consisted entirely of convinced Spiritualists. They were to be screened as potential minilab agents because they already accept the existence of psi, are often psychically gifted and practised – and they are more likely to experience and recognise teleportation than others.

In the British project, the preparatory minilab experiments, which are very simple and nontechnical, are described on a set of information sheets; these are given to anyone who reports frequent teleportation and who is interested in controlling the phenomenon. Target objects – preferably ones that have been acted upon by PK before – are put in specific places and a written log is kept recording their movements, including any disappearances and reappearances; this effectively sidesteps faulty memory. The objects are checked every few days.

The next step involves the use of two shoeboxes as 'coffee boxes' set up in the same manner as those used in the US experiments. A

Levitation

Three notable members of London society witnessed, on 16 December 1868, an incident so extraordinary that it is still the focus of controversy. Viscount Adare, the Master of Lindsay and Captain Wynne saw the famous medium Daniel Dunglas Home rise into the air and float out of one window in a large house in fashionable London and then float in at another – over 80 feet (24 metres) from the ground it is claimed. D. D. Home became known primarily for his levitations, of himself and of objects – on one occasion a grand piano – but he was not alone in having this 'impossible' ability to defy the law of gravity.

St Joseph of Copertino (1603–1663) flew into the air every time he was emotionally excited. Being of an excitable nature, he often made levitations, and they were well witnessed by a surgeon, at least two cardinals and one pope (Urban VIII).

Most levitators are believers in one particular system, be it Christianity, Hindu mysticism, ancient Egyptian mysteries or Spiritualism. It was to this last category that D. D. Home belonged.

Born in Scotland and brought up in America, Home was a puny, artistic child. At the age of 13 he had a vision of a friend, Edwin. Home announced to his aunt's family that it must mean that Edwin had been dead for three days. This was proved to be true. Home's career as a medium had begun – but it was not until he was 19 that he was to defy the law of gravity.

Ward Cheney, a prosperous silk-manufacturer, held a seance at his home in Connecticut in August 1852. Home was there to keep the guests entertained with the usual Spiritualist manifestations such as table-turning and rappings, but something happened, completely unannounced, that made his name overnight. He floated up into the air until his head was touching the ceiling. After this Home's career advanced rapidly; he was lionised in seance parlour and royal court alike. He came back to Europe to inspire adoration and scepticism (Robert Browning's satirical poem 'Mr Sludge' was based on his own biased view of the medium). Wherever he went there were bizarre phenomena – winds howled in still rooms, apports of fresh flowers fell from the ceiling, doors opened and shut, fireballs zigzagged around the room – and Home levitated.

The famous occasion already mentioned when he floated out of one window and in through another, is still the subject of heated debate, particularly since the incident was documented by respectable witnesses. Sceptics tried to disprove this levitation, although none of them was among the witnesses. Some implied that Home's levitations were nothing

Above: medium and psychic Daniel Dunglas Home (1833–1886) was primarily famous for his spectacular levitations, but his talents also included incombustibility, bodily elongation and the manifestation of apports

Right: a levitation performance carried out by an Indian yogi, Subbayah Pullavar, before a large number of witnesses. The photograph was taken by the Englishman P. Y. Plunkett and a friend, and published in the Illustrated London News. *Here the yogi is shown at the height of his levitation, grasping the cloth-wrapped stick which he holds throughout the performance. The relaxed position of the hand on the post suggests that the body of the yogi was indeed very nearly weightless during the performance. Afterwards, his body was so stiff that five men could not bend his limbs*

more than hallucinations produced by his hypnotic suggestion, rather in the same manner that the Indian rope trick is said to be a mass hallucination, the secret being in the magician's patter.

But even in the face of extreme hostility, Home remained a successful levitator for over 40 years. Among his witnesses were Emperor Napoleon III, John Ruskin and Bulwer Lytton – and many hundreds more. Moreover during that long span of time and mostly in broad daylight, Home was never proved to be a fraud.

Although in his mature years Home could levitate at will, he apparently also levitated without being aware of it. On one occasion, when his host drew his attention to the fact that he was hovering above the cushions of his armchair, Home seemed most surprised.

When we examine the phenomenon of levitation, it is clear that one of two things must be happening: either the levitators do not rise into the air at all (that is, witnesses suffer a mass hallucination) or they rise aided by invisible machinery.

Of course, Home and other Spiritualists would also attribute their feats of apportation or levitation to 'invisible machinery' – but in their case the machinery would be the agency of spirits.

And yet we do not refer in this spiritualistic way to the 'unseen power' that keeps us *on* the floor. Every schoolboy knows about Newton and his discovery of the law of gravity. But psychical research points to the relative ease with which certain sensitives can turn this law on its head.

In her book *Mystère et magique en Tibet* (1931), Madame Alexandra David-Neel, the French explorer who spent 14 years in and around Tibet, told how she came upon a naked man, weighed down with heavy chains. His companion explained to her that his mystical training had made his body so light that, unless he wore iron chains, he would float away.

A unique series of photographs appeared in the magazine *Illustrated London News* on 6 June 1936. They showed the successive stages in the levitation of an Indian *yogi*, Subbayah Pullavar – thus proving that, whatever else it was, this phenomenon was not a hypnotic illusion.

A European witness of the event, P. Y. Plunkett, sets the scene:

> The time was about 12.30 p.m. and the sun directly above us so that shadows played no part in the performance. . . . Standing quietly by was Subbayah Pullavar, the performer, with long hair, a drooping moustache and a wild look in his eye. He salaamed to us and stood chatting for a while. He had been practising this particular branch of yoga for nearly 20 years (as had past generations of his family). We asked permission to

take photographs of the performance and he gave it willingly. . . .

Plunkett gathered together about 150 witnesses while the performer began his ritual preparations. Water was poured around the tent in which the act of levitation was to take place; leather-soled shoes were banned inside the circle, and the performer entered the tent alone. Some minutes later helpers removed the tent and there, inside the circle, was the fakir, floating on the air.

Plunkett and another witness came forward to investigate: the fakir was suspended in the air about a yard from the ground. Although he held on to a cloth-covered stick, this seemed to be for purposes of balance only – not for support. Plunkett and his friend examined the space around and under Subbayah Pullavar, and found it innocent of any strings or other 'invisible' apparatus. The yogi was in a trance and many witnesses believed that he had indisputably levitated, although it has been suggested that he had, in fact, merely passed into a cataleptic trance. The famous photographs were taken from various angles during the four minutes of the performance, and then the tent was re-erected around the fakir. Evidently the 'descent' was something very private, but Plunkett managed to witness it through the thin tent walls:

After about a minute he appeared to sway and then very slowly began to descend, still in a horizontal position. He took about five minutes to move from the top of the stick to the ground, a distance of about three feet [1 metre] . . . When Subbayah was back on the ground his assistants carried him over to where we were sitting and asked if we would try to bend his limbs. Even with assistance we were unable to do so.

Ridicule has long been poured on the notion that people can free themselves from the force of gravity: this cartoon (left), entitled 'The Day's Folly', was published by Sergent in 1783. Alexandra David-Neel (below), however, came back from 14 years in Tibet with no doubt that adepts could achieve weightlessness

The yogi was rubbed and splashed with cold water for a further five minutes before he came out of his trance and regained full use of his limbs.

The swaying motion and horizontal position that Plunkett witnessed seem to be essential to true levitation. Students of transcendental meditation (TM) are taught, under the supervision of the Maharishi Mahesh Yogi at his headquarters in Switzerland, to levitate. One student described this 'impossible' achievement:

People would rock gently, then more and more, and then start lifting off into the air. You should really be in a lotus position to do it – you can hurt yourself landing if you've got a dangling undercarriage. To begin with it's like the Wright brothers' first flight – you come down with a bump. That's why we have to sit on foam rubber cushions. Then you learn to control it better, and it becomes totally exhilarating.

So can *anyone* induce levitation? The TM students believe they can, after a stringent mental training; the disciplines, both spiritual and physical, of the yogis seem to prepare them to defy gravity. It is fairly easy to induce a state of semi-weightlessness, as this account of a fat publican – a perfectly ordinary person – being raised in the air as a party trick shows.

The fat man sat on a chair and four people, including his small daughter, demonstrated the impossibility of lifting him with their index fingers only, placed in his armpits and the crooks of his knees. They then removed their fingers and put their hands in a pile on top of his head, taking care to interleave their hands so that no one person's two hands were touching. The four concentrated deeply for about 15 seconds; then someone gave a signal, and quickly they replaced their fingers in armpits and knees – and the fat publican floated into the air.

Sceptics might point to the intervention of non-spiritual spirits, considering the location

Far left: the Transcendental Meditation movement claims that this photograph shows students levitating. It is alleged that, under the supervision of tutors, the students achieve weightlessness through meditation

of the event, but the same phenomenon has been witnessed hundreds of times in pubs, homes, and school-yards. If it works – and one must assume it does – then how is it possible?

The sudden burst of concentration of four people with a single, 'impossible' target could, some people believe, unlock the hidden magic of the human will. Or it has been suggested that a little-known natural force, perhaps the same one that guides the dowser's rod, intervenes to achieve the miracle of nullifying the force of gravity.

Like many inexplicable phenomena, levitation seems to be singularly useless. The distance covered is rarely more than a few feet or, at the most, the height of a room – useful only for dusting or decorating the home. But some people believe that the ancients could levitate quite easily, and did so to design certain enormous earthworks that can be appreciated only from the air, such as some of the white horses of the chalk downland in England and the desert patterns in Peru.

The limitations of modern levitation need not have applied to the ancients – perhaps they had developed the art to a high degree and could soar into the sky at will. Like other psychic faculties, it appears that levitation is an art, once almost lost, that is now being re-learned, so that one day modern levitators will 'fly' as the ancients supposedly could.

With a few exceptions, it seems that one can levitate only after long periods of training and discipline: in this way, the body is mysteriously 'given permission' to defy the law of gravity. Perhaps there is a law of levitation with a secret formula – an 'Open, Sesame' – which the initiate uses before rising off the ground.

Certainly levitation is a rare phenomenon, but when considered with other accounts of equally rare and bizarre human attributes, such as incombustibility, it must be taken seriously. Perhaps we are intended to be able to defy gravity at will. Until we understand the nature of the phenomenon it must remain one of Man's mysterious hidden powers.

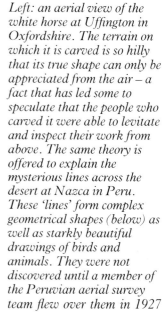

Left: an aerial view of the white horse at Uffington in Oxfordshire. The terrain on which it is carved is so hilly that its true shape can only be appreciated from the air – a fact that has led some to speculate that the people who carved it were able to levitate and inspect their work from above. The same theory is offered to explain the mysterious lines across the desert at Nazca in Peru. These 'lines' form complex geometrical shapes (below) as well as starkly beautiful drawings of birds and animals. They were not discovered until a member of the Peruvian aerial survey team flew over them in 1927

The human salamander

The belief that the blacksmith is 'Master of Fire' is common in both ancient cultures and modern primitive societies, and at various times has been current in central Europe, Asia, Africa and North and South America; a fact that lends extra interest to an extraordinary story published in the *New York Herald* of 7 September 1871.

Nathan Coker was blacksmith in Easton, Maryland, and had long held the reputation of being immune to heat. A committee of local citizens and members of the press asked if they might put him to the test, and he agreed. First, a shovel was heated in his forge until it became white-hot and incandescent. Coker 'pulled off his boots and placed the hot shovel on the soles of his feet, and kept it there until the shovel became black.'

Next, lead shot was heated until molten. Coker swilled it around his teeth and tongue like a mouthwash, until it solidified. Then Coker plunged his hands into the blazing forge and calmly picked out glowing coals, which he showed to the onlookers on the palms of his hands. Finally, he handled a piece of red-hot iron.

'It don't burn,' he told the reporter nonchalantly. 'Since I was a little boy, I've never been afraid to handle fire.'

Coker was neither a showman nor a religious fanatic. To him, the startling phenomenon was simply a fact of life.

The immunity of certain people to extreme heat – whether cultivated, as in the case of shamanist societies, for instance, or apparently fortuitous, as in the case of such individuals as Nathan Coker – has been a source of wonder and bafflement to observers of the phenomenon for centuries. The biblical story of Nebuchadnezzar's burning fiery furnace and its three intended victims Shadrach, Mesach and Abednego, for example, strikes a familiar chord when compared with modern firewalking in Trinidad or Polynesia. Plato and Virgil recorded instances of people walking unscathed on hot coals, while the annals of the Church are littered with accounts.

In 1637 the French Jesuit, Father Paul Lejeune, was very impressed – although at the same time considerably annoyed – by what he saw among the Huron Indians near Quebec. Lejeune was heading a mission to the Indians, but the tribal medicine men were in no mood to be converted and put on what appeared to be a special show for him in which they drew glowing stones from the fire, put them in their mouths and rubbed them against the bodies of the sick without any effect.

Above: Jatoo Bhai, a 'fakir' from Calcutta, dances in the midst of a blazing fire – and later emerged unscathed. As part of the 'fireproofing' process, he works himself into a state of religious ecstacy

The famous English diarist John Evelyn wrote of seeing 'Richardson the fire-eater' perform after dinner at Lady Sunderland's house in London on 8 October 1672. He reported a fantastic performance in which Richardson chewed and swallowed brimstone, ate melted glass and placed a raw oyster on a piece of flaming coal on his tongue, leaving it there until the oyster was not only hot but completely cooked.

Another celebrated 'after-dinner' performer whose feats attracted considerable attention in Victorian society was the medium and levitator Daniel Dunglas Home. Lord Adare, an army officer and war correspondent, and H. D. Jencken, a barrister, told how, at a seance in 1868, Home stirred up a glowing fire in the grate and 'placed his face right among the burning coals, moving it about as though bathing it in water'. It seems that Home could confer his immunity to onlookers too; he would hand them burning embers, yet they suffered no injury.

Even while Home was startling many establishment figures, tales of firewalking and fire-handling feats from far-flung corners of the Empire were becoming commonplace. Basil Thompson, for instance, in his *South Sea yarns*, related how he watched a group of Fijiian islanders walking over red-hot stones.

Anthropologically, it is possible to trace the activities of most fire ritual societies back to a probable central source – the Iron Age shamanists of central Asia. These, Tartars, Mongols and Yakuts, thought of fire as one of the greatest of nature's mysteries.

Over the course of centuries the knowledge and practice of firehandling filtered out from Asia during prehistoric migrations. By about 500 BC, it had spread to China, Japan and Tibet, and it was easily absorbed into the practices of Hinduism on the Indian sub-continent, where it is often mastered by *sadhus*, those who have attained *samadhi*, the eighth stage of hatha yoga.

The majority of *sadhus* seem content to remain in one place and quietly meditate. It is the more eccentric 'fakir' types who capture the popular imagination. Some of these are undoubtedly sincere, setting themselves dramatic but apparently pointless tasks in their search for holiness, such as permanently clenching their fists so that their finger nails grow into the palms of their hands. Some, on

Below: before he steps into the flames, the fakir begins by handling fire

Bottom: though often displayed in a sensational way, immunity to fire is clearly a reality

the other hand, set out on what amounts to a deliberate circus career, and it is from among these that most of the fire masters of India are drawn. To devout and sophisticated Hindus these 'showmen' are anathema, and yet the genuineness of their powers is never doubted: a contradiction that has caused a good deal of Western scepticism. It is almost as if a medieval saint were to have levitated, exhibited stigmata, and performed miracles of healing in the market place for cash.

A fakir will arrive at a village and order the trench to be prepared and filled with hot stones. He then leads the 'faithful' across. There are many accounts of Europeans having joined in the walks, and remarkably few instances of serious injury. 'The idea is,' explained one commentator, 'that the *sadhu* takes on all the pain to himself and then negates it by willpower. The stones are genuinely hot, the bodies of the walkers untreated by any artificial preparation. There seems to be no rational explanation. . . .'

Significantly, it is among the Hindu sects that the firewalkers of Polynesia, Malaya and Tahiti flourish. But the Buddhists of China, Tibet and Japan go in for almost exactly similar practices, while in Hong Kong firewalking feats are an out-and-out tourist attraction. Shintoism, the ancient worship of the Japanese, also has its firewalking devotees.

There is a strong element of showmanship about many of the voodoo rituals of the West Indies, in which fire mastery in various forms plays an important part. In Trinidad, fire-eaters and firewalkers abound, but it is in Haiti, where voodoo still forms the basis of most political, social and religious activity, that fire masters are most spectacular.

Dr William Sargant, author and psychiatrist, made Haitian voodoo the subject of close study for several years. Briefly, he came to the conclusion that most of the phenomena took place after the participants had worked themselves into a state of deep trance. Interestingly, Haitian voodoo practices can be traced back by way of the African Congo, Arab traders, Asia Minor and Persia to the Mongol and Tartar shamans.

Members of one secret society dance on live coals and drink prodigious quantities of fiery white rum into which ground cayenne pepper has been liberally poured. At one all-woman ceremony, Dr Sargant saw the participants not only consume this apparently lethal mixture without collapsing, but rub it into their open eyes without damaging their sight in any way.

The North American Indians are a Mongol race in origin; their prehistoric ancestors were nursed in the same Asiatic cradle as the Tartars, and carried shamanism and its accompanying fire mastery with them from Siberia to Alaska and from there down the American continent.

We know that mastery of fire is practised in many cultures, but exactly how it is achieved cannot yet be explained by modern science.

Andrew Lang, a prominent late-Victorian historian and anthropologist, pointed out that there was not necessarily anything 'psychical' in firewalking or firehandling, and as far as anyone knew it might well be a trick. But 'as a trick it is so old, so world-wide, that we should ascertain the *modus* of it.'

In September 1935, an attempt was made to organise a truly scientific experiment with firewalking under the aegis of the University of London. A 24-foot (7-metre) fiery trench was prepared at Carshalton, Surrey – its average temperature being 800°F (430°C). A young Indian Moslem named Kuda Bux strode across the length of the trench four times, and again was found to be free of any artificial protection. Despite the stringent tests made to guard against trickery, the onlookers included several diehard sceptics. An unnamed doctor sneered to observer Harold S. W. Chibbett that 'anyone could do it'. Invited to try, he replied that he was not suitably dressed.

In the face of the cumulative evidence, such jibes and ill-informed 'rationalisations' are meaningless: certain people, individually and in groups, do have a mysterious ability to walk on hot coals and handle burning embers without mechanical trickery being involved. But does the secret lie in a 'trickery' of the mind – perhaps using self- or mass-hypnosis?

There are several recorded instances of the officiating priest or shaman taking on the pain of the walkers himself, and in such circumstances it would appear that the officiant is able to hypnotise – or literally entrance – his followers: if the spell wears off or faith wavers, the fire resumes its power to burn.

Many of the North American Indian rituals involve preparations of dancing, chanting and either feasting or abstinence. Hindus,

Buddhists and followers of Shinto call upon their gods, saints, and ancestors. Every year on the feast days of St Constantine and St Helena, Greek villagers of Langadas perform a firewalk over hot coals while holding icons of the two saints aloft, thus ensuring themselves protection. In these cases a form of self-hypnosis seems to play a major role.

That there could be substance in the 'natural ability' explanation of fire immunity is borne out by John Evelyn's description of Richardson, the fire-eater, who made no claim to magical or spiritual powers – but could quite simply eat fire.

The sceptic's biggest stumbling block is not the immunity of the fire handler himself, but that of his clothes, which is sometimes the case. A state of trance hypnosis may well protect a person's skin, but how does one hypnotise a pair of socks and shoes?

Dr W. T. Brigham of the British Museum consented to go on a firewalk on the volcanic island of Kona in the South Seas. It was a walk with a difference, for the volcano had just erupted, and his protectors, three Kahunas or local magicians, proposed that he should stroll with them across the glowing, molten lava. First, they suggested, he should take off his boots, as they would not be covered by the magical protection. The professor hesitated, and finally the magicians pulled him onto the lava with them. He was forced to walk across 50 yards (46 metres), while the three magicians laughed heartily at the glowing scraps left behind as his boots and socks burned off. His feet – and the rest of his clothes – were completely unharmed.

After his experiments in Fiji, one noted researcher reported that neither psychical nor psychological theories alone can account for what happens in the case of fire immunity, and that some physical phenomenon takes place that is yet to be explained.

Top left: the Buddhist firewalking festival hi watari, *which is held every year at Mt Takao in Japan. The ceremony is dedicated to prayers for peace – and to the health of the onlookers, who rub their ailing parts with boards before throwing the boards on to the fire*

Top: an early 19th-century engraving showing a Thai firewalker treading a pit of red-hot stones. Only those who are born incombustible or who undergo secret rites – perhaps involving auto-hypnosis – can be exposed to intense heat with no ill effects

Above: an Indian fakir exhibits his technique of mind-over-matter by hanging over a fire

CHAPTER THREE

Creatures
of Myth and Mystery

*Mysterious man-beasts, Sea monsters,
Merfolk, Loch Ness monster, Fish falls,
Toads in rocks, Werewolves*

Mysterious man-beasts

Everyone has heard tales of the 'abominable snowman' or 'yeti' of the Himalayas, and the 'bigfoot' in North America. But sightings of these mysterious beings – 'wild men of the woods' – have been reported from all over the world: China, Australia, Africa, the wastes of Siberia and the Amazon jungle. Stories of astonishing similarity are filed regularly, not only by scientists, but more often by ordinary people who have encountered some form of human animal that bears no resemblance to anything they can identify.

Most often these sightings take place in forested mountains, jungles or wilderness areas that are rarely penetrated and could easily conceal a hitherto unidentified life form. Every continent has some areas like this, though Europe has the smallest proportion of uncivilised territory, which explains why man-beast reports are almost non-existent there. Naturally, the more remote the region, the less likely it is that stories about such encounters will get out. Conversely, the most numerous and best documented sightings come from North America, where huge unexplored regions are interspersed with media-saturated towns and cities. Encouragingly, there has been a considerable increase in the number of reports on file over the last 20 to 30 years. Although this is obviously due in part to the greater publicity, does it also mean that man-beasts are being

Background picture: a dramatic view of the Himalayas, looking down from Khumbu glacier in Nepal. These isolated mountains are the traditional home of the yeti, or abominable snowman

Insets: two stills from the only cine film ever taken of a bigfoot, at Bluff Creek, California, in 1967. Rigorous analysis has not proved the film to be a fake – but sceptics still insist that the creature is a large actor dressed in animal skins

seen more frequently? Since their habitat must gradually be shrinking as civilisation advances, it would be reasonable to expect their numbers to be declining. Perhaps it is this very pressure on living space that forces them to visit settlements for food and this might explain the increased number of reported sightings.

In 1967, the bigfoot-hunting fraternity was thoroughly shaken by the appearance of 30 feet (9 metres) of wobbly 16-millimetre colour film taken by Roger Patterson, who in October that year was riding through the remote forests of the Bluff Creek area of northern California with a friend on the lookout for signs of bigfeet. Their horses reared in fright when they suddenly came across a bigfoot, clearly female,

squatting beside a creek. Patterson leapt down, grabbed his camera and began to run after the retreating figure, filming as he went. Before the bigfoot was lost to sight among the trees, it turned to look back at the men. The famous strip of film has been analysed many times since 1967, but no one has been able to prove it a hoax.

Encounters in which the witness is able to get a long, close look at the creature are the most interesting; a perceptive and unflurried witness can add greatly to our knowledge of the creature. One of the best reports of this kind was made by William Roe, who saw a bigfoot on Mica Mountain in British Columbia in October 1955.

Roe was hidden in a bush, so the bigfoot, a female about 6 feet (1.8 metres) tall and 3 feet (1 metre) wide and weighing around 300 pounds (135 kilograms), came towards him unaware she was being watched. When the

bigfoot was 20 feet (6 metres) away, she squatted by the bush Roe was hiding in.

He later wrote a careful description of the bigfoot's head, face and hair, of the shape of her body and the way she walked. His report concludes:

Finally, the wild thing must have got my scent, for it looked directly at me through an opening in the bush. A look of amazement crossed its face. It looked so comical at that moment I had to grin. Still in a crouched position, it backed up three or four short steps, then straightened up to its full height and started to walk rapidly back the way it had come. For a moment it watched me over its shoulder as it went, not exactly afraid, but as though it wanted no contact with anything strange.

Roe considered shooting what would be a unique specimen, and even raised his rifle. But he could not fire. 'Although I have called the creature "it", I felt now that it was a human being and I knew I would never forgive myself if I killed it.'

Human or animal? The witnesses are not sure, and neither are the researchers. 'If only we had a corpse to examine,' they cry. But those who feel that the priority is to kill a bigfoot and thus prove its existence once and for all are opposed by those who feel equally strongly that the creature should be left in peace. What gives Man the right to commit murder simply to satisfy his curiosity?

In late 1968 Dr Bernard Heuvelmans, a Belgian zoologist who had long specialised in investigating mysterious animals, stumbled on an extraordinary find. Having heard reports about a curious fairground exhibit – some kind of 'hairy man' – he set out with his friend and colleague, zoologist, writer and bigfoot expert Ivan T. Sanderson, to investigate. They found the creature on the farm of a showman named Frank Hansen, who kept it inside a large freezer compartment in a caravan parked near the farmhouse.

The two visitors were astonished to find a creature completely unknown to science. They immediately set about drawing and photographing it, and making notes.

It was about 5 feet 10 inches (1.8 metres) tall, and covered in long brown hair – except for its face and its groin, which were hairless. Testicles and a narrow penis were visible, leaving no doubt about its sex at least. The creature's left arm was thrown up above its face and was obviously broken. One eye socket was empty and the eyeball of the other had been pushed out and lay on the cheekbone. The back of the head seemed to have been shattered. This was clear, bloody evidence that the creature had been shot through the head, vainly defending itself from attack with its arm. The blood was clearly visible to the scientists. They could detect, too, the distinctive

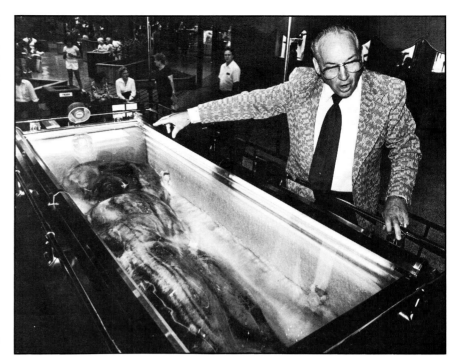

sweet smell of decomposition. On one foot, visible through the ice, they could see the grey-tinged evidence of rotting flesh. They mentioned this to Hansen, who was disturbed by the news.

The beast's torso was broad and muscular. Apart from its hairy coat, the most remarkable feature was its upturned nose, which gave it a pug-like appearance. The legs were short, and the feet were broad and flat. The big toe lay

Above: showman Frank Hansen with his 'iceman'. He tells scientists that his exhibit is a model, while hinting to the public that it is genuine. He once claimed to have shot the creature himself, while hunting in the Minnesota woods

Left: a line of footprints said to have been made by a yeti. An alternative explanation however, is that they were made by a mountain goat. The sun then melted the snow around the hoof marks, enlarging them

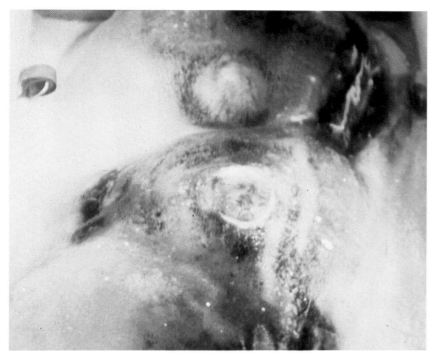

Above: the iceman was viewed by thousands of Americans every year. According to one account, it was found floating at sea, encased in a block of ice, but the body did not resemble any known living species

Far right: the creature as reconstructed from the photographs and drawings made by zoologists Ivan T. Sanderson and Bernard Heuvelmans in December 1968. The owner apparently replaced the corpse with a model, leaving only the evidence of the two scientists to prove it had ever existed

by a yeti and in 1978 Lord and Lady Hunt, revisiting Nepal to commemorate the 1953 ascent of Everest, saw and photographed large tracks in the snow around their huts.

Although less famous, the man-beast of China seems to be fairly active in some areas, particularly Hopeh and Shansi provinces – forested, mountainous country in the north.

Particularly impressive was the report made by 33-year-old Pang Gensheng, a commune leader, in June 1977. Pang was chopping wood

alongside the small second toe, as it does in human beings – there was no gap, as there is in other primates.

Heuvelmans was fascinated, and wanted the press, the public and the scientific community to take his find seriously, but all he achieved was exaggerated, sensational newspaper reporting, and when he tried to subject the 'iceman' to proper investigation, Hansen had taken it on the road again. The affair was never satisfactorily resolved.

Another report, dating from 1924, describes what, if it is true, is the most dramatic bigfoot encounter on record. Albert Ostman claims to have been kidnapped by a bigfoot and held captive for several days before he managed to escape. The kidnap took place near Toba Inlet in British Columbia, when Ostman was prospecting and camping in the mountains. An 8-foot (2.4-metre) bigfoot picked him up in his sleeping bag one night and carried him across country for what seemed to the hot and cramped captive like three hours.

It was still dark when they arrived at their destination, but when it got light Ostman saw there were four bigfeet, male and female adults and male and female children. He finally escaped by feeding the 'old man' a huge quantity of snuff and thereby incapacitating him. While the bigfoot rushed to find some water, Ostman grabbed his belongings and ran for his life.

A few similar reports have emerged from the Himalayas, traditional home of the abominable snowman, even though this is a remote part of the world. These often describe strange footprints in the snow or, less frequently, distant sightings of what is taken to be the yeti itself. In 1974, a Nepalese girl guarding a herd of yaks 14,000 feet (4250 metres) up in the mountains near Mount Everest was attacked

73

in the Taibai Mountains of central Shansi province when he saw a 'hairy man':

> It came closer and closer. I got scared and kept retreating until my back was against a stone cliff and I couldn't go any further. The hairy man came up to 7 or 8 feet [2.1 or 2.4 metres], and then to about 5 feet [1.5 metres] from me. I raised my axe, ready to fight for my life. We stood like that, neither of us moving, for more than an hour. Then I groped for a stone and threw it at him. It hit him in the chest. He uttered several howls and rubbed the spot with his left hand. Then he turned left and leaned against a tree, then walked away slowly toward the bottom of the gully. He kept making a mumbling sound.

The 'man' was about 7 feet (2.1 metres) tall, with a sloping forehead and deep-set black eyes. His jaw jutted out, and he had broad front teeth. Dark brown hair hung long and loose over his shoulders, and his body and face were covered with short hair. His long arms reached below his knees, and he walked upright with his legs wide apart.

Researchers at the Institute of Palaeoanthropology and Vertebrate Palaeontology of the Chinese Academy of Sciences have been investigating such reports, but so far have not been able to solve the riddle of the 'wild man'. Even so, it is significant that the detailed description given by Pang Gensheng is similar to those given by witnesses elsewhere in the world. And the creature's behaviour is quite typical.

Research in the Soviet Union has unearthed numerous sightings in the Caucasus Mountains (where the creature is called an 'almas') and in the Pamir Mountains, where huge footprints have been found.

Near the river Ob in Siberia, a hunter saw two 'wild men' one day in the early 1960s while he was walking with his dogs. The animals were terrified, a common feature of encounters in which dogs are involved; in America bigfeet seem to dislike dogs and have been known to injure or even kill them. The Siberian hunter noted that the wild men were covered with dark hair, had long arms and turned their feet outwards when walking. Their eyes glowed dark red – yet another characteristic that indicates a similarity with bigfeet.

In the 1920s, a chuchunaa ('outcast') was seen by villagers out berry-picking in eastern Siberia. Busily picking and eating the fruit as well, he was very tall, but otherwise quite human looking, except for his tiny, protruding forehead and large chin. The interesting feature of this sighting was that the creature was dressed in deerskin.

In America, too, bigfeet have been seen eating berries, and there have even been occasional reports of them actually wearing clothing.

Reports sometimes surface from seemingly unpromising areas. Our Western image of Japan as a small, industrial nation leaves little room for remote uninhabited country able to support a population of man-beasts. Yet in the early 1970s there were several sightings of the Hibagon (as the beast became known) on Mount Hiba near Hiroshima. Farmer Albert Kubo saw this 5-foot (1.5-metre), big-eyed, smelly creature in 1974 when he was out in his rice fields spreading fertiliser. It was standing on a path, and Mr Kubo began to approach it before he realised what it was.

He said: 'I was petrified, but the stench was what really got me. He must have bathed in a septic tank and dried off with cow dung. I nearly passed out. Luckily enough, though, I managed to turn and run before it realised

Below: this 'man-beast' was shot by Swiss geologist François de Loys on the borders of Colombia and Venezuela in 1917. It is now thought that it might have been a kind of spider monkey

Left: a footprint, allegedly of a yeti, found near the Menlung Base of the 1951 Himalayan expedition. It is regarded as the best piece of photographic evidence for the existence of the yeti

Far right: Igor Bourtsev, a Russian 'snowman' hunter, holding a cast of a footprint found on 21 August 1979 in the Gissar Range of the Pamir-Alai Mountains, Tadzhikistan, in central Asia. The footprint, believed to have been made by an almas, measures 13.5 inches (34 centimetres) long and 6.5 inches (16 centimetres) wide at the toes. It is very nearly the same size as 'yeti' footprints found in the Himalayas

I was there. I ran 5 miles [8 kilometres] straight home without ever looking back over my shoulder.' The strong smell of many North American bigfeet is often described by witnesses in equally graphic terms.

Australia has thousands of square miles of territory rarely visited by Man, as might be expected, it too has its man-beast. The Aborigines, who were apparently well aware of its existence, gave it many different names, but today it is usually called the yowie. Sightings have been regularly reported, especially in New South Wales and Queensland, since the late 18th century. One 19th-century encounter involved two men who, after shouting several warnings at a hirsute, bellowing creature, fired a bullet straight into it; it turned and fled. That the men saw no evidence of the bullet having struck its target does not necessarily mean that they missed. There is some evidence from North America that ordinary guns are useless against the hairy giants, either because they are not powerful enough, or for some stranger reason.

Australian yowie researcher Rex Gilroy has collected more than 3000 sighting reports and, as in North America, there was a big increase in reports during the 1970s. A particularly close sighting, where the witness was able to get a good look at a yowie of 7 feet (2.1 metres), was reported by a National Parks worker in the Springbrook area of Queensland in March 1978. Hearing a grunting sound, he thought a pig was loose and went into the forest to look for it.

Then something made me look up and there, about 12 feet [3.7 metres] in front of me, was this big black hairy man-thing. It looked more like a gorilla than anything. It had huge hands and one of them was wrapped round a sapling.

It had a flat, black shiny face, with two

big yellow eyes and a hole for a mouth. It just stared at me and I stared back. I was so numb I couldn't even raise the axe I had in my hand. We seemed to stand there staring at each other for about 10 minutes before it suddenly gave off a foul smell that made me vomit – then it just made off sideways and disappeared.

Both its appearance and behaviour suggest that the yowie is a close cousin to the North American bigfoot.

The riddle of the bigfoot is not an easy one to solve. It is not simply a question of ascertaining whether or not the creature exists and, if it does, whether it is human or animal. Some reports, especially the more recent ones, have features that seem to deepen the mystery.

The average height of a bigfoot seems to be

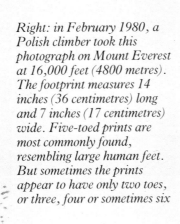

Right: in February 1980, a Polish climber took this photograph on Mount Everest at 16,000 feet (4800 metres). The footprint measures 14 inches (36 centimetres) long and 7 inches (17 centimetres) wide. Five-toed prints are most commonly found, resembling large human feet. But sometimes the prints appear to have only two toes, or three, four or sometimes six

between 6 and 7 feet (1.8 and 2.1 metres), though smaller and larger ones are sometimes reported.

We have seen that some bigfeet have a revolting smell; it has been suggested that they can release this at will, perhaps to ensure that people keep their distance. Another strange feature is that some bigfeet have exceptionally large and frightening eyes which seem, uncannily, to glow.

As we have seen, a significant number of reports, many of them made by experienced huntsmen, tell of a particularly disturbing phenomenon: some bigfeet are apparently completely unharmed by bullets.

There seem to be three possible explanations: the guns used are just not powerful enough to tackle such a creature, or the witness in his excitement did not aim properly (although some shots were fired from very close range) – or bigfeet are not made of flesh and blood.

If the theory that bigfeet are not composed of flesh and blood sounds incredible, there is some even more extraordinary evidence that tends to support it: the claim that some bigfeet are apparently able to disappear or dematerialise. A Pennsylvanian woman, confronted by one on her doorstep one night in February 1974, shot into it from a distance of 6 feet (1.8 metres). She was astounded to see it disappear in a flash of light! Other eyewitnesses have reported signs of insubstantiality in the bigfeet they have seen.

In the Pennsylvania case the witness's son-in-law, who came to help on hearing the shot, saw other bigfeet at the edge of nearby woods. He also saw a bright red flashing light hovering over the woods. There are a number of other cases in which UFOs and bigfeet are reported as having been seen at the same time and in the same area. Coincidence? Or are they both part of the same phenomenon?

A similar incident took place on a farm in Pennsylvania in 1973. It involved a large red luminous ball and two ape-like creatures with green glowing eyes and long dark hair standing near it. Shots were fired, to which the beasts seemed impervious. After this sighting, investigators found a glowing area where the UFO had been.

A related theory is that man-beasts could be holograms, three-dimensional images projected from space. If so, who is projecting them – and why?

Bigfoot cases with such bizarre details are by no means widespread, and not always properly investigated since some veteran bigfoot hunters and investigators are sceptical of apparent paranormal cases, possibly feeling that they do not wish to become involved in fringe eccentricities. At any rate, the chances of tracing a flesh and blood man-beast are remote enough since the creatures are reputed to possess intimate knowledge of the terrain they inhabit so

Above: bigfoot hunter Rene Dahinden stands beside a statue of a bigfoot, sculpted by Jim McClarin at Willow Creek, California. The figure, modelled on descriptions of bigfeet seen in the area, is 8 feet (2.4 metres) tall, 41 inches (1.04 metres) wide at the shoulder, and has feet measuring 18 x 10 inches (46 by 25 centimetres)

Left: 16-year-old Tim Meissner (left) estimates the height of a bigfoot he saw and shot at near his home in British Columbia, Canada, in April 1979. The creature, about 9 feet (2.7 metres) tall, was standing beside this tree when Tim saw it. Later he fired at the creature. It went down on one knee as if it had been hit, but then got up and ran away

that they can travel through it far quicker than a man ever could and yet remain completely concealed.

Most of the time, all the intrepid bigfoot hunter can do is interview witnesses, examine footprints, and collect newspaper reports; and without high-quality photographs, a corpse or a skeleton, or even part of one, all that scientists can do is speculate about possible explanations. Man-beasts may be some form of giant ape or perhaps an early form of man-like ape, *Gigantopithecus*, or they may really be men, prehistoric survivals that have managed to stay concealed against all the odds.

Some people have argued that man-beasts are some kind of paranormal phenomenon. They may come into being when certain types of energy are available (electrical, nuclear or psychic, for example). Bigfeet have sometimes been reported near energy sources.

All we know for certain is that large, human-like footprints have been found in large numbers in remote areas – and not all of them are likely to be hoaxes or misidentifications – and that well over 1000 people in North America alone have reported seeing tall, hairy man-beasts.

Investigators differ in their interpretations of the data, and perhaps no one explanation can account for all the reported sightings. It is most likely that the term 'man-beasts' covers a wide range of phenomena that, for unknown reasons, appear – or seem to appear – in similar guises.

Bigfoot hunters who believe in the creature and want to convince the world of its existence have a hard task since, despite the mass of data, few professional scientists will give their work a glance. This may be due to natural caution or to the curious, yet to them powerful, argument that 'Bigfoot can't exist, therefore it doesn't.' Meanwhile, the man-beast continues to appear regularly, to alarm but not hurt witnesses, and to puzzle all who ponder its presence.

Above: a sea serpent in the Gulf of Suez, sighted by HMS Philomel *in 1879. Once common in mariners' reports, such sightings have declined, especiallly since the second half of the 19th century*

Left: when the crew of a French ship were saved from death at the hands of a monster, they gave a painting of the event, in thanksgiving for their deliverance, to a church in St Malo. The original has disappeared, but the French naturalist, Denys de Montfort had a copy made in the 1790s (shown here), as he felt it confirmed the existence of giant sea monsters

Monster of the deep

With more than 60 per cent of the Earth's surface covered with water, it is hardly surprising that sightings of giant underwater monsters have been reported since antiquity. Even today, marine biologists, who have long been aware of the vast unexplored depths of the Earth's oceans, cautiously accept that the numerous reports of sea monster sightings seem to provide evidence that many creatures, at present unknown and unclassified, may be living in the dark and hidden waters.

A 16th-century cleric, Olaus Magnus, described a sea serpent 200 feet (60 metres) long and 20 feet (6 metres) thick, which plucked animals and men from boats. Interestingly, Magnus described the serpent as being black, having hair hanging from its neck (or mane), shining eyes, and putting its 'head on high like a pillar', characteristics that also appear in recent sighting reports.

On 6 July 1734 a monster appeared off the coast of Greenland, and was reported by a Norwegian missionary, Hans Egede. In 1741 he wrote that its body was as bulky as a ship and was three or four times as long, and that it leapt from the water and plunged back again.

In 1752, the Bishop of Bergen, Erik

Army officers and a military store-keeper were out for a day's fishing when they saw an 80-foot (24-metre) long serpent swim by, not more than 200 yards (180 metres) away. This was at Mahone Bay, 40 miles (65 kilometres) west of Halifax, Nova Scotia, and so convinced were they of the importance of their sighting that they all signed a statement and added:

There could be no mistake, no delusion, and we were all perfectly satisfied that we had been favoured with a view of the 'true and veritable sea-serpent', which had been generally considered to have existed only in the brain of some Yankee skipper, and treated as a tale not much entitled to belief.

Pontoppidan, who had a great interest in the mystery of the sea serpent, arranged for a letter from Captain Lorenz von Ferry to be read to the Bergen Court of Justice, in which was described a sea serpent that the Captain and his crew had seen in 1746 while rowing ashore to Molde in Norway. He said it had a grey head like a horse, large black eyes, a black mouth and a long white mane. Behind the head seven or eight coils could be seen above the water. Captain von Ferry fired at it and it sank below the water and did not reappear. Two of his seamen, who had also been witnesses, swore on oath that the contents of the report were true.

In 1848 Sir Richard Owen, a conservative scientist and opponent of Darwin, conducted a correspondence of some acerbity with Captain Peter M'Quhae, through the columns of *The Times*. Their debate concerned the 60-foot (18-metre) sea serpent that the Captain and his crew had seen in the southern Atlantic from the deck of HMS *Daedalus* on 6 August that year. Although Owen used the sceptic's customary ploy of interpreting the report to fit his own preconceptions (in this case his identification was a sealion), Captain M'Quhae would have none of it and firmly maintained that he had seen a sea serpent.

In May 1901, when the officers on the bridge of the steamer *Grangense* in the western Atlantic saw a monstrous crocodile-like creature with 6-inch (15-centimetre) long teeth, splashing about on the surface, the Captain refused to note the encounter in the ship's log, saying: 'They will say we were all drunk, and I'll thank you, Mister, not to mention it to our agents at Para or Manaus.'

But there were others who were perhaps less careful of their reputation, such as Lieutenant George Sandford who, as captain of the merchant ship *Lady Combermere*, in 1820 reported seeing in mid-Atlantic a serpent 60 to 100 feet (18 to 30 metres) long, spouting water like a whale. On 15 May 1833 four British

Above: one of the sea monsters described by Archbishop Olaus Magnus and illustrated in his history of Scandinavia (1555)

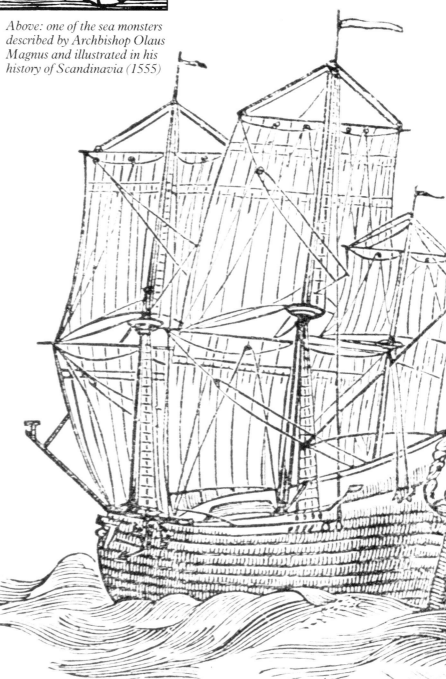

Another sighting of the crocodile-like type of sea monster was made by the captain and crew of the *Eagle* on 23 March 1830, a few hours before they docked at Charleston, South Carolina. Captain Deland sailed his schooner to within 25 yards (22 metres) of the basking creature and fired a musket at its head. When the bullet hit, the monster dived beneath the ship and struck it several times with its tail, blows strong enough to damage the craft if not to sink her.

Since these sightings, sea monsters have continued to surface before startled onlookers. The intrepid trans-Atlantic rower Captain John Ridgway saw a monster just before midnight on 25 July 1966. His companion, Sergeant Chay Blyth, who has since become a world-famous yachtsman, was asleep. As Ridgway rowed he heard a swishing noise and a 35-foot (10-metre) long sea serpent outlined in phosphorescence, 'as if a string of neon lights were hanging from it', came swimming towards the boat. It dived underneath and did not reappear on the other side.

An active monster of recent years, sighted off the coast of Cornwall, England, is known as Morgawr (Cornish for 'sea giant'), and another strange creature has been seen in the waters of Cardigan Bay off the west coast of Wales. On 2 March 1975, six local schoolgirls were walking along the beach at dusk when 200 yards (180 metres) away a creature moved across the

Right: a recent find that attracted world-wide attention was the carcase hauled on board the Japanese trawler Zuiyo Maru *in 1977. Concerned that the carcase might contaminate his catch, Captain Akira Tanaka had it photographed, then threw it back in the sea*

beach towards the sea. They perceived it as being 10 feet (3 metres) long with a long neck and tail and large green eyes. Later they described it to their art teacher, Colin Palmer, who drew the creature. When he showed his sketch to the crew of a fishing boat, who had seen a monster when they were fishing off Bardsey Sound, there was 'instant recognition'.

The sceptical scientist asks for physical remains to examine, and periodically, strange, large carcases are washed up on beaches.

The large decomposing 'glob' that was washed up on a remote beach in western Tasmania in July 1960 received little official

Below: a 'most dreadful monster' seen near Greenland in 1734 by Hans Egede, a Norwegian missionary who took a keen interest in natural history

Left: this strange-looking carcase with its huge head and duck-like beak was washed up on the rocks at Santa Cruz, California in 1925. Decomposition made the specimen hard to identify but, after examining the skull, the Museum of the California Academy of Sciences showed that the carcase was that of an extremely rare beaked whale

Inset: an ornate sea-dragon figurehead from a 9th century Viking burial ship. Norse and Celtic mythologies are full of legends about serpents in the seas of northern Europe

attention until March 1962. Then scientists from Hobart located the exact spot from the air and a group went to investigate. Helicopters were used to carry away samples, and the official statement said that the object was 'a large lump of decomposing blubber, probably torn off a whale'. However, the other biologists who had been following the case thought this was unlikely.

Some of the most convincing evidence for the existence of sea monsters comes from those areas where they have been sighted repeatedly over decades or even centuries. In the Strait of Georgia between Vancouver Island and British Columbia, off the west coast of Canada, the creature known locally as Cadborosaurus or Caddy was sighted by the Indians long before the arrival of the white settlers.

In this century an early sighting of Caddy was made by F. W. Kemp, a local government official. On 10 August 1932, Mr Kemp was with his wife and son when they saw it swim at terrific speed through the water. Caddy was seen frequently during the 1930s and in 1950 was sighted by Judge James Brown and his family, when it appeared as a 45-foot (14-metre) long serpent that rose out of the water several times. Mrs R. A. Stewart, who saw it in 1963 when fishing with her husband, was terrified by its wide-open jaws.

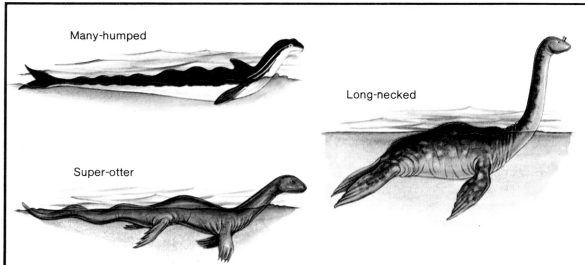

Many-humped

Super-otter

Long-necked

Three of the most common sea serpents classified by Dr Bernard Heuvelmans. The many-humped serpent and the super-otter are both 60–100 feet (18–20 metres) long, while the long-necked type is between 15 and 65 feet (5 and 20 metres)

Further south on the American west coast is San Clemente Island, a favourite area for deep-sea angling and an area where water monsters have been seen frequently throughout this century. When technical fishing writer J. Charles Davis interviewed numerous independent witnesses, he found their descriptions tallied to an amazing degree. Many of the witnesses were wealthy members of the big-game fishing clubs, who knew what to expect from the sea and had no desire to lay themselves open to ridicule.

why does the sea serpent still remain comparatively unknown? One reason might be that although more than 60 per cent of the Earth's surface is covered by water, very little of it is travelled over by commercial shipping, which follows fixed and narrow routes. The vibrations made by engines and bow waves are sufficient to keep timid sea creatures away from these areas, in contrast to the days when sailing ships relied on wind and currents and were often driven well off their routes.

All the evidence points to there being more than one type of sea monster. In 1965, Belgian zoologist Dr Bernard Heuvelmans completed the most detailed and exhaustive work on the subject in recent times – *In the wake of the sea-serpents*, a book that has been of great value to all modern writers on water monsters. In it, Dr Heuvelmans describes and analyses more than 500 reports, dating from 1639 to 1964. Leaving out obvious hoaxes and red herrings, there were 358 genuinely unexplained sightings with various characteristics of appearance and behaviour that could be divided into nine types. These range from the most frequently seen 'long-necked' sea serpent, which has a cigar-shaped body, four webbed feet and is a fast swimmer, to the very infrequently seen marine saurians that look like crocodiles 50–60 feet (15–18 metres) long and have only been seen in mid-ocean tropical waters.

The other types Dr Heuvelmans names informally as merhorses, many-humped, super-otters, many-finned, super-eels, fathers-of-all-the-turtles and yellow-bellies. He has also found a group he calls 'ambiguous periscopes', which might be either long-necked monsters or super-eels. He considers the long-necked serpent and the first four categories above to be mammals, while the super-eel might be a fish. As we will see when attempting to categorise the Loch Ness monster, however, such speculation raises as many questions as it answers.

The world beneath the sea has still not been fully explored and, despite the sceptics, there appears to be abundant evidence for the existence of large, unknown sea creatures. Scientists believe that before long they will have a much more detailed knowledge of life in the ocean depths – indeed, new species are being discovered every year, so perhaps they will soon find the answer to the mystery of the underwater monster.

Merfolk

Half human and half fish, mermaids and mermen of legend stretch back into antiquity and can be found in the folklore of almost every nation in the world. Merfolk have been seen and vouched for down the ages by witnesses of attested integrity – and they continue to be seen today.

Fish-tailed deities can be found in almost every culture of the ancient world and Pliny the Elder (AD 23–79), a Roman administrator and writer, was convinced that merfolk were not only completely real but that they were seen regularly.

In the late Elizabethan, early Jacobean age belief in the mermaid waxed and waned. Men such as Frances Bacon and John Donne gave rational explanations for many natural phenomena, including the mermaid – yet it was also a time of blossoming maritime travel and some of the great seamen of the age told of personal encounters with merfolk. In 1608 Henry Hudson, the navigator and explorer (after whom the Hudson Bay territories are named), made the following matter-of-fact entry in his log:

This morning, one of our companie looking overboord saw a Mermaid, and calling up some of the companie to see her, one more came up, and by that time she was come close to the ship's side, looking earnestly on the men: a little after, a Sea came and overturned her: From the Navill upward, her back and breasts were like a womans (as they say that saw her), her body as big as one of us;

Above: the sirens attempt to lure Ulysses and his crew to destruction with their irresistible singing. Seen here as mermaids, they are also often portrayed as half woman, half bird

Below: the manatee, or sea cow – a plant eating mammal confined to shallow tropical waters. It is thought that sightings of such creatures may have given rise to the legend of the mermaid

her skin very white; and long haire hanging down behinde, of colour blacke; in her going downe they saw her tayle, which was like the tayle of a Porposse, and speckled like a Macrell. Their names that saw her were Thomas Hilles and Robert Raynar.

Hudson was a very experienced seaman who surely knew the calibre of his men and presumably would not have bothered to record a blatant hoax. Also, the report itself shows that his men were familiar with the creatures of the sea and were of the opinion that this creature was exceptional.

In 1809 a respected schoolmaster named William Munro wrote an extensive and detailed letter to *The Times* concerning the sighting near Reay, in Scotland, of a mermaid, sitting on a rock, combing her hair. Whatever it was that William Munro saw and described in such detail, he was not alone, for he adds that several people 'whose veracity I never heard disputed' had claimed to have seen the mermaid, but until he had seen it himself he 'was not disposed to credit their testimony'.

Phineas T. Barnum (1810–1891), the great American showman to whom are attributed two telling statements – 'There's one [a sucker] born every minute' and 'Every crowd has a silver lining' – bought a mermaid that he had seen being shown at a shilling a time in Watson's Coffee House in London. It was a dreadful, shrivelled-up thing – probably a freak fish – but Barnum added it to the curiosities he had gathered for his 'Greatest Show on Earth'.

A comparatively recent sighting was reported by a fisherman on the Hebridean island of Muck: his mermaid was sitting on a floating herring box, again combing her hair. Until his death in the late 1950s the fisherman could not be persuaded that he had not seen a mermaid.

In 1978, a Filipino fisherman, 41-year-old Jacinto Fatalvero, not only saw a mermaid one moonlit night but was helped by her to secure a bountiful catch. Little more is known, however, because having told his story, Fatalvero became the butt of jokes, the object of derision – and, inevitably, hounded by the media. Understandably he refused to say another word.

One major theory is that the mermaid legend sprang from the misidentification of two aquatic mammals, the manatee and dugong, and possibly seals, but this does not account for sightings by experienced seamen, who would be familiar with these creatures.

One suggestion is that merfolk are the descendants of our distant ancestors, some of whom came ashore from the sea. This theory is supported by the fact that human embryos have gills that usually disappear before birth, but some babies are born with them and they have to be removed surgically.

But, whatever she is, the mermaid has a long history of sightings and continues to be seen. For this we should be thankful; the romance and folklore of the sea would be all the poorer without her.

Top left: mermaids, mermen and mer-children disport themselves in the turbulent sea

Top: the 'Fejee mermaid' that was the star attraction of Phineas T. Barnum's touring show in 1842. Barnum, a cynical American who coined the phrase 'every crowd has a silver lining' advertised the creature with posters depicting misleadingly voluptuous creatures

Above: the mermaid as erotic fantasy figure. She was widely believed to prey on drowning sailors, making them her sexual slaves

Loch Ness monster

Although for hundreds of years local legend contained many tales of mysterious creatures in the Scottish lochs, the modern obsession with a 'monster' lurking deep in the dark and brooding waters of Loch Ness began with a very ordinary set of circumstances in 1933. In that year a road was blasted along the north shore of the lake and trees and undergrowth were cut down, giving a much better view of the massive expanse of water. Among the more obvious effects of this development was the influx of visitors to the area – and so the 'sightings' of the Loch Ness 'monster' increased dramatically. The first widely publicised sighting was made on 14 April 1933 by Mr and Mrs Mackay and reported in the *Inverness Courier*. 'The creature disported itself for fully a minute, its body resembling that of a whale.' This sighting was swiftly followed by others – and so Loch Ness became a sensation throughout the world.

Situated in the Great Glen, a tear in the Earth's surface cutting across the centre of Scotland, Loch Ness is a relatively unexplored region. At its deepest point there is possibly more than 985 feet (300 metres) of water, a depth exceeding that of the sea surrounding our shores; it stretches over a length of nearly 22 miles (35 kilometres), and because of the fine deposits of peat in the water, underwater visibility is very poor. Investigation of an area such as this requires more than human will-power or physical prowess: only the most sophisticated technological aids will – perhaps – finally unravel the mysteries of this, the largest body of fresh water in Britain.

The Scottish lochs all originate from the same period as the fjord-like lakes of Scandinavia and Ireland. Glaciers from successive Ice Ages deepened existing valleys, including the Great Glen fault line of Loch Ness, until about

Below: deep and murky Loch Ness, with Castle Urquhart on its lonely promontory in the background

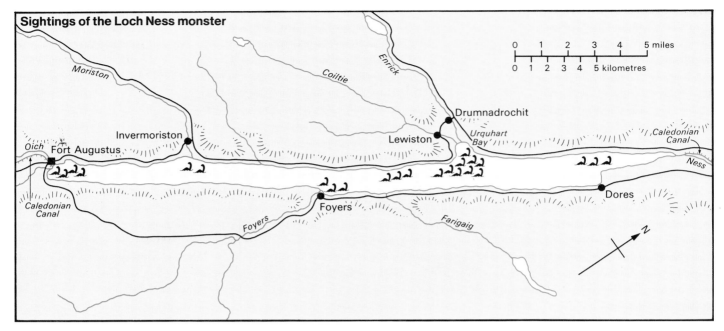

Sightings of the Loch Ness monster

Above: a simplified distribution map of the recorded sightings of the Loch Ness monster. The monster is most often seen near the mouths of rivers

Right: the kelpie, the malignant water-sprite of the Scottish lochs, which was said to lurk by the waterside, disguised as a horse, waiting for human victims. Some of the people who live near Loch Ness can remember, as children, being told not to bathe in the loch for fear of the kelpie

10,000 years ago, when the ice retreated for the last time. For a while some of the lochs remained open to the sea, which had risen slightly owing to the water released by the melting ice. Then, relieved of the weight of the ice, the land rose steadily and the surface of Loch Ness now lies about 52 feet (16 metres) above sea level and is connected to the sea only by the River Ness.

Because of the link between these waters and the sea, it is interesting to recall some 'sea monster' tales that bear certain similarities to the 'monsters' mentioned in eyewitness accounts at Loch Ness.

In Scandinavia many lakes have traditions of animals occasionally surfacing; these include Lake Suldal and Lake Storsjö, where implements made at the end of the 19th century to catch the 'animal' can still be seen. Similar stories involve Lake Okanagan in North America, the Lagerflot in Iceland and the Connemara loughs in Ireland which are inhabited by the pooka, kelpie or *each uisge* – 'water-horse' in Gaelic.

The kelpie and water-horse appear in the folklore of the Scottish Highlands. Strangely, however, although the first written account of a water monster in the River Ness concerns an incident in AD 565, no particular importance was given to reports from Loch Ness until quite recently. That first account was drawn from St Adaman's *Life of St Columba*, which talked of 'the driving away of a certain water monster by the virtue of prayer of the holy man'.

There were a number of sightings during Victorian times and, much more recently, the author Gavin Maxwell, who chose to exile himself on the west coast of Scotland, gave several accounts of similar creatures seen by friends and employees both in the sea and the sea lochs. These accounts come from skilled seamen with a lifetime's knowledge of the wildlife of the west coast, but the major difficulty in evaluating all eyewitness accounts and evidence is one of subjectivity; without very specific experience, it is extremely difficult to judge time, size, distance or speed with any accuracy, especially over water.

The loch itself presents problems because it plays tricks on the eyes. It is a large mass of water sometimes completely calm in a way that the sea, for example, rarely is, and its high shorelines cast deep shadows and reflections. In these conditions you can get a visual impression totally out of proportion to the actual cause – of small animals, water birds, boat wakes and wind. The wakes from boats passing through the loch, for example, can be reflected from the shores to form a standing wave in the centre of the loch after the particular boat has passed out of sight.

Despite these problems, thousands of eye-

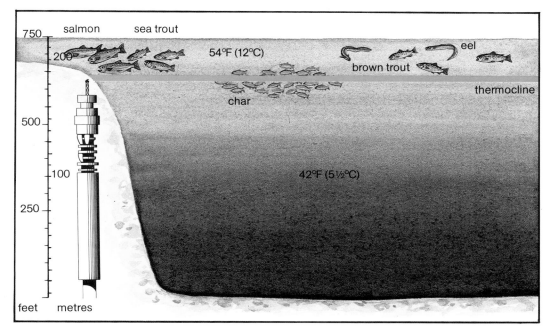

Left: a section through Loch Ness, showing its depth and its fish life, which is concentrated close to the surface in summer, when the temperature may rise as high as 54°F (12°C). The cold, peaty water in the main body of the Loch varies in temperature by no more than half a degree throughout the year and supports virtually no animal life. The official estimate of the phenomenal depth of the loch is 754 feet (230 metres) although some sources claim it is as much as 975 feet (297 metres) deep. It is less than 1 mile (1.6 kilometres) wide, and the sides plunge unusually steeply from the shore. But perhaps the most astounding feature of the loch is the sheer volume of water it contains – large enough to hold the population of the world, the loch has plenty of room for unknown creatures

witness sightings are now on record, thanks to the press, individual authors and investigative organisations such as the Loch Ness Investigation Bureau, which was active between 1962 and 1972. The descriptions are remarkably consistent, and describe a long-necked, hump-backed creature that sometimes moves at speed, both with neck raised and lowered, and at other times simply appears for a while and submerges quietly.

The first chronicler of the Loch Ness sightings was Lieutenant-Commander Rupert Gould who, in his book *The Loch Ness monster* (1934), described 42 sightings from 1923 to 1933 in a well-presented case. He felt that the creature was an isolated specimen that had become trapped in the loch. He was followed by Mrs Constance White, wife of the manager of the Caledonian Canal; her book *More than a legend*, published in 1957, contained references to over 60 sightings. She established that the phenomenon had not ceased after 1934 as some had believed and that sometimes more than one animal was seen at a time – suggesting a resident population. More recent authors include Tim Dinsdale, Ted Holliday, Peter Costello and Nick Witchell, all of whom have added more examples of eyewitness evidence; much of this is drawn from the extensive files of the Loch Ness Investigation Bureau, which collected reports at the loch side.

From these we have learned that there are more sightings in the summer months, particularly at the mouth of rivers, and certainly more on calm, hot days. But clearer weather conditions and the fact that summer marks the height of the tourist season must be taken into account.

Besides eyewitness evidence, there are the photographic records of surfacings. Although the photographic image may appear irrefutable, and may be seen to present measurable

evidence that can be independently assessed, the limitations of the lens in fact make any such assessment very difficult. Photographs taken with ordinary equipment give far less information than the naked eye – and, sadly, the photographic print process is very easy to manipulate in order to produce fakes. Loch Ness is, naturally enough, fair game for hoaxers of all kinds.

From time to time, however, photographs are produced that stimulate real interest. The 'classic' pictures must be included in any discussion of the Loch Ness phenomenon, although very few are now considered significant evidence by the current Loch Ness and Morar Project. Not only do they differ markedly from one another, but none of the pictures taken during the comprehensive surface study by the Loch Ness Investigation Bureau over a

Below: a still from Tim Dinsdale's famous film of 23 April 1960. It is very probably genuine – and, like most genuine photographs of the Loch Ness monster, it shows very little detail

Above: Vickers Oceanics' submersible Pisces *being lowered into Loch Ness. In 1969, while hovering close to the loch floor in water 520 feet (170 metres) deep, Pisces made sonar contact with an object that fled when it was approached*

Below: investigation techniques of yesterday and today. Main picture: surveying Loch Ness with binoculars and camera on a cold day in 1933. Inset: Tim Dinsdale with his sophisticated Cyclops *camera rig in 1968*

10-year period shows anything like the amount of body seen in the 'classic' photographs, although some show low-lying humps and wakes.

Ciné films are far harder to fake than still pictures; so, although their subject matter may still be open to debate, they do provide more valuable evidence. Two film sequences in particular are exceptional.

The first was shot on 23 April 1960 by Tim Dinsdale from the mouth of the River Foyers. It shows a hump moving slowly away from him and then fast across his field of vision while submerging.

The second film, shot by Richard Raynor during the Loch Ness Expedition of 1967 on the morning of 13 June, is exceptional for its technical quality. The film, taken from opposite Dores at the north end of the loch, shows a wake, at the head of which a solid object appears from time to time; the object sub-

merges as a boat enters the field of vision. Raynor is quite ready to accept the possibility that the animal was an otter (the object was definitely animate); this is really the only possible candidate apart from an unknown animal. However, the Joint Air Reconnaissance Intelligence Centre (JARIC) – especially likely to be accurate in view of the photographic quality – estimates a possible length of 7 feet (2 metres) for the part that breaks the surface; an otter of this size would be, to say the least, remarkable.

This film seems to be the best we can expect from surface observation and photography. Although these better examples do suggest that a large animal is involved, they also demonstrate the limitations of this kind of evidence in terms of identification; aquatic creatures cannot be studied on the basis of what proportions of their body are by chance exposed above water.

It was not until 1970 that underwater photography was used as an investigative method. Its potential is enormous, since it should allow a complete profile view of the target to be obtained; in practice, however, the peaty water and limitations of normal underwater equipment reduce the range and coverage drastically. This makes interpretation of underwater pictures very difficult.

Some interesting shots were taken by Dr Robert Rines of the Academy of Applied Science, Boston, Massachusetts, USA, in 1975, showing six images other than the underside of the boat from which the camera was slung; and it has been suggested that two of these are animate. One object, the 'head', has sufficient symmetry to suggest a living creature, with horns used for breathing without creating ripples, although this is obviously a matter of individual interpretation.

Without doubt, however, the most important class of evidence is that of the echo

sounder and sonar. Developed during the Second World War as a submarine detection device, sonar relies on the reflection of transmitted sound waves by underwater targets. It is the only really effective instrument for 'seeing' underwater, particularly where the water is not clear, and by 1960 had been refined to a stage where it was used commercially in fishing – and in the Loch Ness investigations. The problem, however, is that it requires some expertise to assess the results, and this expertise is not generally found among zoologists. Also, because living tissue has a density very close to that of water, it gives little or no echo, so the air cavities within any creature have to

be relied on to give a reflection of the sound waves. For this reason, sonar cannot provide an exact representation, and identification by this means alone is not possible. In addition fish shoals, temperature changes and rising gases are all possible causes of sonar contacts. On the positive side, with sonar it is possible to follow the movements of a target under water and to judge from this whether or not it is animate and even to gain some hints as to its identity.

So far teams from Oxford and Cambridge in 1962, Birmingham University in 1968–69, Vickers Oceanics in 1969, the Loch Ness Investigation Bureau between 1969 and 1970, Klein Associates and the Academy of Applied Sciences between 1970 and 1977 and the Partech Company in 1976–77 have all produced results that they consider indicate the presence of an animate contact larger than a salmon and displaying movement and diving rates different from those expected of fish.

If there are indeed strange creatures in the loch, when could they have become established there, how could they exist and – most importantly – what could they possibly be?

There is no question of Loch Ness being an evolutionary cul-de-sac, since any creatures that live in the loch must have arrived there after the retreat of the ice 10,000 years ago – a mere blink of the eye in the time-scale of evolution.

Far left: Dr Robert Rines of the Massachusetts Institute of Technology examines one of the underwater cameras used during the Loch Ness expedition of 1972–73

Below: is this the head of the Loch Ness monster? This photograph was taken by Dr Rines during a later expedition in 1975. Although the peaty waters of the bottom of the loch make it difficult to identify what the photograph represents, it has been argued that the symmetry of the object shows it is animate; on the other hand, many experts hold that the photograph shows merely the bottom of the loch. Inset: an artist's impression of the object in Dr Rines's photograph. Some people believe the horns may be used by the monster as snorkel tubes to enable it to breathe without surfacing

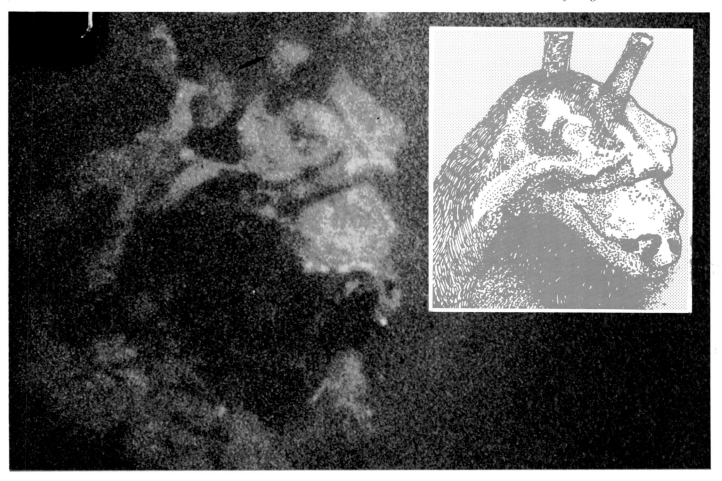

It seems unlikely that any large creature could have entered the loch from freshwater areas – there are not, and never have been, any nearby, and travel to Loch Ness would have entailed considerable distances overland. Thus – and bearing in mind reports of a 'monster' sighted off the coast of Scotland – it seems reasonable to look to the sea for the origins of our creature.

Food for thought

Our next clue may be found by looking at the creature's possible sources of food; those available within the loch are plants, plankton, detritus (organic constituents of sediment) and fish. The dark, peaty water, steep sides and short summer restrict the growth of rooted plants, which are limited for the most part to the first 10 feet (3 metres) of water. Concentrations of bulky plants are close to the shore, so any creature feeding off these would be seen more often than recorded sightings suggest. All herbivorous animals require a very considerable volume of food to survive and the scarcity of aquatic vegetation in the loch rules out these species.

Some of the world's largest animals are plankton feeders – for instance, the largest mammal, the blue whale, and the largest fish, the basking and whale sharks – and it could be that the 'monster' also feeds on plankton. In general, however, the Scottish lochs are very deep in relation to their surface area and are characterised by relative sterility. They also have sparse amounts of plankton compared to other lakes without 'monster' traditions, such as those in the Lake District. Plankton feeders exhibit physical adaptations for capturing and straining plankton from the water. Whales, for example, have baleen brushes and some fish have gills adapted as strainers. These feeders also possess large mouths to take in the greatest possible volume of water, which by all accounts does not seem to apply to our long-necked animal. They also display a great deal

Below: from the series of underwater photographs taken by Dr Robert Rines (see also page 87), an artist was able to build up this picture of what the Loch Ness monster might look like. It shows the long neck, small head and flippers mentioned in so many reports of sightings

Bottom: a model of the plesiosaur, the reptile that seems most nearly to fit the descriptions of the Loch Ness monster. The plesiosaur is thought to have been extinct for the past 70 million years – but that in itself does not automatically rule out the possibility that this is the monster. A rare fish, the coelacanth, was also thought to have been extinct for millions of years – until one was found in the Indian ocean in 1938

of surface activity, since it is near the surface that plankton is concentrated; this is also contrary to the evidence we have so far of our unknown species.

It seems to rest with the salmon and sea trout to provide a solution to the food supply problem. The salmon hatch in rivers entering the loch and remain in fresh water for the first two years of their life, and mature salmon are present virtually all the year round, since they enter at different times – although mainly in spring and summer.

Some aspects of reported behaviour support the theory of a fish-predator. Sightings are frequently made off the mouths of rivers in spate, when the salmon are running up to spawn, and recorded bursts of high speed would be consistent with an animal chasing the fish.

One objection to the existence of a Loch Ness 'monster' has always been the absence of floating or beached remains, and certainly such a find would help us identify it. Yet there are few records of strange carcases being found at Scottish lochs – and none of them recent. The lochs are deep, steep-sided and cold, and it is particularly the last factor that is relevant

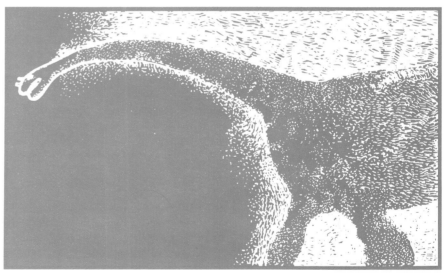

since the cold water would slow down decomposition and allow time for eels to dispose of the remains. This probably accounts for Loch Ness's reputation for 'never giving up its dead'.

Many reptiles and mammals have the curious habit of swallowing small stones, which they use as ballast, particularly when swimming near the surface where pressure due to water is insufficient to keep the animal submerged. If the 'monster' follows this pattern, its body will sink to the bottom of the loch after its death.

Exactly what the 'monster' is – if it exists at all – is the most interesting question of all. The presence of an adapted marine fish-predator within the loch is not, in itself, particularly

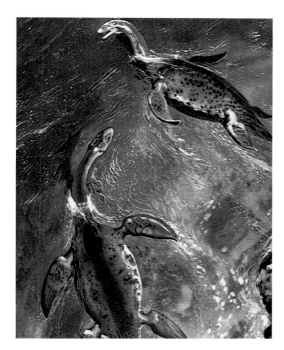

remarkable. What is remarkable is that it seems to be an unknown animal. Furthermore, some of its 'characteristics' raise difficulties no matter what class of animal is considered.

Reptile, mammal or fish?

Certainly the most popular theory is that the 'monster' is a reptile. However, the biological objections are strong. The temperature of the loch would seem too cold for a reptile to remain active. Also a reptile would have to surface in order to breathe and would be expected to come ashore to lay eggs. Of course there are always exceptions to prove the rule. Freshwater 'turtles', for example, can sometimes be seen swimming beneath the ice covering North American lakes (although Loch Ness itself does not freeze). The reptile most often suggested as fitting the descriptions is the plesiosaur, previously thought extinct, which could have adapted to cope with the difficulties of the loch already mentioned. Secondarily aquatic reptiles and mammals have waterproof skins and lungs as opposed to gills, which make long-term adaptation to fresh water easier.

From an environmental point of view, a mammal is a more probable bet. Most seals, for example, are perfectly at home in low temperatures, and a long-necked seal could account for some of the sightings. The problem of reproduction remains, however, since seals breed – and in general give birth – on land. And the need to breathe frequently – and therefore to surface – should not allow a population of this kind to remain so elusive.

The least unlikely solution would be a fish, which would certainly account for the rare surface appearances and take care of the reproduction as well. Unfortunately, most sighting reports do not seem to describe a fish, although there could be something in the opinion among locals that the 'monster' is a large eel of known or unknown species. Some of the sonar evidence suggests that contacts rise and return to the bottom, which is consistent with the behaviour of the eel or of the European catfish, both of which become active at night. The apparent tendency to surface in calm, hot weather, which was first noted by Pontoppidan of the 'sea serpent' in 1752 and is supported by testimonies at Loch Ness, is consistent with the behaviour of bottom-dwelling fish. At least they make rather 'extrovert' surface appearances in response to barometric pressure changes.

The famous 'flipper' picture taken in 1972 by Dr Robert Rines (and later enhanced by computer) is interesting, if it is indeed part of an unknown animal. The flipper or fin is of a rhomboid shape, which led Rines and Sir Peter Scott, the naturalist, to suggest the scientific name *Nessiteras rhombopteryx* for the animal. But it has been pointed out that the shape of this 'flipper' makes it inefficient for aquatic propulsion.

If the flipper is considered as part of a fish, however (in which case it would be appropriate to call it a fin), the position is different. Accepting the objection that the fin is inefficient for aquatic propulsion, fish are anyway almost always tail-propelled and many species have put their fins to other uses apart from swimming, so the 'flipper' is more likely to be the fin of a bottom-roving fish than the propulsive flipper of a reptile or mammal.

Whatever the Loch Ness 'monster' may turn out to be, there will be some very interesting questions to be answered, far more interesting than the mere discovery of a 'monster'. If it is an amphibian, how did it invade the loch in the first place? If a reptile, how does it cope with the cold? If a mammal, how does it remain so elusive? And if it is a fish, it is indeed a very strange fish.

Far left: two plesiosaurs of the Jurassic era. If these creatures have survived their supposed extinction, they could be the monsters of not only Loch Ness, but North American and Irish lakes as well

Below: Dr Rines's famous 'monster flipper' photograph, taken in 1972. If this is indeed part of the Loch Ness monster, it provides some interesting information about what kind of creature it is. The photograph shows a rhomboid flipper with a clear central 'rib' – which, experts agree, is not an efficient design for swimming

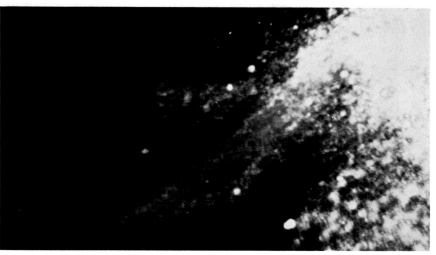

Fish falls

On 16 February 1861 a violent earthquake shook the island of Singapore. For the following six days, rain fell in torrents. Then, on the morning of the 22nd, after a last furious downpour, it stopped. François de Castelnau, a French naturalist staying on the island, reported what happened next to the Academy of Sciences in Paris, later that year.

At 10 a.m. the sun lifted, and from my window I saw a large number of Malays and Chinese filling baskets with fishes which they picked up in the pools of water which covered the ground. On being asked where the fishes came from they answered that they had fallen from the sky. Three days afterwards, when the pools had dried up, we found many dead fishes.

Nearly a century later, on 23 October 1947, Dr A. D. Bajkov, an American marine scientist, was having breakfast with his wife in a café in Marksville, Louisiana, USA, when shortly after a sudden shower of rain, he noticed fish lying in the streets: 'sunfish, goggle-eyed minnows and black bass up to 9 inches [23 centimetres] long.' More fish were found on rooftops, cold and dead, but nevertheless still fit to eat.

No one has yet discovered how often fish falls occur. The records are widely scattered and there is not a full study available that has collected *all* known reports.

One of the best attested cases to have occurred in Britain was at Mountain Ash, Glamorganshire, Wales, in 1859. At 11 a.m. on 9 February, John Lewis, working in a timber yard, was startled by small objects falling out of the sky, one of which fell down the back of his neck.

On putting my hand down my neck I was

surprised to find they were small fish. By this time I saw that the whole ground was covered with them. I took off my hat, the brim of which was full of them. They were jumping all about.... They came down in the rain in 'a body like'.

A similar experience happened some 85 years later to Ron Spencer of Lancashire, while serving with the RAF at Kamilla, India, near the Burmese border. He loved going out into the monsoon rains to wash himself, and on one occasion he was standing naked in the middle of this ritual when

Things started to hit me, and looking round I could see myriads of small wriggling shapes on the ground and thousands being swept off the roofs, along channels and into the paddy fields.

They were small sardine-sized fish.

Attempted explanations for this perplexing phenomenon include the suggestion that it is

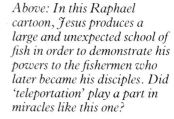

Above: In this Raphael cartoon, Jesus produces a large and unexpected school of fish in order to demonstrate his powers to the fishermen who later became his disciples. Did 'teleportation' play a part in miracles like this one?

Left: one of the most reliably recorded incidents of falling fish in Britain involved a timber yard worker, John Lewis, of Mountain Ash, Glamorganshire. He was hit on 9 February 1859, as illustrated in Charles Tomlinson's Raincloud and snowstorm *(1864)*

Right: one popular theory is that fish are gathered up and deposited elsewhere by tornadoes, like this one photographed in Nebraska. This explanation does not cover all types of falls however. The Mountain Ash fall, for example, was found to contain mostly sticklebacks with just a few minnows. Sticklebacks live in fresh water streams and do not congregate in shoals. How could a whirlwind scoop out such a vast quantity of sticklebacks together from a single source and deposit them all in one place? Another curious feature is the absence of all accompanying debris

caused by fish 'migrating overland'; that fish-eating birds regurgitate or drop their food; that fish are left behind by ponds and streams overflowing; and that fish hibernating in mud are brought to life again by rain. But these do not account for the variety of eyewitness reports, the assortment of species found in the same place, the variety of terrain where fish have been found and the sheer number of fish involved in some cases.

One of the most plausible explanations is that fish falls are caused by whirlwinds, tornadoes and waterspouts, and certainly there are well-documented cases of fish being transported by these means, but this hypothesis is inadequate to cover *all* cases. For one thing, these freak wind conditions tend to pick up anything in their way and scatter it widely. This conflicts dramatically with the great majority of cases of fish falls. In the Mountain Ash case, for example, the fall was restricted to an area 80 yards by 12 yards (73 metres by 11 metres). In addition, whirlwinds move continuously. There is considerable evidence that fish falls have lasted much longer than the time possible for them to have been caused by a whirlwind, and even if whirlwinds retrace their path, some fish falls have occurred in

such a rapid succession that they could not have been caused by one whirlwind.

The length of time during which fish have been transported through the air seems, according to the evidence, to vary considerably. In many accounts, the fish are alive and thrashing when found on the ground; in other cases they have been found dead, but fresh and edible. It is difficult to believe that fish could be hurled against the ground and not be killed, but the evidence suggests that even those found dead were not killed by their fall.

More puzzling still are the falls of dead fish. On two occasions in India, at Futtepoor in 1833 and at Allahabad in 1836, the thousands of fish that fell from the sky were not only dead, but dried. It is difficult to imagine how a whirlwind could keep so many fish in the air long enough for them to have dried out. But, despite widespread publicity in the Indian press at the time, no one came forward to report that a whirlwind *had* snatched up a valuable heap of dried fish!

In the falls of other animals and insects there is a tendency for only one species to descend at any one time, but fish falls seem to be equally divided between falls of a single species and mixed falls. Up to six different species have been identified in a single fall, lending support to the idea that the phenomenon is caused by a waterspout scooping from seas and lakes.

Objects caught up in the currents of a whirlwind might be expected to be hurled out at different times and distances according to their mass, size or shape. Contrary to this expectation, however, fish falls often involve many different sizes of fish.

Charles Fort suggested that fish falls are the result of what he called 'teleportation', a force that can transport objects from place to place without traversing the intervening distance. Through this agency fish are snatched away from a place of abundance to a point in the sky, from which they fall.

Fort further suggested that fish falls might be the result of a new pond 'vibrating with its need for fish'. There is the case of Major Cox, for example, a well-known writer in England after the First World War. In an article published in the *Daily Mail* on 6 October 1921, Cox reported that the pond at his Sussex home had been drained and scraped of mud. The pond was then left dry for five months before refilling with water in November 1920. The following May, it was teeming with tench.

Most fish falls occur during heavy rains, so the whirlwind theory seems to be partially acceptable. A look at the range of reported cases, however, shows that a number of falls have occurred in cloudless skies and quite independently of any accompanying strong wind. But if teleportation seems too far-fetched – and it is difficult to believe that fish can disappear from one place and reappear in mid-air – what other explanation is there?

Toad in the hole

In the winter of 1856, French workmen were blasting a tunnel when they came across a 'monstrous form' in the darkness. They had just split open a huge boulder of limestone, when the thing staggered from a cavity within the rock, rattled its wings, gave a hoarse cry, and died.

In the nearby town of Gray, a naturalist, versed in palaeontology, immediately recognised it as a *Pterodactylus anas*.

The rock strata from which it had come tallied with the era in which pterodactyls flourished, and it was noted that the cavity whence it had emerged formed an 'exact hollow mould of its body, which indicates that it was completely enveloped with the sedimentary deposit.'

The story of the French pterodactyl was perhaps the most dramatic of a series of accounts concerning living creatures immured for thousands of years in solid rock that set the fringe of Victorian science in quiet disarray and caused entrenched taking of sides.

The foundations of the 'suspended animation' controversy were laid in 1761 with the publication of the *Annual Register*, which that year devoted its pages to accounts – some from antiquity, some from more recent times – of living creatures, usually small reptiles or shellfish, having been found sealed in stone. Reports of this kind, which carried on into the Victorian era, were remarkably consistent.

There can have been few more academically respectable accounts, for example, than that given by the geologist Dr E. D. Clarke during a lecture at Caius College, Cambridge, in February 1818. Dr Clarke had been supervising the digging out of a chalk pit in the hope of finding fossils, and at a depth of 45 fathoms had uncovered a layer of fossilised sea urchins and newts. Three of the latter appeared to be in perfect condition, and Dr Clarke carefully excavated them and placed them on a piece of paper in the sunlight. To his astonishment, they moved. Although two of them died shortly afterwards, the third was placed in pond water and 'skipped and twisted about, as well as if it had never been torpid' and became so active that it escaped. Dr Clarke tried, without success, to match the bodies with those of live newts, and the Reverend Richard Cobbold, who attended the lecture and saw the newts, said 'They are of an entirely extinct species, never before known.'

On 8 April 1865, the august and sober *Leeds Mercury* reported the finding of a living, embedded toad during the excavation of Hartlepool Waterworks. Quarrymen, under their foreman Mr James Yeal, found the creature in a block of magnesian limestone 'at a depth of twenty-five feet [8 metres] from the surface of the earth and eight feet [2.5 metres] from any spring water vein.'

As in many similar instances, the toad's body had been perfectly moulded into the rock, 'and presented the appearance of being a cast of it. The toad's eyes shone with unusual brilliancy, and it was full of vivacity on its liberation. It appeared when first discovered,

Below left: Dr Edward Clarke, who in 1818 discovered three 'fossilised', but living newts

Bottom left: a fossilised pterodactyl, more than 100 million years old. In France in 1856 one was reported to have stumbled from the middle of a boulder – alive

desirous to perform the process of respiration, but evidently experienced some difficulty, and the only sign of success consisted of a "barking" noise. . . .'

This was not surprising, as its mouth proved to be completely closed and the 'barking' came from its nostrils. The paper reported that though at first it had been as pale as the stone from which it came, it later changed colour to a fine olive brown. Apart from these facts, and the 'extraordinary length' of its hind claws, it was quite normal. The Rev. Robert Taylor, vicar of St Hilda's and a local geologist of renown, estimated that the magnesian limestone in which it was found was at least 200 million years old. Yet the toad stayed alive for some days.

Examining this phenomenon in his *History of the supernatural* (1863), William Howitt pointed out that frogs and toads sink themselves into the mud at the bottom of ponds to pass the winter. If frogs could live six months in a nearly solid casing of viscous mud, why not six or any number of years?

In time, of course, the mud would become rock; but the great question remained: could frogs and toads survive the enormous pressure involved, let alone the vast geological time spans, before such a metamorphosis could take place?

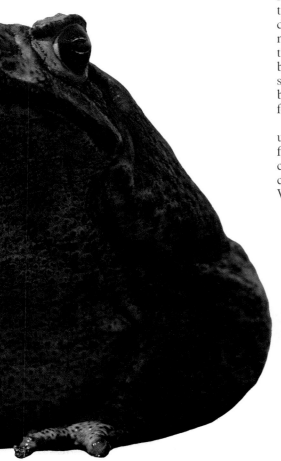

The answer to the first point seemed to be that the frail bodies could indeed survive; the great 18th-century naturalist Gilbert White, among others, had recorded finding a mummified frog in a stone – mummified, not fossilised. And this question of surviving the pressure seemed to depend on the fact that the rock, in its plastic state, was moulded to the body of the frog or toad as neatly as a nutshell to the kernel; a Monsieur Seguin of France, according to *The Times* of 23 September 1862, had encased 20 toads in a block of plaster of Paris, which was then allowed to set and was buried. After 12 years, four were still alive.

These and similar stories, although delighting the sensation-hungry general public, upset the scientific flock no end. The vast majority of doubting scientists refused to look into the matter at all. They fell back on the theory that the witnesses, many of them workmen, had been dishonest, credulous, or both. But why should a man such as Dr Clarke of Cambridge lay his reputation on the line, as it were, for the sake of sensation?

The pros and cons continued to be argued until the end of the century, when the issue finally all but died. It did leave behind one curious culinary legacy, that indigestible concoction of sausage and batter that the Victorians dubbed 'toad in the hole'.

Left: the common frog (Rana temporaria) *can survive for months buried in mud*

Below: Gilbert White, the great 18th century naturalist, claimed to have found a mummified frog inside a stone

Bottom: this mummified toad in a flint nodule was discovered by workmen in Lewes, Sussex. It is probably the only existing example of the phenomenon and is now preserved in the Brighton Museum

Werewolves

In 1598, in a wild and desolate area near Caude, France, a group of men stumbled across the horribly mutilated, blood-spattered body of a 15-old boy. A pair of wolves, which had been devouring the corpse, ran off into a nearby thicket as the men approached. They gave chase – and almost immediately they found a half-naked man crouching in the bushes, sporting long hair and an unkempt beard and long, dirty claw-like nails, which were clotted with fresh blood and the shreds of human flesh.

The man, Jacques Rollet, was a pathetic, half-witted specimen under the curse of a cannibal appetite. He was in the process of tearing to pieces the corpse of the boy when disturbed by the countrymen. Whether or not there were any wolves in the case, except what the excited imaginations of the men may have conjured up, it is impossible to determine. But it is certain that Rollet supposed himself to be a wolf, and killed and ate several people under the influence of the delusion. He was sentenced to death, but the law courts of Paris reversed the sentence and charitably shut him up in a madhouse – an institution where most suspected werewolves should have lived out their days rather than being executed, as often happened.

Another significant werewolf case occurred in the early 17th century. Jean Grenier was a boy of 13, partially idiotic and of strongly marked canine physiognomy – his jaws stuck forward, and his canine teeth showed under his upper lip.

He attacked a little girl one night when she was tending her sheep; she mistook him for a wolf and beat him off with her sheep-staff. When the identity of her assailant was discovered, and he was brought before the courts of Bordeaux, he confessed that he had killed and eaten several children.

A careful investigation by the court indicated that the missing children were eaten by Jean Grenier, and there is no doubt that the half-witted boy was convinced he was a wolf.

Above: little Red Riding Hood and the wolf, in an illustration by Doré. Elements of the werewolf legend have passed into this fairy story; but curiously, Red Riding Hood does not draw the obvious conclusion – that her grandmother is a werewolf

In more recent times, three werewolves were said to haunt the forested Ardennes area of Belgium just before the First World War, while in Scotland at about the same time a hermit shepherd in Inverness-shire was rumoured to be a werewolf.

In America, in 1946, a Navajo Indian reservation was frequently plagued by a murderous beast that was widely reported as a werewolf (Navajo traditions are rich in werewolf tales). Three years later, in Rome, a police patrol was sent to investigate the strange behaviour of a man suffering from werewolf delusions – he regularly lost control at full Moon and let out loud and terrifying howls.

In 1975, Britain's newspapers were full of extraordinary reports about a 17-year-old youth from the village of Eccleshall, Staffordshire who, in the awful belief that he was turning into a werewolf, terminated his mental agonies by plunging a flick-knife into his heart. One of his workmates told the inquest jury that the youth had made a frantic telephone call just before his death. 'He told me,' said the witness, 'that his face and hands were changing colour – and that he was changing into a werewolf. He would go quiet and then start growling.'

The werewolf tradition may be built on ignorance but its influence on the minds of the weak has always been powerful.

Most people's conception of a werewolf is of

Left: a man being pursued by a rabid wolf, from an illustration by Howard Pyle for Harper's Monthly Magazine *of December 1909. Being bitten by a werewolf, tradition has it, will make the victim a werewolf; and being bitten by a rabid wolf will make the victim rabid. Imagine the dilemma of the rustic mind, for whom a rabid wolf was quite simply a raging werewolf; if he were subsequently attacked by the diseased animal and developed the symptoms of rabies, he was, to observers, a werewolf*

an excessively hairy and ferocious man-beast that walks upright on two legs, growls and foams at the mouth, and displays large, dirty-looking lupine teeth. This, of course, is the now familiar portrait represented by late-night television movies like *Curse of the werewolf*, *The wolf man* and *Legend of the werewolf* – and it is inaccurate in all essentials.

History and mythology are quite clear in describing a man transformed into a werewolf as being little different from a natural wolf, except perhaps slightly larger than the wild species.

Those unfamiliar with the subject also tend to bracket werewolves with lycanthropes and talk about them as if they were one and the same thing. They are not.

A *lycanthrope* is a mentally sick person who believes that he has assumed the shape, voice and behaviour of a wolf, although he has not actually undergone any physical transformation. In the 15th and 16th centuries it was believed that the werewolf's fur grew on the inside of his skin; and many a lycanthrope has given this explanation when asked why, if he is a wolf, he still looks exactly like a person.

A *werewolf*, on the other hand, is traditionally a man who, by the agency of magic or by natural inclination, possesses an ability to change his shape to that of a wolf. All the characteristics associated with that animal are readily displayed. He may remain in his animal form for a few hours, or even permanently.

According to tradition, the methods used by werewolves to effect their transformations differed widely. Sometimes the change was spontaneous and uncontrollable; sometimes, as in the transformations described in the Norse and Icelandic sagas, it was achieved simply by assuming the skin of a real wolf; but in many cases all that was needed was the use of a charm that, while involving no actual change in the

human body, caused all onlookers to imagine that they really saw a wolf. Some of the transformed men claimed they could regain human form only by means of certain medicines or herbs such as aconite or hemlock, or by rubbing ointments on their bodies as did Scandinavian and central European werewolves from the 15th century onwards.

Another theory was that the possessed person had merely to put on a wolf's skin in order to assume instantly the lupine form and character. There is a vague similarity here with the alleged fact that the berserker – the Scandinavian bear-man or *werebear* – haunted the shadowy woods at night clothed in the hides of wolves or bears to acquire superhuman strength by transformation.

Such a wolfskin was kept by Jean Grenier. Jacques Rollet on the other hand, confessed to using a magic salve.

A further method of becoming a werewolf was to obtain a girdle, usually of animal origin, but occasionally made from the skin of a hanged man. Such a girdle was fastened with a buckle having seven tongues. When the buckle was unclasped, or the girdle cut, the charm was dissolved.

As for the werewolf proper, two qualities were said to remain when a man was transformed into a wolf: his human voice and his eyes. But in all other respects the metamorphosed werewolf was entirely animal: he had the hairy skin and claws of a wild wolf.

In his human form, however, a number of physical characteristics distinguished the werewolf from his fellow men. His eyebrows were said to meet on the bridge of the nose, and his long, almond-shaped fingernails were of a

Below: Nebuchadnezzar, from an engraving by William Blake. The great Babylonian king suffered a strange kind of malady: after having incurred the wrath of God, he was 'driven from men, and did eat grass as oxen, and his body was wet with the dew of heaven, till his hairs were grown like the eagles' feathers, and his nails like birds' claws'

Inset: a medicine man of the Blackfoot American Indian tribe, in an illustration of about 1830. It is easy to see how the habit of dressing up in animal skins for ritual purposes may have given rise to stories of were-animals

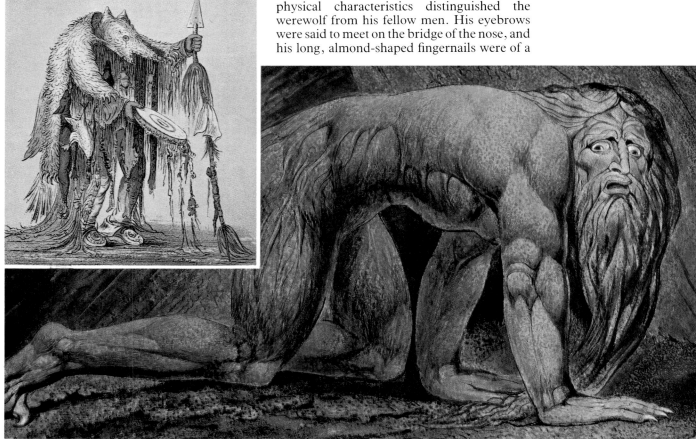

Below: the figure of the werewolf appears in legends throughout the world. By the Middle Ages in Europe, werewolves were generally believed to be real – as records of executions of supposed werewolves attest. It was believed that the creature could be found out if his clothes were hidden, making it impossible for him to resume human form

Above right: Assyrian mummers dressed in lion skins, in a relief from the eighth century BC. Dressing up in animal skins – for ritual purposes, as here, or for camouflage – may have given rise to the werewolf legend

sickening' blood-red tinge; the third finger, in particular, was always very long. The ears, which were positioned rather low down and to the back of the head, and a tendency towards hairiness of the hands and feet, were also clear identifying marks.

There are traditionally three principal types of werewolf. The first was the *hereditary werewolf*. His involuntary malady was passed down from one generation to another as a consequence of some terrible family curse. The second was the *voluntary werewolf*. His depravity of mind led him by choice to the realms of black-magic ritual, and to the use of all manner of terrible charms, potions, ointments, girdles, animal skins and Devil-worship incantations to bring about the desired metamorphosis. And the third was the *benevolent werewolf*. This gentle, protective scion of the werewolf family is almost a contradiction in terms. He felt nothing but shame for his brutal appearance and wished that no harm should befall man or animal.

Although the ancient Greeks and Romans and, to some extent, the ancient Arabs, believed in the occasional, localised existence of werewolfism, the situation was quite different in the Middle Ages in Europe. At this time the process of man-to-beast was supposed to be a phenomenon of daily occurrence. So genuine was the belief in the werewolf transformation that, in the 15th and 16th centuries, werewolves throughout Europe were regarded in the same light as witches and wizards, and anyone suspected of being a werewolf was burnt or hanged with the utmost cruelty, especially in France and Germany. Even today, in remote regions of Europe and Scandinavia, the superstition has not entirely lost its old power to grip the imagination of simple country folk.

Modern science finds in werewolfism little

that can be readily explained, and much that cannot be explained satisfactorily: the superstition, stemming from a period 1000 years before Christianity, contains a great deal that cannot be rationalised by modern thought.

The starting point of the superstition may have been the habit primitive people had of disguising themselves as animals when roaming the countryside as foragers or scouts. Or it may revolve around those born, even in civilised countries, with bestial appetites and cravings, a delight in fiendish cruelty and a liking for human flesh. Ancient medicine could easily have confused the lycanthropic form of psychosis with contagious canine rabies.

Theosophists today believe that during the Middle Ages, when public execution was common, many people sank so low morally that their astral bodies, the human spirits that we are said to use after death, actually linked with an animal. This explains why, if the astral body were to manifest itself in the form of a wolf, and it were subsequently wounded – its paw cut off, say, by a hunter – that wound would be duplicated on the werewolf's physical body in its human form: that is, one of the hands would be badly wounded or missing when the werewolf reverted to its human state. This is known as wound-doubling, and killing a werewolf in this way has always, by tradition, been the most favoured means by which to force him (or her) to resume his natural form on the spot, or lead to his speedy detection.

There are scientists today who have not completely rejected the possibility that werewolves may have existed; for is it really reasonable to suppose that legend, if it has no factual basis, can survive on fancy alone? If it is so much nonsense, this perennial belief in animal metamorphosis, why should learned men of science and medicine in all ages have spent so much time studying it?

CHAPTER FOUR

Belief
and Beyond

*Spiritualism, Psychic art,
Cross-correspondences, Life after death,
Stigmata, Holy incorruptibles,
Images that bleed and weep, Turin Shroud*

Survival of death

What happens when we die? Nothing? Complete bliss – 'eternal life'? Or a vague, insubstantial something?

Materialists and atheists would answer 'nothing'. For them life is a purely biological process; when the body dies the personality dies with it, just as electricity stops being generated when a battery fails. To such people life cannot 'go somewhere else'.

These rationalists frequently point out that the age-old belief in an afterlife is merely a reflection of Man's terror of death, of personal oblivion. Throughout history he has either avoided the unthinkable or surrounded it with ritual and a childish optimism. The materialist believes this to be craven and intellectually dishonest – we ought to face 'the facts' – after all, it is true to say that the one fact of life is death.

What of the concept of 'eternal life'? Nearly all religionists have preached that we survive bodily death – in one form or another. It is probably true to say that the more sophisticated the religion, the more certainly it envisages *some* form of 'life everlasting' for some

deathless element of the individual, whether in a kind of paradise or amid the torments of hell.

If the materialist is correct, no further enquiry need be made. If the religionists are correct, then it surely behoves each individual to look to his or her salvation. But in the context of religion, belief in the afterlife must remain a matter of faith, and only the experience of our own death can prove us right or wrong.

But what if neither of these rigid concepts is correct? What if something – some life-spark, vestige of the human personality – survives and enters a new kind of existence, not as a form of reward or punishment, but merely obeying a natural law? Today many psychical researchers feel that the balance of evidence suggests that 'something' does survive, not necessarily for very long after death, nor necessarily the whole personality. According to them, parts of an individual's memory-system and personality traits sometimes seem to survive for a long time, enabling his disembodied self to be recognised by the living who knew him, but later perhaps to disintegrate forever.

The objective analysis of purported evidence for human survival is a major concern of the Society for Psychical Research (SPR), founded in London in 1882. But the founding of the SPR would probably never have happened but for events of a generation earlier –

The plains of heaven *by the English painter John Martin, 1853. Hosts of the blessed rejoice in a dramatic landscape worthy of the mid-Victorian Romantic poets. These angels, some of them winged, play the traditional harp*

events that were to mark the beginning of the modern Spiritualist movement, whose adherents were to swell to millions around the world.

In March 1848 the home of the Fox family in Hydesville, in the state of New York, was disturbed by unaccountable shakings of the walls and furniture, by the sound of footsteps and knockings on the walls and doors.

One night Catherine, aged 12, tried to imitate the raps by clapping her hands. Almost immediately, according to a statement made by her mother, 'the sound followed with the same number of raps'. Mrs Fox then began to question the unseen rapper, using an alphabetical code by means of which it was established that the rappings were done by a spirit; eventually the entity identified himself as a pedlar who claimed to have been murdered and his remains buried in the cellar.

Neighbours were called in to verify the proceedings and, urged by the spirit, some men

Doris Stokes (box)

An astonishingly successful British clair-audient is Doris Stokes. She lives with her husband John in a modest London flat and regards herself as a very ordinary person. Yet she has an unusual gift that sets her apart from others: she claims to be able to speak with the dead.

Both on public platforms and in private houses, Doris acts as a 'go-between', relaying names and information to the living that she says are given to her by the dead. The messages she relays are usually made up of trivia, but the accuracy of the names and details leaves her recipients in no doubt that they are witnessing a paranormal phenomenon. Guesswork alone would not explain the content of the messages. But is it really communication with the dead?

Doris's gifts were apparent from an early age when she found herself describing – or predicting – things that she could not have known normally. This worried her mother, but her father – a natural psychic like his daughter – understood

started digging in the cellar to see if the story could be substantiated. Later reports suggest that parts of a body were indeed found, but Mrs Fox does not mention this in her statement.

The noises went on for several months; and when Catherine and her sister Margaretta, aged 14, went to stay with their sister Leah in Rochester, the rappings travelled with them. And although others were soon to discover that they, too, had some of this 'medium power', the spirits themselves confirmed that the Fox girls were specially endowed. Repeatedly, the messages insisted: 'You have been chosen to go before the world to convince the sceptical of the great truth of immortality.'

In November 1848, the sisters began to give demonstrations of their powers, and large numbers of people came to witness them. By now other mediums were emerging in emulation of the Fox sisters. The phenomena developed from rapped questions and answers to automatic writing and spoken utterances, culminating in direct voice communication in which the mediums were 'taken over' by the alleged entities. All kinds of physical phenomena accompanied the messages – movement of furniture, teleportation of objects, levitation of sitters or the medium herself, all kinds of noises and a wide variety of luminous phenomena. It was quickly apparent that public opinion was sharply divided between enthusiastic adherents, who had been awaiting just such 'proof' of the survival of the spirit, and no less determined sceptics who

Far left: the Fox sisters – Margaretta (top), Leah (centre) and Catherine (bottom). The strange phenomena at their home at Hydesville, New York, were taken by many to be the long-awaited proof of communications from the dead

and did nothing to discourage her. It was not until after Doris was married and her father had died that her psychic powers grew strong: and her experiences left her in no doubt that she was in contact with people who had died.

Her most dramatic personal experience occurred during the Second World War. Her husband John was reported 'missing in action' and a medium 'confirmed' that he had been killed. Doris returned home in a state of shock, but that day an apparition of her father appeared in her bedroom, saying that on Christmas Day she would receive proof of the fact that her husband was still alive. And, just as he had predicted, Doris learned that John was still alive, though wounded and a prisoner of war, on Christmas Day.

What raises Doris Stokes above the run-of-the-mill Spiritualist medium is her extraordinary down-to-earth attitude. To her the spirit world is as real as this one – and her firm conviction of survival after death communicates itself to her audience. Her specific and often deeply personalised messages frequently offer urgent advice: one deeply depressed widower was told by his wife not to take the overdose he was planning. He was impressed by the fact that no one knew of his intentions except himself – that, and the anger Doris conveyed from his wife. 'Your wife is very anxious about you. She says that is not the way. You must wait until your time comes.

Many a medium could have trotted out that advice – for almost all religious people are opposed to suicide – but Doris backed this up by 'proving' the continued existence of the man's wife through conveying many personal pieces of information known only to the man and his wife.

It is difficult to deny that Doris Stokes does receive information by some means inexplicable in terms of our present knowledge. If this information does not come from the spirits, is it possible that she obtains it by reading the minds of her sitters, by some form of ESP?

'No,' says Doris. 'If I thought that, I wouldn't do it any more. Because that would be an invasion of privacy. I don't think God would allow that.'

Doris Stokes 'performs' before the studio audience of Tyne Tees Television's Friday Live *programme in December 1979*

Below: the Fox family home in Hydesville, as depicted in a 1930s postcard. The original building was destroyed by fire; today an exact replica, built in the 1950s, stands on the site

saw these manifestations as imposture at best, at worst as the work of the Devil.

It was in this climate of extremes that the Society for Psychical Research was set up. The founder members were a group of British intellectuals who objected to the entrenched positions of 'believers' and 'sceptics' and who felt that the objective assessment of unusual phenomena was long overdue. The material collected by the British SPR and similar societies in other countries provides the strongest clues for the serious enquirer into the question 'What happens when we die?'

The huge body of material collected since 1882 includes much information on the activities of mediums – or, as they are better named, sensitives – who, according to their specific gifts, are generally classified into 'mental' and 'physical' sensitives.

'Physical' mediums are those in whose presence, whether they go into trances or not, physical phenomena occur. These may include loud raps from the seance table or from various points around the room; sometimes they seem to be in an intelligent code as if trying to convey some message. Also common are psychokinetic phenomena (solid objects moving as if handled by an invisible person); levitation, of the sensitive and of objects; the playing of musical instruments by unseen hands, and materialisation of spirit forms.

Sadly, in the short history of Spiritualism, many of these phenomena have been faked, but there still remain many cases of genuine physical mediumship that defy 'rational'

On January 30, 1925, Patience Worth gave the following inscription for "Hope Trueblood"—

"Ye see I hae witched thee by strummin' the tenderest chord in womankind, the mither-chord. Ye see I hae witched thee by a wee lassie who lived laughin' through woein'. . . . This be the zest o' life—Pennin' 'wit aneath the cowl o' sorrow."

HOPE TRUEBLOOD

"A Mid-Victorian Novel by a Pre-Victorian Writer"

By PATIENCE WORTH

Edited by CASPER S. YOST

Hope Trueblood differs materially from the previous productions of Patience Worth. In this she abandons her archaic dialect and constructs her story in standard English of the present day, free from grammatical irregularities. Modern in its language, the story is relatively modern in its time, which is about the middle of the nineteenth century—"a mid-Victorian novel by a pre-Victorian writer."

It is a simple tale of life in an English village, the autobiography of Hope Trueblood, born in that village without the knowledge of a father and suffering the tortures which that stain applies to a sensitive soul in a narrow community. One gets but a glimpse of Hope's mother, but the sweetness of her personality is a dominating influence throughout the story. It is filled with a delightful mingling of humor and pathos, and it has the quality of apparent reality that is so remarkable in "The Sorry Tale." A tantalizing mystery holds the reader in suspense to the end of the tale. There are vivid sketches of scenes, and there is much characteristic beauty of thought and of diction.

Patience Worth Publishing Co., Inc.
31 Tiffany Place,   Brooklyn, New York City.

TELKA

An Idyl of Medieval England

By
PATIENCE WORTH

AUTHOR OF "THE SORRY TALE," "HOPE TRUEBLOOD," "LIGHT FROM BEYOND" (SELECTED POEMS), "PATIENCE WORTH" (WITH SPIRIT PORTRAIT), "THE POT UPON THE WHEEL," ETC.

Edited with a Preface by
HERMAN BEHR

NEW YORK
PATIENCE WORTH PUBLISHING CO., INC.
1928
LONDON

Top: Mrs Pearl Curran, who allegedly took dictation from the spirit of a 17th-century Quaker named Patience Worth. Although the books communicated by Patience won critical acclaim, Mrs Curran's own literary abilities were negligible and her education limited. It seems impossible that Mrs Curran could have deliberately invented the ghostly Patience – but there is no evidence to show that Patience ever existed as she claimed

who want to believe will believe anyway. However, sensitives often have striking gifts of extra-sensory perception.

Sometimes they communicate with alleged spirits through the ouija board, or planchette, and perhaps the most remarkable illustration of this is the case of 'Patience Worth'. Purportedly the spirit of a 17th-century Englishwoman who had emigrated to America where she was killed by Indians, 'Patience' dictated a mass of material to Mrs Pearl Curran of St Louis, in the southern USA. From 1913 until Mrs Curran's death in 1938 she 'dictated' a colossal number of words, mostly of a quality that can fairly be described as 'literary'. She composed poems, novels and plays. One of her full-length novels, *Hope Trueblood*, was published in England under the name 'Patience Worth', with no explanation of the bizarre circumstances surrounding its composition. It won acclaim from the totally unsuspecting critics and public alike.

Patience's epic 'Golden Age' poem *Telka* contained 60,000 words and made astonishingly accurate use of Middle English phraseology. Her book *The sorry tale* told in 325,000 words the story of a contemporary of Christ whose life ran parallel to his and who ended by being crucified beside him as one of the thieves. *The sorry tale* was written extremely rapidly – in an evening's work of only two hours, Patience Worth could produce an average of 3000 words. In addition, no research was necessary. The details of social, domestic and political life in ancient Palestine and Rome, and the language and customs of Greeks, Arabians, Romans and several sects of Jews are rich and convincing. They could have been set down only by a highly knowledgeable scholar who had specialised in the history of the Middle East of 2000 years ago.

This could not have been Mrs Curran. She had been to Sunday School and that was the limit of her knowledge of the Bible lands. She was not fond of reading and had finished her school education at about 15 years of age. She had never left St Louis and, indeed, had rarely left St Louis. Until the appearance of Patience Worth she had concentrated her energies on being a housewife and an amateur singer of some talent. She knew little poetry and the verses she composed as an adolescent were no worse – but certainly no better – than those of any other girl of her age and background.

Naturally enough, 'Patience Worth' was intensively investigated by psychical researchers as well as academics. Members of the Boston Society for Psychical Research searched Mrs Curran's house for books of esoteric knowledge that could have been incorporated, consciously or unconsciously, into such works as *The sorry tale*. They found none. They also noted that the few books of poetry in the Currans' meagre library were unthumbed, and in one the pages were uncut.

explanation. Many tests have been set up to try to trap the frauds, and, to a lesser extent, to determine the extent of the phenomena.

A 'mental' sensitive may go into a trance, in which a 'control' ('controlling spirit' or 'spirit guide') speaks through her (sensitives are more often women than men), frequently in a voice entirely different from her own, and occasionally even giving her a different appearance, so that a European woman may temporarily take on the likeness and voice of, say, a Chinese man.

Through the sensitive the control may introduce other alleged spirits, recognisable by voice, gesture, or the nature of the private information they give to one of the sitters.

Another type of sensitive is the 'direct voice' medium, who does not, as a rule, go into a trance and from whose vicinity voices of both sexes and different kinds speak in various accents, and sometimes other languages.

Such so-called spirits may seem extremely convincing, though it must be said that those

The investigators tested Mrs Curran's own ability to write by asking her to produce short stories and poetry. These reveal a style that might be expected from a housewife unused to putting her thoughts on paper. Her personality shows through sufficiently to make any connection with the serious attitudes of Patience Worth seem positively ridiculous.

At first Mrs Curran produced automatic scripts on a ouija board. This, however was soon found to be too slow and clumsy as a means for taking down Patience's dictation, and Mrs Curran began automatic writing proper. This involves resting a pen or pencil,

Above: Mrs Rosemary Brown, who believes she is an amanuensis for long-dead composers, being filmed by a television company in 1980. During the filming Mrs Brown 'wrote' Mazurka in D flat (left), which she claims was inspired by Chopin. Beethoven (far left) apparently contacted Mrs Brown in 1964; he told her he was no longer deaf and could once again enjoy listening to music

held lightly in the hand, on a piece of paper. If one is so gifted, the pen will begin to write of its own accord. But soon even this method became too restrictive for the prolific outpourings of Patience Worth, who began instead to communicate directly with Mrs Curran's mind. She 'spoke' her poetry through Mrs Curran, who at the same time witnessed beautiful, atmospheric visions. Mr Curran took down Mrs Curran's/Patience Worth's words in longhand, and they were then typed.

Patience admitted to having burning literary ambition – and also acknowledged that in some way she might be a messenger of God. Perhaps she was suggesting that the mysterious phenomenon she was causing could guide people to God and a belief in eternal things. She wrote: 'I weave not, nay but neath these hands shall such a word set up, that Earth shall burn with wonder.'

Long-dead painters and composers, too, allegedly prove their continued existence by carrying on their arts through mediums.

The best known of those who claim to be amanuenses for long-dead composers is London housewife Rosemary Brown, who acts almost as an agent for Liszt, Beethoven, Brahms, Debussy, Chopin, Schubert and, more recently, Stravinsky. She is an unassuming, middle-aged lady with only a rudimentary musical background and she is the first to acknowledge that the works 'dictated' to her are beyond her everyday musical capacity. Mrs Brown sees herself merely as the humble scribe and friend of the late composers.

The idea of survival beyond death is not, however, strange to this Balham housewife. As a young girl she had visions of an elderly man who told her repeatedly that he and other great composers would befriend her and teach her their wonderful music. It was only many years later, when she was a widow concerned mainly with the struggle of bringing up two children on very limited means, that she saw a picture of Franz Liszt (1811–1886) and recognised him as her ghostly friend.

In 1964 she was contacted by other great composers – including Beethoven and Chopin – and her life work began in earnest: taking down their 'unfinished symphonies' and sharing her belief that there is no death – the great musicians are still producing.

The pieces transmitted to her are no mere outlines: they are full compositions, mainly for the piano but some for full orchestras. Mrs Brown says the music is already composed when it is communicated to her: the musicians dictate it as fast as she can write it down.

Indeed, observers of the process are amazed at the speed with which Rosemary Brown writes the music – and the standard is far beyond her conscious capacity or even her conscious knowledge.

Psychic art presents many of the same questions to the psychical researcher that are posed by the prize-winning literature of Patience Worth or Beethoven's 1980 symphony. Is the painting, poetry or music, believed by many to be evidence of the artists' survival beyond the grave, merely an exhibition of the medium's own repressed creativity, finally finding expression? Or is it really as simple as the psychics would have us believe – that the world's great musicians, writers and artists are 'proving' their continued existence by carrying on their arts through selected 'sensitives'?

But some examples of 'automatic' or psychic art are impressive, both in their own right and, more significantly, as examples of the styles of the great painters. Some collections of psychic art are also impressive in their diversity of style and their sheer quantity.

It was Matthew Manning's enormous collection of sketches, paintings and drawings,

Above: the style is unmistakably that of Toulouse-Lautrec, but this portrait was painted by the Brazilian trance artist Luiz Gasparetto. He produces vast numbers of 'old masters': some are painted with both hands simultaneously, some with his toes; almost all are completed within a few minutes. In a state of normal consciousness, Gasparetto says, he cannot paint at all

Left: a painting in the style of the great French impressionist Claude Monet, 'communicated' to the British psychic Matthew Manning. Does such work provide evidence of the artist's survival beyond the grave?

produced psychically by him as a teenager in the early 1970s, that convinced his publisher that he was a very special young man.

Matthew Manning's intelligent, articulate and objective approach to all the strange phenomena in his life makes fascinating reading. In his first book, *The link*, he discusses his method of 'contacting' dead artists. He simply sat quietly with a pad and pen in his hand and concentrated on the artist. He never went into a trance and was always aware of everything going on around him. Almost immediately the pen would begin to move, usually starting in the centre of the page and finally filling the page with what seemed like a well-planned work of art. Almost always the result was recognisably in the style of the artist he had been concentrating on – sometimes it was even signed. Occasionally, although bearing a strong resemblance to the style of the artist he had wanted to 'get through' to, the pictures were not signed. It seemed to Mr Manning that some other discarnate artist, perhaps even a pupil of the greater one, had intervened.

Among the signed works in his collection are drawings recognisably in the styles of Arthur Rackham, Paul Klee, Leonardo da Vinci, Albrecht Dürer, Aubrey Beardsley, Beatrix Potter, Pablo Picasso, Keble Martin and the well-known Elizabethan miniaturist Isaac Oliver.

Sometimes a finished picture would be very similar to a famous work by that particular artist. Matthew Manning often recognised them as 'copies' but occasionally the remarkable similarities had to be pointed out to him. A virtual reproduction of Beardsley's famous *Salome*, for example, took place under his eyes as he concentrated on Beardsley. But what value did these copies have – except to prove perhaps that the artist was alive and his style unchanged? Were they meant, in fact, to establish his identity?

Fragments and allusions

The deaths of the SPR's founder members, notably that of F. W. H. Myers in 1901, were followed by a new phenomenon in survival research, that of the 'cross-correspondences'. These were fragmentary messages received at different times and places through two or more sensitives unconnected with each other. The messages, often apparently nonsensical taken separately, made perfect sense when fitted together. The compiling of the cross-correspondences took over 30 years. The timing of their beginning, coinciding as it did with the deaths of those whose main preoccupation in life had been to understand the mysteries of death, seems to many investigators to prove beyond doubt who was behind the experiment. It seemed as if the founders of the SPR had a meeting beyond the grave and said, 'Any

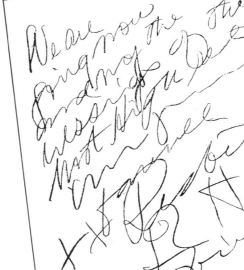

Right: Frederic Myers, a founder member of the Society for Psychical Research, apparently tried to prove his survival after death. He supposedly sent messages through various mediums, in different parts of the world, by means of automatic writing, which he had studied intensively in life.
The fragment below was produced by the medium Leonora Piper, in a hand markedly different from her normal script

Above: the celebrated medium Mrs Leonora Piper. Several researchers who studied her, including Myers, allegedly communicated various messages through her after their deaths

normal message we send will be ascribed to thought transference. Let us devise a method of communication that will not be open to such an interpretation.'

Certainly no messages easily ascribable to thought transference had ever been communicated in fragments to different mediums before. And the subject matter of the messages – poetry and erudite classical allusions – was highly characteristic of the group of dead SPR members. Many researchers believe that the cross-correspondences are the best evidence yet of survival. But even so, all they do is attempt to convince us, in as many ingenious ways as possible, of the continued existence of certain individuals. (The dead Myers is alleged to have found the effort of communication trying, and 'endlessly presenting my credentials' frustrating in the extreme.) But even assuming its authenticity, this massive, painstaking experiment tells us little of what happens when we die except that we retain something of our earthly habits of thought and some traits of personality.

The disembodied self

Since the 1960s research has been carried out into the experiences of people who have clinically 'died' – often on the operating table – and who have come back to life. They nearly all report approximately similar experiences, whether they had previously believed in survival or not. They were conscious of leaving their bodies and passing through a dark tunnel with a light at the end. When they emerged from the tunnel they were met by a radiant figure, often too bright to be seen clearly. This being they identified differently, according to their religious 'vocabulary'; for the Westerner he is usually taken to be Christ. They may also be aware of the presence of dead friends or relatives, and are filled with tremendous peace and joy. Yet they are told that their time has not yet come and they have to return. With the greatest unwillingness they re-enter their body.

One person who has had this kind of experience is Durdana Khan. In 1968, when she was about two and a half years old, Durdana became dangerously ill and 'died' for a quarter of an hour. According to her own account, she then went to a new world in the stars, met long-dead relatives and had an interview with God – whom she could describe only as 'blue'. Durdana painted some pictures of the scenes she saw during the time she was apparently dead, and these were subsequently shown in an interview she gave on the BBC-TV programme *Pebble Mill at one*. The next day,

Durdana's father was contacted by a Mrs Goldsmith, who had seen the programme; it turned out that she had had an experience of near death similar to Durdana's. 'I nearly jumped out of my chair when I saw this picture on the television,' she said about one of the paintings. ' "My God," I said, "I've been to this place . . ." '

Astonishingly, it appeared that she had visited the actual spot that Durdana had painted. Mrs Goldsmith recognised everything that was in Durdana's picture, and also

Above: Durdana Khan, aged two and a half, on her way to recovery after having 'died' for 15 minutes as the result of a neural illness. She said that she had heard her father's voice calling her – and had asked God if she could return. When asked what God was like, she could only say 'blue' (top: Durdana's impression of God)

described things that were not shown. They talked about what was round the bend in the stream that Durdana had painted, and about the location of the other streams that Durdana had described to her mother.

Where was it that Durdana spent her quarter hour of death? Durdana herself believes that her experience somehow reflects her own expectations. 'If I had been a Martian, perhaps I would have been sent to a replica of Mars. There perhaps, God would have appeared red.' And yet Durdana's experience must be more than a dramatisation of her own imagination – for Mrs Goldsmith recognised the very same place.

The stages of death

Almost everyone in the Western world is afraid of dying. The fear itself is natural enough – but what exactly are we afraid of? The answer differs greatly from one person to another. One fears the pain and indignities that terminal illness may bring; another fears divine judgement, while someone else, on the contrary, is afraid that there is nothing after death but oblivion. But to most people death is simply the 'unknown', too fearful to be contemplated. The result is a taboo on the discussion of our own deaths.

This conspiracy of silence adds to the burdens of those who are approaching their deaths: they are facing the greatest trauma of their lives, yet all too often no one will even talk about it. A new profession has been created to meet the needs of the terminally ill: counsellors to the dying. And one of the most remarkable workers in this field is Dr Elisabeth Kübler-Ross, an American who has been counselling the dying, from tiny children to old people, since the 1960s. In 1974 Dr Kübler-Ross made this uncompromising statement: 'Before I started working with dying patients, I did not believe in life after death. I now believe in it beyond a shadow of a doubt.'

Extraordinary personal experiences convinced her of this. But before they occurred, what she had seen of the deaths of others sometimes suggested that they marked the transition to a new life.

She observed that there are five stages that a terminally ill person can go through. The first is denial, accompanied by avoidance of other people. This is followed by anger. The third stage is bargaining, then comes depression. Finally comes the stage of acceptance.

In her work Dr Kübler-Ross encountered many such cases. She also talked to many patients who had clinically 'died' and had been resuscitated. Their stories of leaving their bodies and experiencing great happiness and even excitement were remarkably consistent. Few wanted to 'come back'. And most significantly, almost everyone who had experienced a short period of 'death' had no fear of dying finally.

The strength of Dr Kübler-Ross's convictions rests on her own amazing personal experiences. In the early 1970s, after a tiring day, she lay down to rest. Suddenly she had the experience of leaving her body. She later learned that someone checked her pulse and respiration at this time and thought she was dead.

When Dr Kübler-Ross 'returned' to her body, she felt that she had discovered that consciousness can leave the body in certain circumstances in life – and presumably does so at death, permanently. She felt that she now knew what it was like to die.

An even stranger and far more traumatic experience was to follow, transforming her outlook on life – and especially death. One night she was finding it difficult to sleep when suddenly:

I had one of the most incredible experiences of my life. In one sentence: I went through every single death of every single one of my thousand patients. And I mean the physical pain, the . . . agony, the screaming for help. The pain was beyond description. . . . I was able to catch my breath for a split second and I pleaded – I guess with God – for a shoulder to lean on.

And a thunderous voice came: 'You shall not be given.'

Figures of angels and the symbol of the cross, found in every Christian graveyard, express a profound hope for a life beyond the grave – a hope that goes hand in hand with a deep fear of death. Yet some who have been on the very brink of dying claim to know that there is an afterlife. One such is Dr Elisabeth Kübler-Ross (below), a psychiatrist who is now acknowledged as a world authority on the counselling of the dying

Gasping for breath, she raged at it: 'I have helped so many and now no one will help me.' But at that moment in place of the unimaginable suffering came 'the most incredible rebirth experience'. She began to see every pebble, leaf and bird – everything that is – as being part of a whole 'alive universe'. She had experienced what the mystics have termed 'cosmic consciousness'. In some way the experience gave her an insight into the continuity of all things, including the spirit before and after death.

The acknowledged expert in her growing field, Dr Kübler-Ross has written a major work, *On death and dying* (1970), which is essential reading for those who are continually faced with the problems of coping with the

Top: the statue of Justice that stands above the Old Bailey in London. The scales and the sword she carries represent the two aspects of justice: mercy and retribution. Absolute justice, however, is said to be found only in the afterlife – where motives are seen for what they really were in life

Above: the traditional Christian belief in a day of reckoning, as portrayed in Fra Angelico's The day of judgement

Right: The garden of earthly delights *by Hieronymus Bosch. He saw the average man's ideal world as totally physical – and, ultimately, totally degrading*

dying. Yet her certainty about the afterlife, her out-of-the-body experiences and her descriptions of cosmic consciousness have proved a shocking embarrassment to the medical profession. Her work is freely quoted and her vast practical experience is drawn on, but very few students care to discuss her spiritual discoveries.

The dying patient who is lucky enough to be counselled by Dr Kübler-Ross may well never hear her speak of an afterlife unless she is specifically asked to do so. But to her five stages in the process of dying, she has privately added a sixth: the afterlife.

The journey of the soul

Evidence for reincarnation not only indicates that we survive and are reborn (perhaps many times), but also offers clues as to why we are born at all. Hypnotic regression into 'past lives'; some children's spontaneous memories of being someone else; the 'far memory' of some adults; some *déjà vu* experiences; all these, though amenable to other explanations, point to reincarnation as a possibility. Many

people believe that we must submit to a string of different earthly lives until we have achieved near perfection of soul, then we become gods or progress on a purely spiritual plane of existence. Some think that not everyone is reincarnated but that we do not understand the rules governing the selection process involved.

Dr Ian Stevenson of the University of Virginia in the United States has made a detailed and scholarly investigation into the evidence for reincarnation. He has amassed hundreds of cases of alleged 'past lives' and came to the conclusion that 'a rational man . . . can believe in reincarnation on the basis of evidence.' However, for the majority of people such a belief will remain a matter of faith alone.

Even among people who believe in some kind of an afterlife, alleged communications from the 'other side' are frequently regarded with suspicion. Perhaps it is natural to ascribe such accounts to the result of wishful thinking or unjustified hopes and fears. For this reason most people are unaware of the enormous amount of material, accrued by the SPR and the College for Psychic Studies, purporting to describe the next world from people *who are now there*. But if, for a moment, we suspend our disbelief, what emerges from this material – which seems to emanate from intelligent and honest sources and has been given to reputable mediums over the past 100 years or so – is not only evidence for an afterlife but an amazingly consistent description of what it is like to be dead.

The first feature of the accounts is that dying is not the absolute event most people fear; largely, it appears to be a state of altered consciousness. Evidence points to it being harder after death to get rid of the old earthly self than we had supposed. The same personal limitations continue until we resolve them. Death does not in itself change us; it gives us a different kind of opportunity to change ourselves.

In spiritualistic communications, life after death is often described as a progress through seven spheres, each of a more rarified and spiritually invigorating nature than the last. The seven spheres basically represent levels of consciousness, and any of these is reached only by a widening and deepening of the moral nature. After death one must realise that life continues as a process of learning.

The discarnate spirit, after meeting the loved ones who had died before him, lives first in *summerland* or *winterland*, both of which he creates from his own habits of thought, respectively good or bad. These are both on what has been called the *ideo-plastic* plane ('ideo-plastic' meaning creation through ideas alone) and seem to serve to break him of his earthly preoccupations and make him yearn for the benefits of higher, more spiritual faculties. But summerland is not 'heaven', nor is winterland 'hell'. Both states exist because of the inner

self of the individual. When he becomes more spiritual they are transcended.

First, however, the spirit must undergo the *judgement* in the *first heaven* and the *second death*, processes that hold a mirror up to the person he was, mercilessly stripping him of his illusions about himself and making him realise – by momentarily *becoming* other people in his life – what his actions and words had done to them. Sir Arthur Conan Doyle, in describing his own posthumous experience, calls this transition 'terrible and marvellous', adding that 'there are no trimmings on a man after the second death.' Yet this traumatic experience prepares the student, shorn of his most dearly held pretensions, for the next stage in his progress: his entry into the *second heaven*.

During his stay in the second heaven the spirit learns from a 'replay' of his past lives to discover his true potential and what steps he should take to fulfil it. Strengthened by the insight and love of a highly important unit known as the *group soul* – friends formed over many lifetimes, with whom he relives ancient memories to which his immediately previous personality had no access – he is now ready for a yet further expansion of his consciousness, which takes place in the *third heaven*.

This is, however, too intense an experience for many spirits to endure for very long, although it is open to them for precisely as long as they can endure. According to the communicators, in the third heaven a spirit comes to the limits of his consciousness. After a brief glimpse of this plane he finds he cannot go further into it than his nature allows. Faced with his limitations he has no choice but to return to earth.

However, if his next incarnation goes well and he grows spiritually as a result, he will find that he can then proceed deeper into the third heaven. This in turn will enable him to make more of his succeeding earth life, for it is in the third heaven that the true nature of the group soul's task unfolds as consciousness expands in the individual members.

But what happens when a person has little more to learn from earth? He can take a leap into the great unknown, leaving this planet and its successive incarnations altogether, and begin again somewhere else. Communications are vague on this point, but they do seem to imply a new cycle of physical lives on another planet. Most spirits, however, prefer to wait, helping others if needed, even if it means being reincarnated on earth yet again. A group soul will move on only when every member is ready to go. No one will be left behind.

People frequently deplore the injustice of 'life', meaning their earthly existence. But if the accounts of the afterlife summarised here are substantially true, then there is such a thing as absolute justice, there is cause for hope, there is free will and ever-expanding consciousness.

Stigmata

One Friday in March 1901 a young Italian girl prayed before a large lurid crucifix, and experienced a vision that changed her life. Her name was Gemma Galgani; she was 23 years old and an orphan. She wanted to become a Passionist nun, but was refused because of her spinal tuberculosis; instead, this simple, quiet and fervently devout girl became a domestic help in the local village. But her vision lifted her out of the ordinary, as she identified with Jesus's suffering, experiencing with combined agony and ecstasy each blow of the lash.

When she was found in her room by her adopted mother, her arms and back were covered with wounds like whip marks and her clothes were soaked in blood. From that day until she died two years later these stigmata appeared with astonishing regularity each Thursday, vanishing the next day. Her biographer, Father Germano di Stanislao, described how her wounds developed at the onset of her ecstasy, reddening slowly on the backs and palms of both hands; '. . . under the epidermis a rent in the flesh was seen to open by degrees . . . after a little the membrane burst and on those innocent hands were seen the marks of flesh wounds.' They were very deep, apparently passing right through the hand itself. They were full of blood, 'partly flowing, partly congealed', and out of consideration for the pain they caused the girl, Father Germano never probed them. On Friday the wounds closed quickly, leaving only a whitish mark by Sunday. The location of the marks varied from week to week, said Father Germano, sometimes appearing on the hands or feet only, sometimes bleeding through an unruptured skin. At other times the appearance of nails with thick heads could be seen in the wounds, formed out of mounds and ridges of darkened flesh and dark, solidified blood.

Despite the scorn of sceptics, there can be no doubt about the reality of stigmatic phenomena. They have occurred too many times under close medical scrutiny to be a fiction. And although the greatest body of evidence lies in the hands of the Catholic Church and is inaccessible, we have more than enough proof of their existence from the testimony of doctors and other impeccable witnesses cited in many official biographies, and in modern times the marks have been photographically recorded.

So what are these marks? Popularly the word *stigmata* is taken to mean the wounds suffered by Christ that are reproduced on the body of the stigmatic. Traditionally these are the wounds corresponding to those made by the nails in the hands and feet, and the spear wound in the side of the chest. There are also supplemental stigmata, often appearing on their own: scourge marks on the body, holes in the forehead as if made by a crown of thorns, a deformed shoulder said to be from the weight of the cross, and more bizarrely, curious symbols were said to be imprinted onto the heart and other internal organs.

Genuine stigmata have very interesting physiological characteristics that differentiate them from ordinary flesh wounds. The blood that flows from them is clean arterial blood with no trace of disease. The wounds may stay open for long periods, sometimes years, with a complete inhibition of normal healing processes, despite which they remain free of infection and inflammation. Most stigmata recur regularly, some during Lent and Easter every year, some on special Church feast days only, and others every Friday, especially Good Friday.

The first recorded stigmatic was St Francis of Assisi who, while praying in 1224, found his hands and feet pierced by nails, the heads of which were clearly visible. His biographer

Opposite page: in his Crucifixion, *Velasquez portrayed Christ's wounds in the traditional places in his palms. We now know that the nails must have gone through his wrists in order to support the weight of his body. Will future stigmata appear in the clinically accurate location?*

describes a nail-like formation of tissue apparently lodged in the wound, and those in the feet protruded so much St Francis could not walk. So bizarre is this detail that many historians have dismissed it as an embellishment, but medical testimony to similar formations suggest its authenticity.

Reports of stigmatism have continued to occur up to the present; indeed, they may even be more frequent today than ever before. An extensive listing of stigmatics was attempted in 1894 by Dr Imbert-Gourbeyre, who reached the total of 321 cases. A survey conducted in the 1930s by the subject's great authority, Father Herbert Thurston, suggests that this figure is conservative.

Another curious statistic is the extraordinary high proportion of female stigmatics; in Dr Imbert-Gourbeyre's figures only 41 were male, and only one of these was stigmatised fully – St Francis himself.

The only other known fully stigmatised man since St Francis has been the Capuchin friar Padre Pio Forgione, most of whose humble life was spent at the monastery of San Giovanni Rotondo at Foggia, Italy, and who died in 1968. In 1915, aged 28, he emerged from a long meditation with a stinging sensation in his hands. Three years later he was alone in the choir, celebrating the Feast of the Stigmata of St Francis, when his piercing cry brought his brothers running. They found him unconscious, bleeding profusely from the traditional sites of all five of Christ's wounds. He begged for this to be kept a secret, but word spread. Regularly, as he lifted the Host during mass, he would pass into ecstasy and a cupful of blood and serum would flow from his wounds every day. He could move only with pain and difficulty but tried to remain private and to conceal his hands; however, public adulation was so great that he was under almost constant observation and pursuit, not to mention the dispassionate scrutiny of the Vatican.

Perhaps the most famous female stigmatic of the 20th century is Teresa Neumann. Like St Gemma, she came from a poor background and took up menial work until mysterious

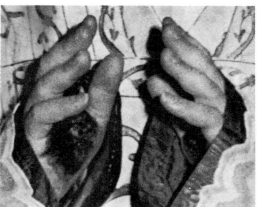

Right: St Francis and St Andrew *by El Greco. The stigmatism of St Francis was the first recorded instance of the phenomenon, yet it did not occur until 1200 years after the crucifixion*

Above, far right: Padre Pio Forgione, who died in 1968, was one of the most revered and best-known of all stigmatics. After he was stigmatised in 1915 at the age of 28, this Capuchin friar sought to hide his terrible hand-wounds (far right), appearing in public only to say mass. There is no doubt that his stigmata were real; doctors examined them over the years and discovered his palms to be permanently pierced right through. Padre Pio suffered constant pain but bore it uncomplainingly

illnesses incapacitated her. In 1926, when she was 28, her afflictions were spontaneously cured after a vision that left her stigmatised. For 32 years she gushed blood from hands, feet, side and forehead during most Fridays – sometimes losing as much as a pint (0.5 litre) of blood and 8 pounds (3.6 kilograms) in weight. Yet she was back to normal by Sunday. For most of this time she was under medical supervision, in the Bavarian village of Konnersreuth, and was also watched closely by the Bishop of Ratisbon. Doctors examined her

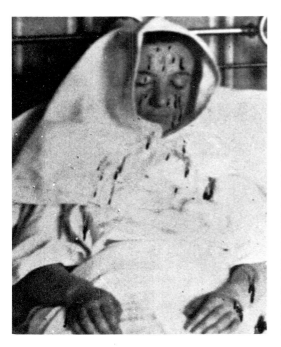

the 'stigmatic complex' corresponds to certain psychoneurotic conditions, particularly that known as 'hysteria'. The major problem here arises over the popular misunderstanding of the meaning of the word. To most people – including most Catholic theologians – it conjures up an image of someone highly excitable and weak-minded.

Uses of hysteria

The clinical meaning of the term is, however, quite different; a hysterical *personality* indulges in the dramatic and exaggerated behaviour commonly associated with 'hysteria' but the *symptoms* described by this word can afflict anyone in circumstances of stress, heightened emotion or inner conflict. There are many cases on record of soldiers in action who are suddenly smitten with inexplicable paralysis or blindness. Tests show that they are not malingering – the symptoms are 'real' –

Far left: Teresa Neumann, the poor Bavarian woman whose mysterious illnesses were banished when she was stigmatised in 1926. Every Friday until her death in 1962 she suffered Christ's Passion; wounds appeared in her hands, her sides and her forehead. She lost weight yet she was always back to normal every Sunday. She also spoke in Aramaic during trances and is said to have taken no food or liquid – except the Communion wafer and wine – for 35 years

Below: weeping blood, a rare phenomenon closely related to true stigmata and equally mysterious

thoroughly – taking advantage of her trances and periods of unconsciousness – and frequently described the appearance of wounds with the nail-like formations first seen in St Francis of Assisi. One observer noted that, as the years went by, wounds that had been on the backs of her hands developed instead in the palms.

According to Johannes Steiner's biography of Teresa Neumann, which was published in 1967, and which includes photographs of her unique rectangular hand wounds, no food or liquid – except the Communion wafer and wine – passed her lips for the last 35 years of her life, and many experiments by different doctors confirmed this astonishing fact. Moreover, her excreta ceased after 1930 and her intestinal tract simply withered – yet despite this she remained fairly active, having ecstasies and visions right up to her death in 1962.

Cases of stigmata continue to be reported. Of the many that could be mentioned, one is of special interest to researchers, that of little Cloretta Robinson, who was 10 when she was stigmatised for 19 days over Easter in 1972. She was studied by two psychiatrists, who reported in *General Psychiatry* (May 1974) that they had seen drops of blood oozing through a discoloured patch of skin on her palms when they put her hands under a microscope. Although her marks did not return, this case is especially remarkable, because not only is Cloretta a normal American girl – she is no brooding mystic – she is also the first known black and non-Catholic stigmatic.

There are sceptical scientists who, without investigation, prefer to dismiss these stories and their frequently unimpeachable witnesses as subject to hoax, delusion and wishful thinking.

However, there are many who believe that

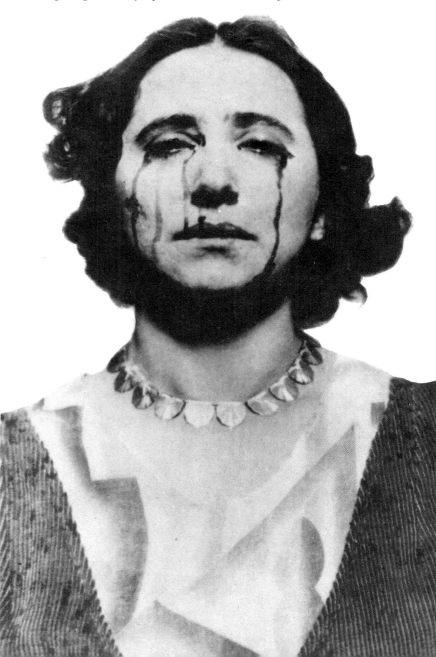

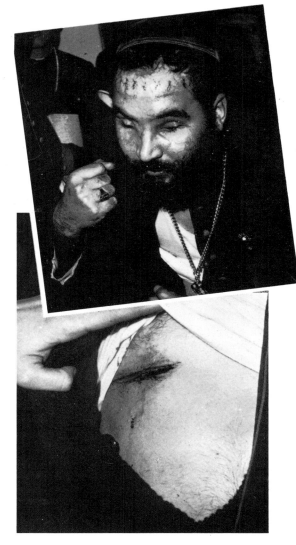

but the cause is discovered to be hysterical. The soldier cannot face the battle any longer but because of his training and fear of being labelled a coward he cannot give in to his fear and run away. Instead his brain resolves the conflict for him, causing his body to cease functioning as a fighting force.

Hysterical symptoms are, psychiatrists agree, not incompatible with ordinary lives nor with those of the highest sanctity. Hysteria does not 'explain away' stigmata, as many Church apologists fear, but it could well describe the mechanism of this bizarre phenomenon.

Yet most Roman Catholics still regard a 'hysterical' explanation of stigmata as an insult and a blasphemy. They point out that stigmatics such as St Gemma Galgani or Padre Pio were humble, quiet and downright unexcitable, therefore obviously not 'hysterical'. But a closer look at the lives of these 'quiet' stigmatics reveals a history of mysterious maladies and an abnormal physical sensitivity. They were subject to a range of inexplicable illnesses including blackouts, fits, paralysis, blindness and so on. Many were victims of tuberculosis, which heightens suggestibility. And, interestingly, the visions that stigmatised them also marked the end of their illnesses.

This subjective element in the patterning of stigmata, and the great variety of forms it takes, would also seem to argue for a hysterical foundation; the wounds themselves differ according to how the stigmatic imagines Christ was crucified. Perhaps significantly, there are no known examples of wounds occurring in the wrists, the site of the wounds suggested by researchers into the Turin Shroud. But now that this is quite common knowledge among the devout, future stigmatics could well exhibit wrist wounds.

There have been many attempts to reproduce stigmata by hypnosis but the only results have paled in comparison to the dramatic piercings and copious bleedings of genuine stigmata, which have defied normal healing processes and stayed with the stigmatics for most of their lives. Yet it cannot be overlooked that there is a high correlation between the histories and phenomena of stigmatics and those of clinical hysteria; the difference is merely one of context and degree.

In many, if not all, cases of stigmata the effects seem to stem somehow from the subconscious mind of the stigmatic. If we could begin to understand the process of cause and effect involved then perhaps many more strange phenomena would be understood.

Right: St Charbel Makhlouf who died in 1898 at the Hermitage of St Peter and St Paul in Lebanon. According to the custom of his order he was buried without a coffin, but several weeks later his superiors ordered an exhumation, since strange lights were seen around the grave. His body was perfectly intact despite the floods that had filled the grave with mud and water. It was washed and reclothed and placed in a wooden coffin in the monastery chapel. Soon an oily liquid – like a mixture of blood and perspiration – seeped from the body copiously and many cures were attributed to pieces of cloth soaked in it. In 1927 the body was placed in a zinc coffin and bricked into a wall. In 1950, pilgrims noticed liquid oozing through the wall and the tomb was opened, revealing St Charbel to be completely lifelike and free from corruption. Every year since then his tomb has been reopened and the body examined. Each time, it is fresh and intact, and the oily exhudation which collects to a depth of about 3 inches (8 centimetres) is drained off to be distributed as a healing cure

Holy incorruptibles

Of the many miracles associated with the saints, none is more dramatic and mystifying than that of incorruptibility – the phenomenon of bodies that do not decompose after death. There has been remarkably little study of this strange subject despite the high quality of the proofs demanded by the Congregation for the Causes of Saints in the process of canonisation. And the Church records demand serious consideration because exhumations and examinations have nearly always been carried out before many witnesses, including where possible doctors and medical specialists. It seems astonishing that so well-documented a fact as the incorruption of certain persons should

have escaped medical scrutiny for so long.

Father Herbert Thurston, the subject's first historian (writing in the late 19th century), describes six types of phenomena associated with cases of incorruption (not all of which may occur in the same case): very often a persistent fragrance is reported emanating from the body; an absence of rigor mortis; absence of putrefaction; sometimes there is a bleeding (from stigmata or wounds suffered in martyrdom, for example) long after death; in a few cases the body is felt to be warm long after death; even more rarely there is some kind of ritualised movement of the limbs (for example, giving a blessing) that cannot be accounted for by mere contraction of muscles. To this we may add another group of phenomena frequently encountered in cases of incorruption: often the secret or long-forgotten burial place of the saint is revealed to his discoverers by a dream or vision; sometimes their first interment is marked by unusual phenomena, like the strange lights that played around the grave of St Charbel Makhlouf; long-dead bodies, or their remaining parts, frequently exude a fragrant clear oil in great quantities, whose origin and composition is a mystery; finally, to this exudation, as well as to the relics of their bodies, blood and clothing, are attributed great powers of healing, the success of which has been established at many shrines by medical case histories.

The only other work of any note on incorruption is that of a New Orleans woman, Joan Cruz, who over many years patiently extended the lists of incorrupt saints begun by Father Thurston, by going through all the generally available ecclesiastical biographies.

Her book, *The incorruptibles* (published in 1977), contains 102 such cases approved by the Congregation for the Causes of Saints of the Catholic Church. There may be a great many others, adds Cruz, lying undiscovered in their graves, or whose details are hidden in the secret archives of the Vatican. Even such a prodigious sweep through the hagiographical literature failed to turn up a study of incorruption by any physician, eminent or otherwise, other than the statements of those doctors who attended specific post-mortem examinations.

One of the astonishing aspects of incorruption is not that it happens at all, but that it frequently happens to bodies under conditions that would encourage the normal processes of disintegration, including that of death caused by disease, and burial in close proximity to other bodies that decomposed normally. Some, again like St Charbel, had been consigned to the bare earth without any ill effect, except perhaps some minor distortion by the pressure of the earth. Others survived – if one may use the word – burial in such damp conditions that their clothes rotted off their intact bodies.

A number of the incorruptibles had been stigmatics during life, and in some cases their mysterious wounds persisted beyond the grave. St Catherine of Siena believed she bore the marks of Christ's Passion invisibly, and on her death the wounds appeared on her hands, feet and side. When her body was examined and parts detached as separate relics – an act called a 'translation' – one such mark was still visible on her perfect left foot in 1597 (217 years after her death).

An even more bizarre case, which defies all the normal expectations, is the martyrdom of the Polish saint, Andrew Bobola, at the hands of the Cossacks in 1657. After a cruel beating he was dragged by horses from one town to another, partly flayed, and had parts of his face and limbs torn away before being dispatched by a sabre. He was hastily buried in a churchyard at Pinsk, during a hot summer, in moist ground and in the midst of many other corpses whose bodies had decayed normally. Forty years later his body was discovered intact (apart from his wounds), and has since been subjected to many medical examinations. In 1917 it was on exhibition, still pliable and well-preserved. In 1922, Red Army troops, hearing of the legend of St Andrew's preservation, surrounded the church at Pinsk and broke open his tomb. After dragging out the body and presumably satisfying their curiosity, they left it on the floor. It was taken to Moscow and returned years later only after a plea by Pope Pius XI. The relic now resides in the church in Warsaw that bears his name.

The phenomenon still occurs today, and not always within a specifically saintly context. In 1977, a family grave in Espartinas, Spain, was opened to inter the body of a local man. The sexton and his helpers were shocked to find that the body of the man's son was still intact after 40 years. The boy, José Garcia Moreno, died in 1937 of meningitis at the age of 11, and the family deny that he was embalmed. Soon the whole village had viewed the body in its rotting grave-clothes – and, believing the boy must have been a saint to be so 'favoured', have begun to petition Rome for his canonisation. However, as Father Thurston points out, phenomena such as stigmata, visions, levitation or incorruption are less important to the

Below: a bizarre example of incorruption, one of the oldest cases, is that of St Cecilia, of a noble Roman family, martyred in AD 177. An inexperienced executioner bungled her beheading, and she lay for three days dying on the floor of her family home, her hands crossed in prayer, her face to the floor and her neck half-severed. Her body was placed in the catacomb of St Callistus in the exact position in which she died. In AD 822, her secret burial place was revealed in a vision to Pope Pascal I, who placed her body beneath the altar of the basilica dedicated to her name. It was rediscovered during restoration work in 1599. The original coffin was found in good condition inside a marble sarcophagus, St Cecilia's body in her dying position and still totally incorrupt after almost 1500 years. The body – with the neck wound plainly visible – went on view for a month before its reinstatement beneath the altar in a special casket commissioned by Pope Clement VIII

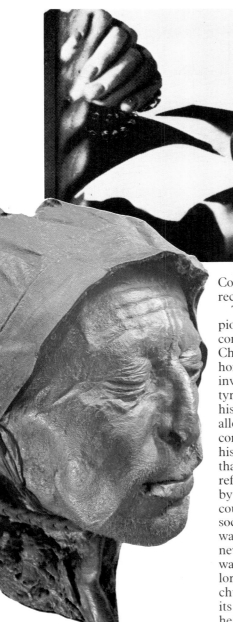

Above: the head of a Tollund man, dating from the Danish Iron Age. A sacrificial victim, killed by strangulation, he has been perfectly preserved – if extremely discoloured – by the natural chemical processes of the bog into which he was thrown. Such corpses are usually very distorted, unlike true incorruptibles

Top: St Bernadette of Lourdes who looks as fresh and lifelike as when she lay dying in 1879. Her face is, however, now covered with a thin layer of wax to prevent discoloration from exposure to the air

Congregation for the Causes of Saints in the recognition of a saint than a life of piety.

There is another case that gives the usual pious morality of these stories a new twist. It concerns the body of a German knight, called Christian Kahlbutz, who bravely defended his homeland of Brandenburg against the Swedish invaders in 1675. But domestically he was a tyrant, who, among other abuses, insisted on his *droit de seigneur* (the feudal custom that allowed a lord to usurp a peasant bridegroom's conjugal rights on the wedding night). Besides his own 11 children, it seems he fathered more than 30 on local girls. It was when one of them refused his advances that he revenged himself by killing her fiancé. The girl took him to court, but he escaped justice because of his social position and by swearing solemnly: 'If I was the murderer, then shall the good Lord never let my body rot.' He died in 1702, and it was not until over 90 years later, when the new lords of the manor were renovating the local church, that his incorrupt body was found in its coffin, and the crime that everyone believed he committed was openly confirmed.

No doubt large parts of this story are a curious mixture of folklore and the opportunism of local moralists, but the unusual preservation of the knight's body seems a verifiable fact. During the 1936 Berlin Olympic Games, coachloads of visitors were taken to the village of Kampehl (now in East Germany) to see the browned and desiccated body in its open coffin. So many people were writing graffiti on the shroud, which had remained intact since his burial, that a glass top had to be placed over the coffin. In 1895, Rudolf Virchow, a well-known pathologist, had carried out an autopsy. He failed to find any trace of embalming preservatives, and confirmed that the internal organs and the general condition of the body were remarkably good. At least one other medical expedition set out from Berlin to investigate and test various alternative theories, but left the riddle as intact as the body.

So what are the hypotheses most frequently put forward as alternatives to the idea of a miracle? To begin with, there are various kinds of embalming, but they can safely be ignored since in most of the fully authenticated cases it is clear from medical examination that no preservatives had been used and none of the viscera removed as is essential in embalming.

A further consideration is the curious natural process known as *saponification*. In this, as the name suggests, the body tissues are turned into an ammoniacal soap beneath a toughened outer skin. This soap-like substance is called 'adipocere' (from the Latin *adeps* for fat, and *cera* meaning wax) – or *gras de cadavre* (French, meaning 'corpse fat') – and is caused by burial in damp soil in the proximity of putrefaction. Why it develops in some cases and not others is unknown, but the plumpness, plus the eyes and hair of bodies preserved in this way can be unimpaired after five years or more. Still, the presence of adipocere is easily recognised and verified by a medical examiner, and without doubt would have been noted in any post-mortem examinations of the allegedly incorrupt since dissection could hardly have failed to reveal it.

Authenticated true incorruption is very rare, and each story has a similar structure. The questions it raises strike to the core of the nature of our physical and spiritual existence, and the nature of reality itself.

Images that bleed and weep

One day in April 1975, just after Easter, Mrs Anne Poore of Boothwyn, Pennsylvania, USA, was praying in front of a 26-inch (66-centimetre) plaster statue of Jesus. 'Suddenly I looked up at the statue,' she later told reporters, 'and my heart stopped beating. Two ruby-red drops of blood had appeared over the plaster wounds in its palms. I was terrified. I could see it was real blood.'

When she recovered from her shock she made the statue the centre piece of a shrine on her front porch. On Fridays and holy days the flow of blood was particularly strong, streaming downwards, in a cyclical recurrence that parallels the regular bleedings of some stigmatics. Eventually the statue was moved to St Luke's Episcopalian Church at Eddystone, Pennsylvania, and installed on a platform 10 feet (3 metres) above the altar.

In this case there is no doubt that a blood-like liquid flowed mysteriously from the sites of Christ's wounds on the statue. But was it actually blood? Dr Joseph Rovito, a respected Philadelphia physician, conducted his own investigation. x-rays could find no trace of a reservoir or other trick mechanism concealed in the statue, but the result of the blood tests was not so straightforward. Although it was identified as human, the low red cell count was curious, and indicated great age. The fact that the blood flowed quite a distance before coagulating indicated that it was fairly fresh, and fresh blood contains millions of red cells. Dr Rovito concluded: 'It's so old we can't even determine the blood type.' Some Catholics believed it to be the blood of Christ.

Such images are almost always objects of worship, and so the mysterious appearance of liquids on or near these images is bound to be interpreted in a religious context.

The allied phenomenon of pictures or statues that appear to weep is equally baffling. An American parapsychologist, the writer D. Scott Rogo, tells the story of the Reverend Robert Lewis, who, on the day of his ordination, recalled how his grandmother – his first spiritual mentor – had wept with joy when he said he wanted to join the ministry. She had died before his ordination and he deeply regretted not being able to share the happiness of his success with her. He glanced at her photograph on his dresser, and suddenly accused his companion of playing a joke. The friend, the Reverend William Raucher, later wrote:

I went over to see what was troubling him. I was astounded. The photo of Bob's grandmother was soaking wet, dripping with a small pool of water spreading on the dresser under it. Examining the picture we found that it was wet *inside* the glass. . . . The back of the picture was so wet the velvet had streaked and faded. When the photo dried, the area about the face remained puffed, as though the water had originated there and run downwards from the eyes.

Rogo suggests that Lewis had unconsciously used a telekinetic ability to project a strong emotion into his immediate environment. 'Lewis underwent a mini-trauma when he passed his ordination exams,' writes Rogo. 'His grandmother often wept with joy . . . He wanted to share his joy with [her]; he wanted to see her cry with happiness, so he used his psychic ability to stage the event.' He makes the further suggestion that this was not a freakish power of one individual, but that we all may possess this ability to cause dogmatic changes in our environment by projecting powerfully felt or suppressed emotions.

It is most often objects of religious worship that issue blood or tears; in the 1950s, an Italian physician, Dr Piero Casoli, made a prolonged study of weeping Madonnas, concluding that they occurred on average about

Below: the 300-year-old wooden crucifix in the church at Porto das Caixas, Brazil, that began to bleed in 1968. The blood was proved to be real, and became the focus for many miracle cures

Below left: Mrs Antonietta Janusso on her sickbed, with her mother wiping away the tears shed by the plaster Madonna. Mrs Janusso had experienced fits and convulsions, with alternating periods of blindness, deafness and dumbness. Doctors could find no cause, but the similarity between her symptoms and those of clinical hysteria have been noted

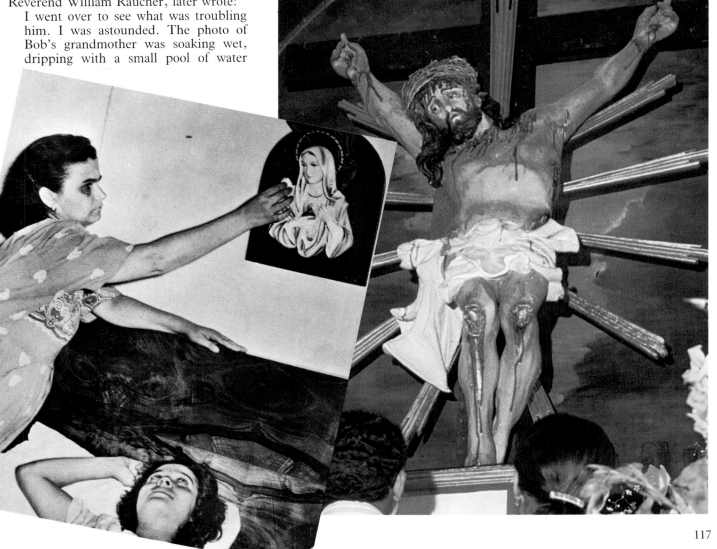

Above: in September 1911, a portrait of Christ in the church at Mirebeau-en-Poitou in France began to ooze blood. By March 1912 the blood was flowing copiously. The phenomenon seemed in some way connected with the parish priest, Abbé Vachère, who revelled in the attention of the pilgrims who flocked to witness the phenomenon. He was eventually excommunicated and the bleeding stopped at his death in 1915

Below: a weeping Madonna belonging to the Catsounis family of New York. In 1960, this was found to shed an 'oily' substance

twice a year in Italy alone.

Once trickery and natural explanations such as condensation have been discounted as an answer to the mystery, and the flow has been established as not coming from inside the statue, then we have to accept that the liquid is appearing on the surface of the object, materialised there from an unknown source by a mysterious force called – for want of a better term – teleportation. The appearances of these liquids are not random; in fact, they are remarkably consistent, for they restrict themselves to the appropriate sites where either faith or legend leads us to expect miraculous happenings. Further regularity is observed in the association between bleeding and images of Christ, and weeping and images of the Virgin Mary. This regular association suggests either that the teleportative force is created by an unknown intelligence or that it acts automatically in response to especially powerful images in the human mind, on an instinctive or unconscious level. It seems probable that the undoubted piety of Mrs Poore brought forth 'real' evidence of the sufferings of Christ.

A demonstrable case of bizarre cause and effect involves the celebrated weeping Madonna of Syracuse, Sicily, in August 1953. The statue was owned by the newly wed Mrs Antonietta Janusso and was in fact a small plaster bust of the Virgin Mary in the style known as 'The Immaculate Heart of Mary', a mass-produced ornament bought locally.

The couple were desperately poor, and sharing rundown accommodation. Mrs Janusso began to suffer mysterious illnesses.

The bedridden girl, in a sorry state, looked up one day to the shelf above the bed where the statue rested, and saw it begin to cry. It continued to do so for many days and was seen by impeccable witnesses. But at the end of the first day, despite the excitement and strain of people crowding into the small room to see for themselves, Mrs Janusso felt considerably better. By the time the statue had stopped crying, she had completely recovered.

To the faithful it was a miracle – to others it was confirmation that her illnesses, genuinely debilitating though they were, had a hysterical origin. Perhaps the unconscious stages such apparently mystical or magical events to break a vicious circle of depression and self-pity.

Whatever the origin of the emotional energy, the facts are suggestive of a teleportation of liquids – but from where? And in the end the value of these phenomena must – like those associated with poltergeists, which are often very similar – be studied in their relationship to the person who proves to be their focus. But the results are very different, for as American psychoanalyst Dr Nandor Fodor observed: 'Religious ecstasy of the Weeping Madonna type restores, whereas the poltergeist senselessly frightens and destroys.'

Turin Shroud

At the end of the 19th century the Vatican issued a proclamation stating that no relic, 'be it the most sacred in Christendom', could be regarded as authentic. This bald edict was made to counter the remarkable assertion of a French scientist and agnostic, Dr Yves Delage of the French Academy of Sciences, that a strip of cloth known as the Holy Shroud of Turin was the genuine winding sheet of Christ.

The Turin Shroud is a rectangular strip of cloth measuring 13½ feet (4 metres) long by 3½ feet (1 metre) wide. On its surface can be seen the faint, yellowish-brown imprint of a human figure, naked and bearded. Darker stains, said to be blood, are superimposed on the image, notably on the head, wrists, feet, and side of the body, and both back and front views of the figure appear hinged, as it were, at the crown of the head, which appears to bear a kind of wreath.

Owned by the Dukes of Savoy since the 15th century, the shroud was kept in a silver frame in a special shrine – Sainte Chapelle – at Chambéry. In 1532 a near-disastrous fire broke out in Sainte Chapelle; the heat melted the silver reliquary, and drops of molten metal burned through the cloth in several places, though water was quickly used to douse the scorching. The worst burns were neatly patched, and both the burns and the water stains were to be of assistance during later scientific investigation. In 1578 the shroud made its last journey across the Alps to Piedmont, where the then Duke of Savoy had set

up his household at Turin. It was lodged in the cathedral, next to the royal apartments and has remained there, apart from a spell in vaults during the last war, ever since.

Until his death in 1983, ex-King Umberto of Italy, Duke of Savoy, owned the shroud. He bequeathed it to the Vatican, but it is still kept in Turin Cathedral and looked after by Archbishop Anastasio Ballestreno.

Although observers had long noticed that there was something indefinably 'wrong' about the image on the shroud, it was not until 1898 that it revealed its first strange secret. It was taken from its silver casket to be put on rare public display, and a Turin photographer, Secondo Pia, was commissioned to take the first photographs of it. As he developed his plates there appeared not the blurred, odd image on the shroud but the perfectly formed features of a man: the shroud itself was a photographic negative.

This discovery led to the involvement of Dr Delage, who was determined to find out how the image had appeared – 500 years before the invention of photography. He experimented with various medieval pigments, but concluded that the image had not been painted on the cloth in any way.

He then began again from the premise that the cloth had been *somebody's* shroud. Further work indicated that the cloth was of a type used in Palestine before the fourth century, and that the stains on it were likely to have been made by the burial ointments common at that time. Furthermore, the marks on the shroud indicated that whoever was buried in it had undergone exactly the same form of torture and death as Christ did, including being scourged, crowned with thorns and pierced through the side with a lance. Delage believed the cloth to be the shroud of Christ, but he stated that this conclusion was not a religious statement, simply the result of identifying a piece of historical evidence. Nevertheless, the predominantly Roman Catholic Academy were nervous of the implications, and rejected his findings – even taking the rare step of suppressing them by refusing to print his carefully mustered evidence in their minutes.

The subject remained in abeyance for 30 years until, in 1932, another Frenchman, a forensic pathologist named Dr Pierre Barbet, began to look at the image from a medical point of view, taking advantage of a much clearer set of photographs taken the previous year.

Left: Jesus is taken down from the cross by his followers and prepared for burial by being wrapped in a single piece of cloth in precisely the manner indicated on the Turin Shroud (right). On this strip of cloth have been formed impressions of the front and back of a man's body, 'hinged' at the head

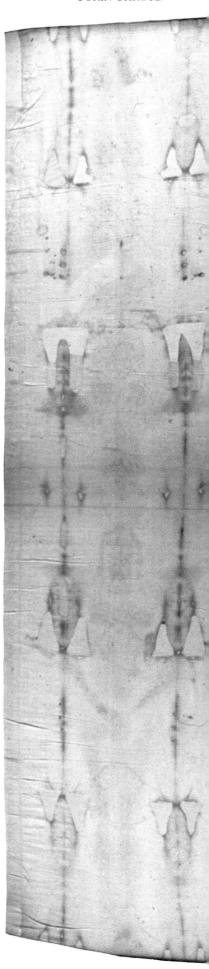

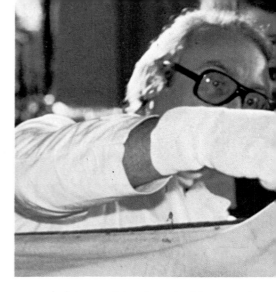

Right: Dr Ray Rogers, Dr John Jackson and Professor Giovanni Riggi, of the Shroud of Turin Research Project, take their first look at the underside of the shroud in October 1978

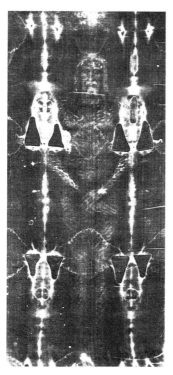

Above: the shroud as it appears on a photographic negative. The distinctive parallel lines of scars that cover the surface of the body are of a type that could have been made by Roman flagrae – two-thonged whips tipped with lead or bone

The first point to intrigue Dr Barbet was the position of the nail wounds in the wrists, rather than through the palms as traditionally depicted. The knowledge that this is indeed what happened in crucifixion is fairly recent and would have been unknown to medieval forgers. Furthermore a nail placed in this way would damage the median nerve, causing the thumbs to retract involuntarily into the palms of the hand – again a little known piece of evidence that was embodied in the shroud figure. The 'blood' stains around the shroud figure's side wound also showed the marks of a clear liquid – tallying with the biblical description of 'blood and water' issuing from Christ's side, and with the medical knowledge we now have about the nature and effect of this form of death.

The next time ex-King Umberto allowed the shroud to be examined was in 1973. By that time the Carbon 14 process had been developed, making it possible to establish a date for the fabric, but since using this process would involve destroying part of the shroud, Umberto was reluctant to give his consent. In addition, the process could not give an exact enough date to justify any destruction, given that a study of the cloth established it as dating from before the fourth century anyway.

Instead, in 1973, two top European scientists were invited to use more orthodox methods. Professor Max Frei, a leading Swiss forensic scientist, and Professor Gilbert Raes, an expert on fabrics from the University of Ghent in Belgium, were given access to the cloth. First, the pair reported that 'the image was completely superficial, in that the topmost fibrils [minute strands] of the threads only were affected. No pigmentation could be seen even under magnification.'

Frei took dust particles for laboratory analysis, and found 48 different samples of pollen. The identification of pollen grains, which survive almost indefinitely even in the most unlikely conditions, is one of the most precise processes of modern forensic science. Most of the seeds were from France and Northern Italy, as expected, but seven proved to be from halophylic (or salt-loving) plants usually found around the Dead Sea and certain other parts of Palestine. Though interesting circumstantially, this was not definite evidence of the shroud's origin, as pollen travels great distances on the wind and may have been transmitted on the clothing of travellers – the image had been openly exhibited during its early recorded history.

Gilbert Raes had removed small samples of threads, however, and his evidence also indicated that the threads were of archaic middle-eastern origin.

In 1974, came a breakthrough as important in its way as the discovery that the shroud was a photographic negative. Two US Air Force scientists, John Jackson and Eric Jumper,

scanned pictures of the shroud with a complex instrument called the VP-8 Image Analyser. Using a computer in conjunction with the VP-8 they were able to build a strikingly lifelike three-dimensional model of the man of the shroud. This was an incredible development since the VP-8 can usually reproduce only *actual* three-dimensional images – not flat, two-dimensional ones like photographs. It was this development that finally convinced a group of US scientists that the shroud was worthy of intensive study, and in March 1977 the Shroud of Turin Research Project was given permission by ex-King Umberto to go ahead with 'non-destructive' tests.

On 8 October 1978, after a public exposition, the shroud was removed from its nitrogen-filled container and taken to the Turin Royal Palace where it was scrutinised by 36 scientists who had brought with them 72 cases of ultra-modern equipment. They included physicists, biochemists, forensic scientists, pathologists, microphotography specialists, analysts and – somewhat incongruously – leading representatives from the US Nuclear Technology Corporation.

After hours of intensive work, the scientists reaffirmed that they could find no evidence that any kind of pigment had been used. One of the principal chemical investigators, Ray Rogers of the Los Alamos National Scientific Laboratory, said in 1980:

Most of us are now convinced that the shroud is not a painting. Except for a small amount of iron oxide we found no pigment whatsoever. And we do not think that either liquid or vapour could have produced the image we see.

Spectroscopist Sam Pellicori of Santa Barbara Research Center added:

The process of the formation of the image on the shroud is baffling. I can best describe it as a boiling up of the surface material of the outer threads. Certain evidence indicates that this may have been caused by a violent burst of radiant heat.

The 'bloodstains' on the image came in, of course, for extensive scrutiny. Dr John Heller

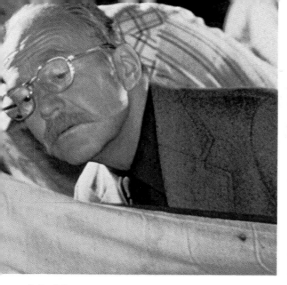

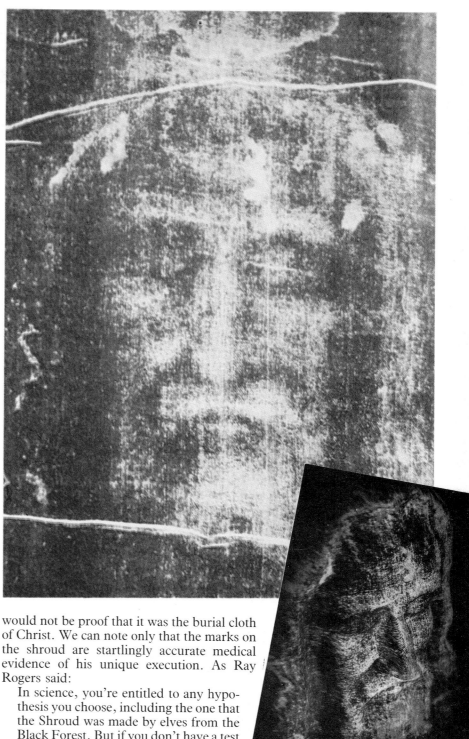

of the New England Institute said that none of the tests had shown that the ancient stains were not blood, but several had indicated that they could be. Most importantly, Dr Heller found tiny crystals between the threads on the blood-stained areas that he considered to be haemoglobin 'altered by age'.

The shape and direction of the stains themselves were 'authentic', as if a newly crucified body had been involved. Stains from the wrist wounds, for instance, ran up the forearms to the elbows – exactly as would occur with the arms in a crucified position. Furthermore blood from the wound in the side had run down and collected under the small of the back – another authentic detail. Finally, the entire surface of the body from neck to ankles was covered in scars in parallel pairs – apparently the marks of a form of scourging that fitted with known Roman practice.

The one dissenting voice among the scientists belongs to Dr Walter C. McCrone, head of a private firm of chemical analysts in Chicago, who was not present at the Royal Palace and apparently worked from samples. In a series of lectures in Britain in September 1980, he said that his microscopic tests revealed stains from iron oxide, a constituent of traditional artist's materials. 'Though how the artist did it I cannot say,' he said. 'I believe the shroud is a fake but I cannot prove it.'

One recent and dramatic development has involved a new image analysis that was begun in June 1983 by Dr Robert M. Haralick, Director of the Spatial Data Analysis Laboratory at Virginia Polytechnic Institute and State University at Blacksburg, Virginia. This study indicates that detailed analysis of the face of the shroud shows signs of broken money-shaped patterns on the eyelids, the imprints on which match those on Pontius Pilate coins.

Testing for Jesus

Ultimately, all the evidence we have is circumstantial. As yet the carbon dating process is not exact enough to justify its use, and even if it could date the shroud accurately, that would not be proof that it was the burial cloth of Christ. We can note only that the marks on the shroud are startlingly accurate medical evidence of his unique execution. As Ray Rogers said:

> In science, you're entitled to any hypothesis you choose, including the one that the Shroud was made by elves from the Black Forest. But if you don't have a test to examine that hypothesis, it's not worth anything. We do not have a test for Jesus Christ. So we can't hypothesize or test for that question.

The other continuing enigma is the cause of the shroud's markings. The scientists can tell us, rather dryly, that the image is made of 'dehydrative acid oxidation of the linen with the formation of a yellow carbonyl chromophore'. But every suggestion as to how it got there has been invalidated by technical data. If it *was* produced by a 'burst of radiant heat', what could have caused it?

Above: a three-dimensional model of the head on the shroud made by photographer Leo Vala in 1963. He projected a photographic negative (top) onto clay and shaped the features according to the depth of shadow projected

121

CHAPTER FIVE

The Spirit World

Ghost hunting, Place-centred ghosts, Glamis castle, Spirit photography, Phantom hitch-hiker, Borley Rectory, Amityville, Enfield, Exorcism, Origins of poltergeists, Rosenheim, Physical effects

A guide to ghosts

'Fear came upon me, and trembling, which made all my bones to shake. Then a spirit passed before my face; the hair of my flesh stood up. It stood still, but I could not discern the form thereof.'

This is how the experience of seeing a ghost is described in the book of Job 4: 14–16. The word 'ghost' comes from an ancient root meaning 'to be scared', and to many, including Job, encounters with ghosts have been literally hair-raising.

The existence of ghosts has been accepted without question in almost all cultures throughout history. Only with the growth of the scientific outlook in the West in the last few centuries have their existence and nature been disputed. But serious attempts to find out what they are and to study their behaviour are surprisingly few. And many people still respond to the idea of ghosts with an irrational blend of fear, ridicule and laughter. We reject what we do not understand, rather than face the possibility that there are indeed more things in heaven and earth than are dreamed of, let alone taken seriously, by the scientific establishment.

Ghosts are even rejected by people who have seen them. 'I saw it, but I still don't believe it!' is a commonly reported reaction, for the human mind instinctively rejects information it cannot assimilate and interpret. Clearly, better evidence, and more of it, is needed before the ghost can find its way into the physics and biology textbooks.

What, to begin with, is a ghost? Dictionaries define it as the supposed disembodied spirit, or soul, of a dead person. The word 'ghost' has also acquired the sense of a vestige of something, as in 'the ghost of a smile'. Frederic W. H. Myers, a leader of early psychical research, echoed this meaning in his characterisation of a ghost as 'a manifestation of persistent personal energy' – a conclusion he had reached after careful study of a mass of evidence.

A great deal of evidence is available, for seeing or hearing ghostly presences is a very common experience. In 1889 the British Society for Psychical Research, of which Myers was a founder member, embarked upon a large-scale survey of experiences of apparitions, asking the question:

Have you ever, when believing yourself to be completely awake, had a vivid impression of seeing or being touched by a living being or inanimate object, or of hearing a voice; which impression, so far as you could discover, was not due to any external physical cause?

Almost 10 per cent of the 17,000 people who replied said 'yes'. Later surveys in several other countries confirm this picture.

Today, the question facing modern parapsychologists and psychophysical researchers tends not to be 'do ghosts exist?', but 'how do ghosts exist?' Are they the spirits of the dead?

Bottom left: Reverend K. F. Lord was amazed to find this form on his picture of his church in Newby, North Yorkshire, as he had not seen it when taking the photograph

Below: two ghostly forms appear behind the figure of an English lady, Miss Townsend, in the Basilica at Domrémy, France, in 1925

Are they the result of telepathy? Are they produced by mass hallucination or self-hypnosis? Advances in psychology over the last few decades have brought us nearer to understanding some aspects of apparitions, but the definitive truth still eludes us.

Those ghosts for which evidence is most compelling, and that critical researchers have concluded are genuine, usually show a number of features. Such a ghost obeys the laws of perspective, looking different to different observers; it appears solid; it is visible when viewed in a mirror; and it makes sounds appropriate to its movements – footsteps can be heard, for example. It generally gives the impression of being as real as a living person, if only for a limited period. A sensation of sudden cold may be felt.

The feeling of coldness is also a commonly reported feature of poltergeist cases, but poltergeists are unlike conventional ghosts: they cause solid objects to move, yet they are not seen doing so. Apparitions have been reported in association with poltergeist activity, but we have yet to see one pick up an object and throw it. Poltergeists are often treated separately from ghosts because they manifest themselves so distinctively that there is a strong argument for suggesting that they are a completely different phenomenon. Later, we shall consider them and several fascinating, well-documented, case histories that question the commonly held belief that poltergeists come from beyond the grave.

When a ghost is seen by only one person, the suspicion arises of hallucination, error or deception – whether practised by the percipient or someone else. But ghosts are often seen by more than one person at the same time, though not necessarily by everybody present. This is often sufficient to rule out the possibility of deception or mistake, but the true nature of the apparition remains unknown. It is not necessarily a disembodied spirit – it could be an 'intersubjective' phenomenon, the joint creation of the percipients' minds.

An apparition may provide some plain evidence of its non-physical nature. It may pass through walls; sometimes it appears and disappears through phantom doors that open and close while 'real' doors stay closed; it may become transparent and fade away.

While the nature of ghosts is still mysterious, their behaviour has been studied in great detail. G. N. M. Tyrell, in his book *Apparitions*, published in 1943, identified several groups by their pattern of activity. The most common were apparitions that haunted specific places and are termed 'place-centred'

Public houses and inns are frequent sources of place-centred ghosts. Britain has hundreds of pubs that feature spirits other than the liquid variety. One is the Busby Stoop Inn in North Yorkshire. So many people who sat in its cursed stoop chair (far left) died soon afterwards that the brewery was forced to remove it from the premises

The Star Inn (below) at Ingatestone, Essex, has a long history of haunting. A ferocious bull terrier once lived in the pub, and when it died in 1914 its head was stuffed and placed above the bar (below left). Its ghost is said to haunt the passage leading to the bar, and one former landlord claimed that his dog always growled and stiffened in fear whenever it went into the passage

Below: Prince Rupert leads his cavalry into the English Civil War battle at Edgehill in 1642, after which mass apparitions were reported. Similar scenes occurred at Naseby, Northamptonshire (above), the sight of another Civil War battle

ghosts. On the whole they do not arouse fear and they sometimes come to be treated as part of the family.

The second category consists of post-mortem apparitions, taking place some time after the death of the person seen, and not related to any particular place or event.

Third, there are crisis cases, in which the apparition is of someone who is undergoing some profound experience at the time (often unknown to the percipient), such as an accident or illness or, of course, death.

Believers in an afterlife assert that place-centred ghosts arise when a spirit is trapped in its earthly environment, perhaps because of some unfulfilled task, or for the purpose of punishment.

By and large, however, parapsychologists tend to theorise that in certain cases a kind of psychic record may be imprinted on a location, perhaps because of some violence or strong emotion generated there. In these cases, the apparition would not be a 'living' spirit, a 'mind', but merely a projection like a cinema film. This certainly seems to be the most likely explanation of, for instance, the Edgehill haunting – a scene of mass apparition in 1642.

On 23 October 1642, Royalist troops under Prince Rupert of the Rhine, nephew of King Charles I, and Parliamentarians commanded by Robert Devereux, third Earl of Essex, fought the first serious battle of the English Civil War at Edgehill, Warwickshire. After the indecisive clash the bodies of some 2000 men lay on the unseasonably frozen slopes of Edgehill.

A month after the battle, a number of local shepherds saw what they at first thought was another fight at the same spot: the thundering cavalry, rolling gunsmoke, flashing steel. And they also heard the neighing of horses, the screams of the wounded and the steady beat of drums. It was only when the whole tableau suddenly vanished that they took fright and ran to tell the authorities in the nearby town. On Christmas Eve the phantom battle was enacted again, and was so convincing that a London printer, Thomas Jackson, interviewed several witnesses and published an account of the phenomenon in pamphlet form on 4 January 1643.

This was drawn to the attention of the King, who was so intrigued that despite his hard-pressed military position he appointed half a dozen army officers to investigate on his behalf. They were led by Colonel Sir Lewis Kirk, former governor of the garrison at Oxford, and a young cavalry captain named Dudley who had ridden at Edgehill.

On their return the officers brought detailed confirmation of the news. Not only had they interviewed the shepherds and recorded their accounts, but on two occasions they had seen the battle themselves, recognising not only a

vanishes into the opposite wall. He has never been known to speak or pay any attention to witnesses, and although he seems perfectly solid, if his way is barred by a living person he dissolves and then reappears on the other side of them.

The identity of the 'man in grey' has never been satisfactorily proven, but a possible clue turned up in the late 1840s, when workmen were making alterations to the wall from which he appears. In a bricked-up alcove they found the seated skeleton of a man, with a rusty dagger between his ribs. A few tattered remnants of cloth clung to the figure but crumbled to dust when touched. At the obligatory inquest it was suggested that the man may have been a victim of Christopher Ricks, the 'bad man of old Drury' who had managed the theatre in the time of Queen Anne and was notorious for his violence. Ricks made constant alterations to the theatre's structure, and could easily have disposed of a body without too much difficulty. However, there was no solid evidence, and after an open verdict was returned the body was given a pauper's funeral at a nearby graveyard.

However, the 'man in grey' continued to be seen throughout the Victorian era and on into the 20th century. W. J. McQueen Pope, theatre critic and historian, saw the ghost many times and made ardent but fruitless attempts to establish its identity. An interesting point was that the ghost appeared regularly

Above left: this is not, as it may seem, final evidence for the existence of ghosts, but a carefully staged visitation photographed for the British Tourist Authority at London's Theatre Royal, Drury Lane. The ghostly apparition is the so-called 'man in grey' who is said to have haunted the theatre for over 200 years

number of the men who had died on the field, but also Prince Rupert, who was still very much alive. Whether or not anyone took notice of it at the time, this last fact carried with it the intriguing suggestion that the phenomenon was a sort of action replay rather than haunting by revenant spirits.

Although Sir Lewis and his colleagues were justifiably startled, they drew no conclusions, merely reporting the facts of what they had seen.

A more recent example of a place-centred apparition witnessed on innumerable occasions by dozens of people is that provided by the so-called 'man in grey' who is recorded as appearing at the Theatre Royal in Drury Lane, London, from the early 18th century until the late 1970s. The accounts are remarkably consistent, although the 'stagey' look of the ghost and the fact that it appears in a theatre has convinced more than one witness that they were seeing an actor dressed for a part.

The figure is that of a man of above average height with a strong, handsome face. He wears a three-cornered hat, powdered wig, long grey cloak, sword and riding boots, and emerges from a wall on the left hand side of the upper circle, walks around behind the seats, and

Bottom left: wreckage scattered over Florida swampland after the crash of Eastern Airlines' flight 401 on 29 December 1972. The ghosts of two crew members who died, pilot Bob Loft (above left) and second officer Don Repo (above), were later seen on other Eastern Airlines' Tri-Star flights (below left)

Below: Glamis Castle - a seemingly peaceful spot, but one which has been dogged by mysterious horrors for nine centuries

in the period between the mid 1930s and Pope's death in 1960, while he was conducting sightseers around the Theatre Royal.

Certainly Pope did not invent the ghost, and its last recorded sighting, by an American who thought he was seeing an actor during an afternoon matinée, took place in 1977.

A more bizarre case consisted of a series of apparitions on board several jumbo jets belonging to an American airline. An Eastern Airlines Tri-Star, flight 401, crashed in December 1972 in a Florida swamp, killing 101 people. The ghosts of the pilot, Bob Loft, and his flight engineer, Don Repo, were seen on more than twenty occasions by crew members of other Eastern Tri-Stars, especially those that had been fitted with salvaged parts of the crashed plane. The apparitions were invariably described as wholly lifelike. They were reported both by men and women who had known Loft and Repo and by others who had not, but who recognised them later from photographs. The haunting became well-known among people in the airline community, and an account of it even appeared in the newsletter of the US Flight Safety Foundation, in 1974.

An author, John G. Fuller, made thorough investigations of the case with the help of several airline personnel. They produced a mass of compelling testimony, including claims that log books recording apparitions had been withdrawn and crew members re-porting them had been threatened with a visit to the company psychiatrist.

But perhaps the most popular conception of a place-centred apparition – and the source of so many fictional ghost stories – is the haunted ancient house. One well-documented example is the famous Glamis Castle, ancestral home of Queen Elizabeth the Queen Mother, which for centuries has had the reputation as a place of strange and awful happenings.

Glamis Castle stands in the great vale of Strathmore in Tayside, Scotland. For hundreds of years the vast fortified house with its battlements and pointed towers – looking like the setting for a fairy tale – has been the ancestral home of the Earls of Strathmore. Their family secret is reputedly hidden within the walls of Glamis.

That there was unpleasantness within the castle's walls is an undoubted historical fact. And that the castle is today the centre of a triangle formed by three biblically named villages – Jericho, Zoar, and Pandanaram – may indicate the terror felt by its minions, for, according to a Scottish National Trust guidebook, the men who built and named them 'had at least some knowledge of the Scriptures and regard for the wrath of God'. That wrath, claim locals even today, was called down on Glamis for the sins of the first dozen or so Lairds. The present, 17th Earl of Strathmore, Fergus Michael Claude Bowes-Lyon, is well-liked by his tenants and there is no evidence

Above: Lady Elizabeth Bowes-Lyon, the future Queen Mother, grew up at Glamis. She is said to have felt the presence of the horror in the Blue Room

Top, far left: the 13th Earl of Strathmore, Claude Bowes-Lyon, was deeply troubled by the tales of strange events at Glamis. One of his friends said that after the secret was revealed he became 'a changed man; silent, moody, looking anxious and scared'

Top centre: the 14th Earl and (top) Mr Gavin Ralston, the estate factor. When told the secret by the Earl, Ralston was so appalled he vowed never to sleep at the castle again

that his immediate forbears were any less affable; but the conduct of at least one of their ancestors called into being what is still known as the 'horror' of Glamis.

It is the nature of the horror that makes it one of the great mysteries. No recent Earl has ever spoken of it to an outsider, except in enigmatic terms. No woman has ever been let in on the secret. It is passed on only to the Strathmore heir on his 21st birthday.

The historical record of horror at Glamis Castle goes back to 1034, when King Malcolm II was cut down by a gang of rebellious subjects armed with claymores, the large broadswords peculiar to Scotland. It was said that every drop of Malcolm's blood seeped from his body into the floorboards, causing a stain that is still pointed out today, in what is called King Malcolm's Room.

The Lyon family inherited Glamis from King Robert II, who gave it to his son-in-law, Sir John Lyon, in 1372. Until then the Lyon family home had been at Forteviot, where a great chalice, the family 'luck', was kept. Tradition held that if the chalice were removed from Forteviot House a curse would fall on the family; despite this, Sir John took the cup with him to Glamis. The curse seemed to have a time lapse, for though Sir John was killed in a duel, this did not occur until 1383.

The 'poisoned' chalice may well have influenced events 150 years later when James V had Janet Douglas, Lady Glamis, burned at the stake in Edinburgh on a charge of witchcraft. The castle reverted to the Crown, but after the falsity of the charge was proved, it was restored to her son. The spectre of Lady Glamis – the 'Grey Lady' as she is known – is said to walk the long corridors even today.

It was Patrick, the third Earl of Strathmore, who made the idea of a Glamis 'curse' wide-spread in the late 17th century; indeed, to many people he seemed the very embodiment of it. A notorious rake and gambler, his drunken debauches were well-known in London and Edinburgh as well as in his home region.

There are many apocryphal stories about Patrick's devilish nature, but the most verifiable one tells of the Earl being the father of a deformed child who was kept hidden somewhere in the castle, out of sight of prying eyes. The story is supported by a picture of the third Earl that now hangs in the drawing room. It shows Patrick seated, wearing a classical bronze breastplate, and pointing with his left hand towards a distant, romanticised vista of Glamis. Standing at his left knee is a small, strange-looking green-clad child; to the child's left is an upright young man in scarlet doublet and hose. The three main figures are placed centrally, but two greyhounds in the picture are shown staring steadfastly at a figure, positioned at the Earl's right elbow. Like the Earl this figure wears a classical breastplate apparently shaped to the muscles of the torso – but if it is a human torso it is definitely deformed. The left arm is strangely foreshortened. Did the artist paint from life – and if so does the picture show the real horror of Glamis?

One story tells – with curious precision – of a grey-bearded man, shackled and left to starve in 1486. A later one, which probably dates from before Patrick's time also, is gruesome in the extreme. A party of Ogilvies from a neighbouring district came to Glamis and begged protection from their enemies the Lindsays, who were pursuing them. The Earl of Strathmore led them into a chamber deep in the castle and left them there to starve.

Unlike the unfortunate grey-bearded man, however, they had each other to eat and began to turn cannibal, some, according to legend, even gnawing the flesh from their own arms.

One or other of these tales may account for the ghost of a skeletally thin spectre known as Jack the Runner. And the ghost of a Negro pageboy, also seen in the castle, would seem to date from the 17th or 18th century, when young slaves were imported from the West Indies. A 'white' lady haunts the castle clock tower, while the grey-bearded man of 1486 appeared, at least once, to two guests simultaneously, one of whom was Mrs MacLagan, wife of the Archbishop of York at the turn of the 20th century. Mrs MacLagan told how, during her stay at the castle, one of the guests came down to breakfast and mentioned casually that she had been awakened by the banging and hammering of carpenters at 4 a.m. A brief silence followed her remarks, and then Lord Strathmore spoke and assured her that there were no workmen in the castle. According to another story, as a young girl Queen Elizabeth the Queen Mother (daughter of the 14th Earl, Claude George Bowes-Lyon) once had to move out of the Blue Room because her sleep was being disturbed by rappings, thumps, and footsteps.

Fascinating as all these run-of-the-mill ghosts and their distinguished observers are, however, it is the horror that remains the great mystery of Glamis. All the principal rumours – cannibal Ogilvies notwithstanding – involve a deformed child born to the family and kept in a secret chamber who lived, according to 19th-century versions of the story, to a preternaturally old age. In view of the portrait openly displayed in the Glamis drawing room, and always supposing that the mysterious child is actually portrayed, the subsequent secrecy seems rather pointless. If Patrick himself was prepared to have his 'secret' portrayed in oils, why should his successors have discouraged open discussion of the matter?

Despite the secrecy, at the turn of the 19th century the stories were still flying thick and fast. Claude Bowes-Lyon, the 13th Earl who died in 1904 in his 80th year, seems to have been positively obsessed by the horror, and it is around him that most of the 19th-century stories revolved. It was he, for instance, who told an inquisitive friend: 'If you could guess the nature of the secret, you would go down on your knees and thank God it were not yours.' Claude, too, it was who paid the passage of a workman and his family to Australia, after the workman had inadvertently stumbled upon a 'secret room' at Glamis and been overcome with horror. Claude questioned him, swore the man to secrecy, and bundled him off to the colonies shortly afterwards. To a great extent the obsession seems to have visited itself upon his son, Claude George, the 14th Earl, who died in 1944.

Unlike his forbears, however, Claude George broke the embargo on the secret by telling it to his estate factor, Mr Gavin Ralston,

who subsequently refused to stay overnight at the castle again.

When the 14th Earl's daughter-in-law, the next Lady Strathmore, asked Ralston the secret, Ralston is said to have replied: 'It is lucky that you do not know and can never know it, for if you did you would not be a happy woman.'

That statement, surely, is the clue to the horror of Glamis. Old Patrick's deformed offspring did not alarm the father because nothing like it had been seen in the family before. Possibly the 'wicked' Earl rather delighted in him. But if the same deformity appeared even once in a later generation, the head of an ancient, noble and hereditary house would certainly have been reluctant to broadcast the fact. Perhaps Claude, 13th Earl of Strathmore, knew of such a second, deformed child in the Bowes-Lyon line, and passed the secret and the fear of its recurrence on to his successors?

The other most frequently recorded form of ghost is the 'crisis apparition', which occurs when a person under great stress – sometimes

Above: the chapel at Glamis where a secret room was discovered in the late 19th century. A workman came upon the door by chance and, finding that it led into a long passage, decided to investigate - but he emerged soon after, shaking with fright. He reported his experience to the Earl who, anxious to preserve the family secret, persuaded the man to emigrate

Inset above: a painting of the third Earl, Patrick, with his children and greyhounds dominates the far wall of the drawing room at Glamis. It is around Patrick that many of the strangest stories revolve

Above and below: cases of crisis apparitions are most common in times of war, when a mother may see her son at the moment of his death on a battlefield. It seems that the shock of death causes some kind of telepathic communication between son and mother. But rarely does the mother have a vision of a dying soldier; in most cases she sees her son as he appeared in normal, everyday life. This further suggests that the vision is not a revenant spirit

on the point of death – appears to someone close to them as a 'vision' or, occasionally, as a disembodied voice.

The majority of crisis apparition cases have tragic overtones. For instance, soldiers have appeared to their mothers or wives at the exact time of their own deaths on faraway battle-fields.

Some investigators have suggested that this form of ghost emerges out of a kind of tele-pathy. Evidence indicates that the person appearing as the ghost – the agent – plays a smaller part in crisis apparitions than does the person seeing it – the percipient. If we look at recorded cases it becomes apparent that the agent rarely appears as he is at the moment of 'transmission' – the percipient does not see a mangled body in a motor car, or a dying

wounded soldier in a trench, but what appears to be a normal image of the agent that, more-over, relates to the percipient's surroundings.

Consider the case of travelling salesman Mr F. G. who, while working in his hotel room in Boston, Massachusetts, USA, suddenly became aware of a presence and looked up to see his sister, who had died nine years previously. As he sprang delightedly to his feet and called her name she vanished, and yet he had time to take in every detail. 'She appeared as if alive,' he said, but added that there was a small red scratch on her right cheek.

Disturbed, Mr F.G. made an unscheduled stop at his parents' home and told them of his experience. When he mentioned the scratch, his mother was overcome with emotion, and said that she had made the scratch on the dead body of her daughter accidentally, as she was preparing it for burial. Two weeks later, the mother died.

In this case the apparition figure was not the corpse with the dull mark on which the mother's regretful thoughts might dwell, but the girl in health and happiness, with the symbolic *red* mark worn as a test of identity.

One of the most famous cases of a collective crisis apparition was reported to the SPR in the late 19th century by Charles Lett, the son-in-law of a Captain Towns of Sydney. One day at about 9 p.m. some six weeks after the Cap-tain's death, his daughter, Mrs Lett, and a Miss Berthon entered a bedroom at his home. The gas light was burning:

And they were amazed to see, re-flected in the polished surface of the wardrobe, the image of Captain Towns. It was . . . like an ordinary medallion portrait, but life-size. The face appeared

Below: an image of an embracing couple not seen by either the photographer or the subject (far left) appeared on this picture taken in a churchyard in 1928 by a Mrs Wickstead. The 'spirits' could not be identified - and the Society for Psychical Research, who investigated the matter, could not explain them

Inset: a number of 'extras' crowd this picture taken by the English medium and psychic photographer William Hope. There is the woman's dead son (in the cloud of ectoplasm), a pony's head to the right of the boy's head (recognised as a dead pet) and the image of an old man to the left of the boy's head (recognised as the boy's dead uncle)

wan and pale . . . and he wore a kind of grey flannel jacket, in which he had been accustomed to sleep. Surprised and half alarmed at what they saw, their first idea was that a portrait had been hung in the room and that what they saw was its reflection – but there was no picture of the kind. Whilst they were looking and wondering, my wife's sister, Miss Towns, came into the room and before any of the others had time to speak she exclaimed: 'Good gracious! Do you see Papa!'

One of the housemaids passing by was called into the room. Immediately she cried: 'Oh miss! The Master!' The captain's own servant, the butler, and the nurse were also called in and immediately recognised him. Finally Mrs Towns was sent for and, seeing the

apparition, she advanced towards it with her arm extended as if to touch it, and as she passed her hand over the panel of the wardrobe the figure gradually faded away, and never again appeared.

Those parapsychologists who lean to the telepathic origin of all apparitions would probably say that the vision was seen first by either Mrs Letts or Miss Berthon, who then passed it on by thought transference to each arrival. But the question remains: where did the vision come from in the first place?

One of the early SPR pioneers, F. W. H. Myers, author of the book *Human personality and its survival of bodily death*, suggested that it was the revenant spirit or 'essence' of Captain Towns taking a last look at his old home six weeks after death.

A more bizarre manifestation of apparitions is the phenomenon of spirit photography, which captures ghosts or 'visions' on film. The most extraordinary spirit photographs have been made in seances, often under rigid test conditions, but a few interesting ones have been made unexpectedly by amateurs. People take a snapshot of a friend, or of an interior, or of a pet, and afterwards find, to their astonishment, the image of a face or figure – sometimes recognisably that of a deceased relative or friend – on the print. This happens rarely, but it does happen; and many examples, with written accounts, have been preserved by archivists and librarians interested in psychic phenomena. The earliest preserved examples of spirit photographs were of this order: they were taken by amateur photographers who had no specialist interest in psychic effects, and who indeed were disappointed that their portraits and landscapes were 'spoiled' by extra images.

Above: the widowed Mary Todd Lincoln with the spirit of President Abraham Lincoln. The picture was taken in Boston, Massachusetts, USA, by William Mumler, the first professional spirit photographer, the year that Lincoln was assassinated

Top right: a typical early photograph by the Frenchman Jean Buguet, who produced a high percentage of 'extras' that were recognised by the living as being of the dead. Buguet was brought to trial and convicted of fraud, but still has many defenders of his abilities as a true psychic photographer

It is generally accepted that spirit photography as such began in Boston, Massachusetts, USA, on 5 October 1861, when William Mumler accidentally produced his first spirit picture. But this date may not be entirely accurate. For, according to an early pioneer of Spiritualism in Boston, Dr Gardner, a few portraits exhibiting a second figure that could not be accounted for had been made before that at nearby Roxbury. The Roxbury photographer was an 'orthodox Christian' who, after hearing about Mumler's pictures, refused to print any negatives containing 'spirits' on the grounds that 'if it had anything to do with Spiritualism, it was the work of the Devil.'

The majority of psychical researchers involved with spirit photography claim it occurs by the direct intervention of the spirits themselves. However, what makes the discussion of spirit photography so difficult is that no one knows how genuine images come to be on plates and film. And no one knows exactly what these spirit images are.

Perhaps the most famous of the early examples of amateur spirit photography is the 'Lord Combermere's ghost' picture. The circumstances surrounding the taking of this photograph have fortunately been well-documented. The picture was a study of the splendid library in Combermere Abbey, Cheshire, taken by Miss Sybell Corbet in 1891 as a souvenir of her visit. She was surprised, if not disappointed, to discover on the plate the transparent image of an old man sitting in a chair at the left of the room.

Only the head, the body and arms of the figure are relatively clear – the legs are missing. Subsequent research by psychical investigators revealed that at the precise time that the plate was being exposed, the body of Lord Combermere was being buried in the local churchyard at Wrenbury, a few miles away from the abbey. Lord Combermere had died in London a few days previously as a result of a road accident. In this accident his legs had been so badly damaged that, had he lived, he would never have walked again.

The subject of spirit photography greatly excited psychical investigators in the 1870s and 1880s, but no organised and sustained study seems to have been made. This period saw the first professional spirit photographers, many of whom were quickly exposed as hoaxers.

The Bostonian William Mumler was almost certainly the first person in the United States to earn a living as a professional spirit photographer. He became very well-known, and it is clear from surviving pictures that his mediumistic abilities were quite remarkable. Several investigations failed to unearth any fraud on his part. Nonetheless, Mumler fell foul of the law in 1869 – but it was as a result of a journalistic campaign whose aim was to create scandal. The spirit photographer was eventually charged as a swindler, but the evidence brought to the court was so overwhelmingly in his favour that the case was dismissed.

Mumler's most famous spirit picture is one taken towards the end of 1865, about four years before his trial. The sitter, who visited Mumler incognito, was no less a person than Mary Todd Lincoln, then recently widowed by the assassination of President Abraham Lincoln. In the print is a recognisable image of Lincoln, standing behind her and laying his hands upon her shoulders.

After Mumler's death in 1884, another spirit photographer came to notice on the west coast of the United States. This was the Californian Edward Wyllie. Dr H. A. Reid, who was a specialist in the history of 19th-century psychic photography, said of him:

As to the work of Edward Wyllie, the medium photographer, the proofs and testimonies that the phenomena were genuine and not trickery, were all so

Far right: Charlie and the 'extra' of his son, taken by Edward Wyllie as a test for psychical researchers. They wondered if a spirit would appear when the sitter was completely ignorant of Spiritualism - and Charlie, who was Chinese, filled the bill exactly

Above: a tiny Cairn puppy that had been dead for about six weeks, makes a curiously out-of-place appearance on this photograph of its mistress and the forlorn-looking wolfhound that had been its constant companion when it was alive

open, untrammelled, fair and conclusive that to reject them is to reject the validity of all human testimony.

The hallmark of the professional spirit photographer is the ability to capture images of the dead that are recognisable to living relatives or friends. The professional with the highest record of such recognitions was the Frenchman Jean Buguet. While Mumler could claim

15 recognitions, and the English photographer Frederick Hudson 26, Buguet could claim 40 recognitions in his spirit photographs. Even had Buguet miraculously discovered a new way of making double exposures that would fool the photographic experts of his day, fraud on that scale would have been almost impossible. For many of the Buguet spirit forms were of people who had died before the invention of photography, so there were no originals to use for double exposures.

Some of the stories attached to recognition photographs are extraordinary. A particularly interesting one concerns the production of a picture of a Chinese man and his son, made by Wyllie for one of the psychical research societies on the west coast of America. The society had expressed a hope that Wyllie might be able to obtain a spirit form on a photograph of someone who was wholly ignorant of Spiritualism. Accordingly, when Charlie, a Chinese laundryman, came in on his usual round, Wyllie asked him if he would like to sit for his portrait.

He was very much scared. I made his mind easy and asked him to come in a few days, and I would give him the picture. When I developed the negative, there were two extras [apparition figures] on it – a Chinese boy and some Chinese writing. When Charlie came round I showed him the print, and he said, 'That my boy; where you catchee him?' I asked him where his boy was, and he said, 'That my boy. He's in China. Not seen him for three years.' Charlie did not know that his son was dead.

The phenomenon is not limited to human manifestations, as there is a collection of animal spirit photographs, mostly taken by surprised pet-owners. An interesting example is

Left: Blue Bell Hill between Chatham and Maidstone in Kent - the site of a famous phantom hitch-hiker story. Here the hiker is thought to be a young girl who was killed at the foot of the hill on the eve of her wedding in November 1965

the picture that was submitted to the British College of Psychic Science in 1927. This was an ordinary photograph of Lady Hehir and her Irish wolfhound Tara taken by a Mrs Filson. The picture proved to be far from ordinary, however. The extra was no semi-transparent wraith but a very substantial puppy head, curiously misplaced at the rear end of the wolfhound. Both Mrs Filson and Lady Hehir recognised this disjointed extra as the Cairn puppy Kathal, which had been a close companion of the wolfhound. It had died about six weeks before the picture was taken.

Some investigators have suggested that spirit photography could be produced by a person willing or thinking an image onto the photographic film. And there is documented evidence of people who have been able to imprint images on film by psychokinesis.

Perhaps this is a plausible explanation, but some psychical experts take the idea further and claim that ghosts themselves are creations of our deep subconscious. They cite as evidence the many recurring ghosts stories – often identical except for superficial details – that have appeared throughout the centuries in widely differing cultures. The story of hitch-hiker ghosts is one example.

The tale of the phantom hitch-hiker is a ghostly classic, an ancient, oft-repeated piece told and retold in many localities. 'People,' declared folklorist and anthropologist Andrew Lang, who became President of the Society for Psychical Research in 1912, 'will unconsciously localise old legends in new places and assign old occurrences or fables to new persons.'

In this way the tales are given new leases of life and are passed from one narrator to another across great distances.

These 'folk ghosts' are the theme of traditional supernatural stories governed by strict narrative conventions. The teller and his audience tacitly agree to suspend disbelief and pretend the tale *may* be true, the 'evidence' for its accuracy being that 'it happened to a friend of a friend' of the narrator. But it does not stand up to cross-examination. If a researcher demands names of witnesses, for example, it usually proves that, like the ghost of the story, these personages have a talent for disappearing without trace. There is nothing to check up on, and the account is reduced to hearsay.

Few ghost stories are as well-travelled as that of the phantom hitch-hiker. The tale is told in Korea, Canada, Malaysia, Sweden, Sicily, Pakistan and South Africa; local specimens occur in most English counties. Of course, details as to age, sex and physical appearance of the hitch-hiker fluctuate, as do the number of witnesses and the type of vehicle in which he or she hitches a ride – a car, a taxi, a motorcycle, a bus, a horsedrawn wagon or carriage and, in one Malayan version, a trishaw. In the most commonly heard form, the hitch-hiker is a young female who, before vanishing inexplicably, gives the driver an address at which he subsequently calls, learning to his horror that the girl has been dead for days, months or years.

Consider the bewildering experience of Roy Fulton, who gave a lift to a phantom hitch-hiker on a foggy October night in 1979. His

Above: carpet fitter Roy Fulton who in October 1979, stopped to pick up a hitch-hiker – who then vanished

Below: a carved figure said to represent Pele, the divine guardian of Mauna Loa, Hawaii, the largest volcano in the world. Pele is the subject of a phantom hitch-hiker folk story: she utters a warning about an impending eruption of the volcano before disappearing

encounter obviously seemed real enough to him, but there was no independent corroborative evidence to give it any objective reality.

Mr Fulton stopped close to the small Bedfordshire village of Stanbridge on his way home from a darts match; the 26-year-old carpet fitter had no reason to suppose the figure at the roadside, thumb upraised in customary hitchers' manner, was anything other than human. True, the pale young man in the white shirt and dark trousers was uncommunicative, merely pointing wordlessly towards Dunstable when asked where he wanted to go, but Mr Fulton knew from experience that some hitch-hikers are like that.

They had been travelling at a steady 40 miles per hour (65 km/h) for several minutes when Mr Fulton decided it was time to break the ice:

> I turned round to offer him a cigarette and the bloke had disappeared. I braked, had a quick look in the back to see if he was there. He *wasn't* and I just gripped the wheel and drove like hell.

Not long afterwards, local police were hearing Roy Fulton's extraordinary story. They formed the opinion that Fulton was reliable, 'an ordinary sort of chap' and not the worse for alcohol. Evidently representatives of police and press were favourably impressed with Roy Fulton as a witness, but does their evaluation mean that we should accept the account as fact?

Britain's most famous phantom hitch-hiker story is set on Blue Bell Hill between Maidstone and Chatham in Kent. There is little hard evidence for a psychical researcher to follow up; witnesses' names are absent, dates left obscure and other important details unavailable. Yet the wealth of anecdotes from this area, only a fraction of which have appeared in print, are assigned with monotonous regularity to the spirit of a bride-to-be, who was killed in a car crash on the eve of her wedding at the foot of Blue Bell Hill back in November 1965. This accident is an historical fact, but in other phantom hitch-hiker tales the connection between the hitch-hiker and a death on the road on which the phantom appears is no more than conjectural. People are prone to think ghosts must be the products of tragedies – and, as the phantom hitch-hiker is popularly assumed to be a ghost, there is a strong temptation to hunt for accidents to account for it.

It is this kind of tempting, if unscientific, deduction that has been the undoing of so

Left: ghost-hunter Harry Price during a radio broadcast direct from a haunted house in Meopham, Kent in 1936

Below: the scene of Price's most famous investigation, Borley Rectory. Most of the phenomena he reported there later turned out to have been faked, and his research was totally discredited by the SPR in 1956; yet stories of strange happenings at Borley continue to be told

many ghost-hunters. Many enthusiasts simply cannot overcome their excitement at discovering possible evidence of a ghost. In their eagerness, many are tempted to make far-fetched assumptions. The conclusions of such investigators are at best speculative, but at worst they can sustain damaging hoaxes ruining the credibility of other researchers.

Serious ghost-hunters and parapsychologists, such as the members of the Society for Psychical Research, are always wary of the temptation to make unfounded conclusions. In fact, the SPR was founded in 1882 'to examine without prejudice or prepossession and in a scientific spirit those faculties of man, real or supposed, which appear to be inexplicable on any generally recognised hypothesis'.

The society's members have often been instrumental in uncovering ghost hoaxes or in exposing poor, unsubstantiated research of less-scientific ghost-hunters. One such legendary ghost riddle was that of Borley Rectory, a case that was first investigated by the zealous and, at times, over-imaginative Harry Price.

'The most haunted house in England' was a local inhabitant's description of Borley Rectory, on the Essex-Suffolk border, when he gave directions to a motorist in 1929. The driver was Harry Price, self-styled ghost hunter and the most energetic and controversial psychical researcher of the century. He made his way to Borley, where he found – or claimed

to have found – the ingredients for a series of books, radio broadcasts and articles that he was to produce for the rest of his life.

The case apparently had everything: ringing bells, strange lights, footsteps, flying stones, a skull wrapped in brown paper, mysterious writing on walls, and, of course, a ghost. Local legend had it that the rectory was built on the site of a monastery, from which a monk had unsuccessfully tried to elope with a young lady from a nearby nunnery. Both had been caught and executed, but the nun and the monk (minus his head) and the coach they used were said to be still around. Borley Rectory, Harry Price said, was 'the best authenticated case of haunting in the annals of psychical research.'

This would be welcome news indeed, for surprisingly, although ghosts have been seen over centuries, very few have ever been investigated thoroughly in order to learn their true nature. But had Price authenticated the Borley hauntings?

Not in the opinion of a team of members of the SPR, who tore the case to pieces in a devastating report published in 1956. Not only, they claimed, was there no proper evidence for any paranormal occurrences at Borley, but some of

Below: a brick thrown through the air at the site of the ruined Borley Rectory is captured on film by a Life *magazine photographer. Harry Price, who was present at the time, later cited this picture as photographic evidence of poltergeist activity at Borley – without mentioning the workman who was demolishing a nearby wall when the picture was taken*

the reported phenomena had very probably been caused by Price himself. They quoted one outright accusation of fraud, made by a *Daily Mail* reporter, Charles Sutton, after Price's death:

> Many things happened the night I spent in the famous Borley Rectory with Harry Price and one of his colleagues, including one uncomfortable moment when a large pebble hit me on the head.
>
> After much noisy 'phenomena' I seized Harry and found his pockets full of bricks and pebbles. This was one 'phenomenon' he could not explain, so I rushed to the nearest village to 'phone the *Daily Mail* with my story, but after a conference with the lawyer my story was killed.

Even some of Price's fellow investigators concluded that he was more interested in a good story than in the truth of the case. A typical example of this was given by a *Life* magazine reporter, Cynthia Ledsham, who visited Borley with Price and a photographer in 1944. The rectory, which had burned down in 1939, was being demolished. The photographer took a distant shot of the ruins, which showed a brick flying through the air. Price later claimed that this could be 'the first photograph ever taken of a Poltergeist projectile in flight'. However, the reporter later admitted to the SPR investigators that while the picture was being taken a workman was dismantling a wall nearby, throwing bricks at regular intervals.

Price's account of the haunting was demolished as surely as the building itself. The rectory had not been built on the site of a monas-

tery after all. The 'nun' who had been spotted by a newspaper reporter 'flitting about in the gloom' was in fact the maid, a lively girl who later admitted to having carried out a spot of poltergeist activity herself. One former occupant of the rectory declared it to have been haunted by no more than 'rats and local superstition'. Another, the source of a great deal of the anecdotal material (which Price himself privately admitted to not believing), turned out to have lived previously near Amherst in Nova Scotia, scene of a well-publicised 19th-century haunting with many remarkable similarities to the alleged happenings at Borley. And so the indictment continues through 180 pages of a special issue of the SPR's *Proceedings* wholly devoted to an exposé of Price's bold claims.

In Trevor H. Hall's *Search for Harry Price* (1948), the 'ghost-hunter extraordinary' is depicted as a publicity-seeking charlatan and an unscrupulous liar. Although argument was still raging in 1980 in the pages of the SPR's *Journal* over both the facts of the Borley case and the

Top: Borley church, the major part of which was constructed in the 15th century

Inset: the Enfield Parapsychical Research Group outside Borley church. Ronald R. Russell (far right), a founding member, sympathises with Price's view of the controversy over Borley's hauntings. But the group found the church itself of most interest and carried out many tests using cameras and sound equipment

Above: Jay Anson, author and script-writer, who wrote a dramatic account of the hauntings at 112 Ocean Avenue (below), from interviews with George and Kathy Lutz, in his best-selling book The Amityville horror

integrity of its investigator-publicist, it cannot be claimed that Price made any useful contribution at all to our understanding of ghosts, or that there is any reason to believe a word of what he wrote about Borley.

Yet, ironically, since the early 1970s unexplained events – many of them recorded on tape – have been monitored in and around the 12th-century Borley church, just yards from the rectory site. These have proved to be far more baffling than anything that happened at the old rectory.

When hauntings become the focus of intense media interest it becomes all too easy to offer the public what it wants – shock, horror and occult thrills. It is much more difficult and costly to do the painstaking work of a good investigator. The late Jay Anson, who scripted the film based on the novel *The exorcist*, made an estimated £3 million from his book *The Amityville horror*, but he had no first-hand experience of this case whatsoever. A researcher who followed up the case, Dr Stephen Kaplan, dismissed the book as 'mostly fiction'.

The story begins, classically, with a horrifying murder. Early in the morning of 13 November 1974 a young New Yorker, 24-year-old Ronald DeFeo, ran screaming and hysterical into a bar near his home in Ocean Avenue, in Long Island's district of Amityville. Someone, he sobbed, had broken into the DeFeo house and slaughtered the six members of his family. When the police reached the house they discovered his mother, father, two sisters and two brothers shot dead in their beds. DeFeo's claim that the crime had been committed by an intruder was not taken seriously; he was arrested, charged with the murders and sentenced to six consecutive life-terms.

When the trial was over, the DeFeo house was put up for sale. It was an imposing three-storey residence built in the Dutch Colonial style in 1928, and with its garage, boathouse and swimming pool made a substantial property that should have commanded a high figure. Instead, in view of its unhappy history, the house agents offered it at the bargain price of $80,000 but, even so, it remained empty for nearly a year before the Lutz family moved in on 18 December 1975.

Recently married, George Lutz was a 28-year-old ex-marine who ran a land-surveying company; his wife Kathy, a divorcee, was fully occupied looking after her two small sons and five-year-old daughter. The large rambling

According to Jay Anson's account, George Lutz (above right) felt continually cold in the house on Ocean Avenue, despite a high level of heating. He began to identify with multiple murderer Ronald DeFeo (above) whom he imagined he resembled physically. His wife Kathy (bottom right) said she suffered from painful red weals over her body, as if she had been burned with a red-hot poker

house seemed the ideal place for a young family. But only a month later the Lutzes were to flee from it – victims, they said, of a relentless, nameless terror.

The full story of their ordeal was told in the book *The Amityville horror* (1978) and was based on many interviews with the Lutzes themselves. This book became a best-seller and was acclaimed as 'one of the most terrifying true cases ever of haunting and possession by demons'.

According to the account in the book, the trouble began with overpoweringly foul stenches pervading the house. The bathroom fittings became stained with a black slime, and no household cleaner would remove the stains. Then came the flies – hundreds of them swarming into a second-floor bedroom. Once, the massive front door was discovered wrenched open and hanging from its one remaining hinge. George felt constantly chilled to the bone, despite the huge blazing fire that roared in the living room. It also seemed that a 4-feet (1.2-metre) high ceramic lion began moving around the house by itself.

Kathy Lutz was the first to be truly terrorised by the entities. Invisible arms embraced her and tried to gain possession of her body; she felt that escape was impossible and that she was going to die. Others, too, claimed to have felt the effects of the 'horror'.

If all this is true, it is a grim and horrifying story. But it is so like fiction that it prompts the reader to ask whether there was ever an authentic horror in the first place. Independent researchers who have investigated the facts have all emphatically answered no.

Dr Stephen Kaplan, the director of the Parapsychology Institute of America, said after months of study and many interviews with those involved in the affair:

We found no evidence to support any claim of a 'haunted house'. What we did find is a couple who had purchased a house that they economically could not afford. It is our professional opinion that the story of its haunting is mostly fiction.

After visiting the house Jerry Solfvin, of the Psychical Research Foundation, wrote that the case 'wasn't interesting to us because the reports were confined to subjective responses from the Lutzes, and these were not at all . . . characteristic of these cases.'

The most damning report of all originated with investigators Rick Morgan and Peter Jordan who visited Amityville and interviewed people mentioned in the book. Among their startling findings was the fact that the police denied ever investigating the house while the Lutzes were in residence, although the book describes Sergeant Cammaroto touring the house and even inspecting a 'secret room' in the basement.

In fact, very little in the book stood up under scrutiny. Local handymen and locksmiths knew nothing of the paranormal damages they were supposed to have repaired. And far from being driven out of the house by hauntings, it appeared that the real reasons for the Lutzes leaving their home were much more prosaic: a cash crisis and a near-breakdown.

Without a confession from the Lutzes it will probably never be quite clear what started the whole thing off. But it is known that the family had grown desperate after several personal and financial crises. It seems certain that although they had problems, none of them were paranormal.

Increasingly, the causes of paranormal phenomena are being linked with the psychological state of the individuals concerned. For instance, most recent theories about poltergeist activity suggest that it may be provoked by some psychological, emotional or physical traumas. However, the idea that poltergeists may be spirits has not yet been laid to rest.

A guide to poltergeists

Below: a saucepan, scissors and a piece of paper leap into the air in a cottage in the French Alps. 'We can't explain what we saw,' said the photographer and his colleague, 'we can only guarantee that none of the pictures is faked'

What exactly is a poltergeist? The name derives from two German words: a folklore term, *polter*, meaning 'noise' and the word for 'spirit', *geist*. The development of psychical research and parapsychology during the last 100 years has introduced into the language a more cumbersome phrase to describe poltergeist phenomena – recurrent spontaneous psychokinesis (RSPK).

Mysterious bangs, loud crashes, objectionable smells, furniture that moves about on its own, sudden cold spells, inexplicable voices, objects that appear and disappear, the uncontrolled levitation of victims – these are all symptoms of poltergeist activity.

Such disturbances have been recorded since at least the 12th century. At one time they were believed to be caused by an evil force, a creature of Satan, though the identity of the force remained a mystery. Writing in the 13th century, Gerald of Wales noted that a 'spirit' was heard to converse with a group of men in an alarmingly aggressive fashion; 300 years later, in 1599, one of the first authentic examinations of this type of incident was undertaken by Martin del Rio. He described 18 kinds of demon, including one that specialised in causing disturbances:

> The 16th type are spectres which in certain times and places or homes are wont to occasion various commotions and annoyances. I shall pass over examples since the thing is exceedingly well known. . . . Some disturb slumbers with clattering of pots and hurling of stones and others pull away a mattress and turn one out of bed.

Although there are still some people today who maintain that RSPK can be attributed to the activity of 'elementals', it is more generally accepted that 'hauntings' of this kind have a 'natural', not a 'supernatural', origin. Yet we still do not understand them.

The most spectacular case of RSPK ever recorded lasted for an 11-month period, from August 1977 to September 1978. During this time a woman and her four children, who were living in a council house in Enfield, on the northern outskirts of London, experienced practically every type of poltergeist phenomenon that has been identified. No fewer than 1500 separate incidents were recorded between August and March, and this astonishing barrage of disturbances mystified all those who were involved in the investigations, including social workers, a speech therapist, photographers, psychologists, priests and two investigators, Guy Lyon Playfair and Maurice Grosse.

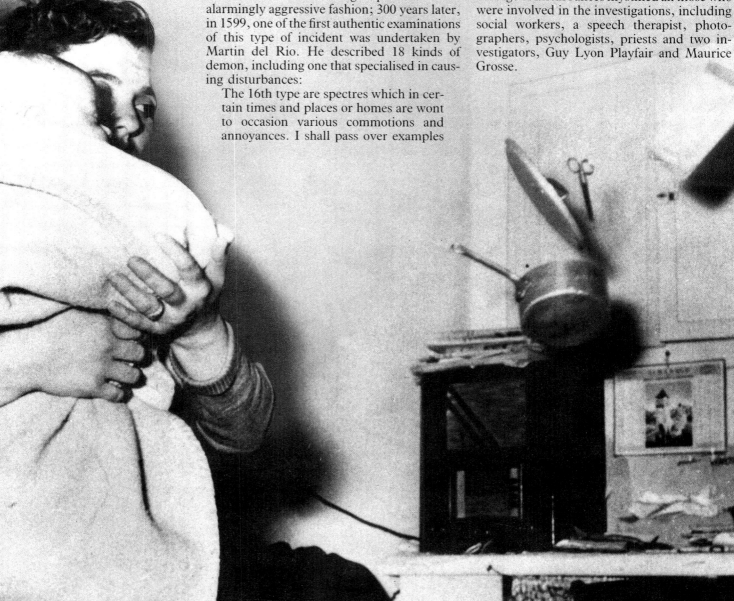

Below: the worried Harper family and their neighbours await the next attack by flying objects. Left to right are: neighbours Mrs Nottingham and her son Gary, Mrs Harper and her children – John, Rose and Janet. Janet was thought to be the focus of the poltergeist activity – although there was great controversy among investigators over whether the activity was genuine. But whatever actually took place in that Enfield council house, the world's press seized on the story avidly (bottom)

The Enfield poltergeist first made itself known at about 9.30 p.m. on 31 August 1977. Mrs Harper, a divorcee in her mid forties, was putting two of her four children to bed in one of the three upstairs bedrooms of her semi-detached council house in Enfield when Janet, aged 11, and her brother, aged 10, complained that something was making a 'shuffling noise'. Shortly afterwards, Mrs Harper was astonished to see a heavy chest of drawers moving about 18 inches (46 centimetres) along the floor, well beyond the reach of either child's feet. She pushed it back into place, but it moved again, as before, and this time it refused to budge when she tried to move it. At about the same time, there were four loud knocks that seemed to come from the party wall.

Mrs Harper, as she recalled about a week later, began literally to shake with fear. She was convinced, as were her usually exuberant children, that something was going on that did not have a normal explanation. Her immediate reaction was just to get out of the house. She thought of calling on her brother John Burcombe, who lived six doors up the road. But her immediate neighbours, Vic and Peggy Nottingham, still had their lights on, so it was to them she first turned for help.

The knocking sounds began again as Vic and his son were making a thorough search of the house. As Vic walked down the stairs, the noise seemed to come from the wall right beside him. He immediately searched both front and back gardens, but saw nobody.

They called the police at about 11 p.m., and in the presence of one of the two constables who were soon on the scene, a chair in the living room slid along the floor more or less as the chest of drawers had done a couple of hours earlier. WPC Carolyn Heeps later signed a written statement to this effect, thereby testifying to at least one genuine phenomenon on the very first day of the case.

The following day, marbles and pieces of toy brick began to fly around the house at great speed. Some, when picked up, were found to be unusually hot. This aerial bombardment went on for three days, and by Sunday 4 September both the Harpers and the Nottinghams were at their wits' end. By then, they had called the police again, sought help from the local vicar and from a local lady who claimed to be a medium, but all to no avail.

The disturbances continued for nearly 11 months. A voice, deep, gruff and crude, was tape-recorded on many occasions. After several attempts had been made to identify it, the voice itself claimed to belong to a 72-year-old man from Durants Park, a nearby road. A listener to a local radio phone-in programme

heard a recording of the voice and identified it as that of her uncle, Bill Haylock, whom she described as 'a gypsy type'. But every attempt to prove the validity of the claims failed – a fairly common experience in cases of this kind.

There were many other inexplicable incidents. On one occasion a toy brick suddenly appeared, 'flew' across the room and hit a photographer on the head. Paper and pieces of cloth caught fire spontaneously, and a box of matches that was lying in a drawer burst into flames, which extinguished themselves without igniting the rest of the contents of the drawer. A message, patched together from lengths of sticky tape, was found on the lavatory door. Cutlery, a metal teapot lid and a brass pipe were all seen to bend and twist of their own accord. Three pieces of stone were found scattered about the house, which were later discovered to be fragments of a single stone that had been split.

The strength of the force at work in the house can be gauged from some of the more impresssive incidents. Part of a gas fire was wrenched away from the fireplace, and its grille was thrown across the sitting-room. Large pieces of furniture, among them a chest of drawers, a heavy sofa and a double bed, were tossed around the house.

Janet Harper seems to have been the focus (the epicentre) of all this activity. It was from her that the deep voice appeared to emanate. It was she who experienced levitation (witnesses on two occasions said that she seemed to be suspended in mid-air). She and her sister Rose were thrown out of bed so often that in the end they decided to sleep on the floor – but that did not put an end to the poltergeist's activities, for Janet was often found, fast asleep, on top of a radio in her bedroom.

Although the family was very frightened at first, as time wore on the children and their mother were mystified rather than alarmed.

However, some researchers had doubts about Enfield and claimed that the two teenage girls were playing practical jokes. This was found to be true on several occasions, although many unexplained incidents still remained. One researcher, Anita Gregory, said she had been excluded from the girls' bedroom or been told to turn her head when the poltergeist phenomena began. She also alleged that when the girls were creating the deep voices, they would cover their mouths with blankets or avert their faces from view. Neighbours had apparently told of Janet's enjoyment of misleading strangers.

Later Anita Gregory said of the Enfield case: 'I talked to Mrs Nottingham, who told me that she thought that what was going on at that time was "pure nonsense", and only being kept going by the interest of the investigators.' And she described the case in the SPR's *Journal* as 'far too sketchy, impressionistic, unsystematic, imprecise, ambiguous,

and confusing, to be seen as a contribution to *research*'.

The Enfield case was certainly remarkable for the extent and duration of the phenomena. But many of its features have been observed by countless people in other places and times.

Mysterious knocking and rappings, for example, are often the first indications of the presence of a poltergeist (though some people notice first that objects are moved from their usual places). An early classic British case of RSPK, which became known as the Drummer of Tidworth, was recorded in 1666 by the Reverend Joseph Glanvill, who lived in a house on the site of the present Zouch Manor in Wiltshire. Two girls occupied a bedroom from which a 'strange drumming sound' seemed to emerge. The noise was traced to a point 'behind the bolster'; sceptics argued that the girls were the cause. But eventually the girls were cleared of suspicion.

In a case in Battersea, in south London, in the 1950s, however, the poltergeist announced its arrival by placing an unidentified key on the bed of a 14-year-old girl, Shirley Hitching. This incident remained as puzzling as Shirley's ability to produce raps, several paces from her body, in answer to questions that she asked her 'polty'. Perhaps to prevent hysteria and mental stress, she and her parents, like many other victims, invented a personality for the poltergeist, whom they called Donald.

Top: poltergeist activity at Enfield sends a settee flying across the room. In other disturbances Janet was often dragged out of bed by an invisible force (above). Even when she took to sleeping on the floor she was still forcibly moved and was often found asleep on top of a large radio. When she was seized by the force it became very difficult to hold her down, as researcher Maurice Grosse discovered (above left)

In these more extreme cases many people, in desperation, turn to exorcism. Those seeking exorcism presumably feel that poltergeists are, in some way, related to spirits of the dead or possession by the Devil. However, there is agreement among those who have been concerned with poltergeists that only about 2 per cent of all reported cases genuinely involve inexplicable phenomena – that is, psychokinetic effects for which no cause can be found in the lives of those affected. While there is as yet no explanation for the means whereby mattresses are slashed, the contents of drawers or wardrobes spontaneously combust, or people and things levitate uncontrollably, the source of most poltergeist activity can usually be traced to some form of emotional disturbance in an individual within the afflicted household.

'Exorcism' takes many forms. If the main object of intervention by a clergyman is to

Above: after a violent spiritual struggle, this Italian woman lies at peace beneath a priest's crucifix at the end of an exorcism

Left: English medium Donald Page performing an 'exorcism' on a woman patient. Whatever explanations are offered for the ritual and its outcome, there is no doubt that a considerable amount of physical energy is expended by the medium

Far left: the New Testament tells how Christ himself expelled demons by a 'word of power', and said that this act was a sign of the coming of God's Kingdom. The evil spirits were believed to issue from the body's orifices, and this decorated initial, from a 12th-century manuscript in Winchester Cathedral library, shows a 'little blue devil' emerging from the mouth of the possessed man

relieve an undefined 'feeling', this can often be achieved through a religious service or blessing, or by encouraging the victim to accept that the 'atmosphere' of the affected room or house is not malign. It may take time to convince the victim, but if the 'exorcist' is caring and patient, this approach can eliminate symptoms of poltergeist activity.

A full 'exorcism' cannot be authorised until a thorough examination of the circumstances of the victim has been undertaken. Normally this process involves obtaining a report from the family doctor, an assessment from the local clergyman and, often, the views of a social worker. Indicating the more balanced approach now being adopted by some respon-

sible members of the Churches, Father Peter Ball, Bishop of Lewes, has said that he would not consider giving his approval to the holding of an exorcism unless a medical expert were present, or had examined the victim and had agreed that such a service might assist. And it should be stressed that a theatrical performance complete with bell, book and candle is usually inappropriate nowadays.

In both the Catholic and the Anglican Church, the ritual of exorcism is based upon the belief that a person or a place may be 'possessed' by an evil spirit or spirits, and that the appropriate words and ceremonies can be used to 'command' the evil spirit to leave. The form of the ritual is very simple, and it appears that the most important element is the strength of personality of the exorcist himself.

Since about AD 250 a ceremony of exorcism has been a part of the baptismal service in the Roman Catholic Church. This does not mean that candidates are considered to be 'possessed'; it is regarded rather as a ceremony to remove the effects of original sin.

In the earliest days of Christianity exorcism was a ceremony that could be practised by anybody. Any major exorcism now requires the authorisation of a bishop before it may be performed, but many parish priests (and also certain specialist practitioners recognised within the body of the Church) have been known to carry out private exorcisms on their own responsibility.

The form of words in the ritual varies considerably. The Rev. J. Christopher Neil-Smith, for instance, begins with the traditional words: 'I rebuke thee! I rebuke thee! I rebuke thee! I abjure thee and summon thee forth from this man. . . .'

This religious ceremony does help many

RSPK victims obtain some relief, although it is by no means certain that the effects are lasting. Unfortunately, just as many people endure even greater suffering in the wake of a request for an exorcism, as there is still a body of fanatics, both clerics and laymen, who have little or no knowledge of psychology or parapsychology and whose ridiculous and scaremongering activities serve merely to increase the distress of those whom they claim to be able to help.

In recent years newspapers have reported a growing number of cases in which unfortunate victims have suffered severe mental (and, indeed, physical) distress; and several people have been found guilty of manslaughter and committed to prison as a result of ignorant attempts to practise something of which they had no understanding or experience.

In Hastings, Sussex, in 1979, for example, a canon so harassed a disturbed victim, who was suffering from the effects of the menopause and a drug problem, that she was admitted to a clinic for three months' treatment. The woman's condition could well have been far more serious if her husband had not stopped the canon in the middle of his 'treatment' and told him to leave. And in 1977 a family in the Midlands was subjected to a horrifying sequence of 'cures'. First, their house was blessed by an archbishop and a local vicar. Then a religious group visited the victimised family (who were suffering from hallucinations) and held a two-hour 'stomping session'. Within a few months two seances had been held in the house, and numerous 'Spiritualist' mediums had called upon the family, each providing a different (and usually nonsensical) explanation for the imagined phenomena. One claimed that the house was haunted by the evil spirit of a tall Negro; another informed the family that the incidents were to be attributed to the influence of a ginger-haired dwarf girl. The family was able to return to normal only after a parapsychologist had spent a few hours with the mentally disturbed wife and made arrangements for a local doctor to visit.

However, the claims for the success of exorcism are declining. A mere 20 per cent of exorcisms are now considered to be successful, and then only after repeated visits by authorised exorcists. As the waning of religious belief makes way for the scientific study of phenomena hitherto regarded as supernatural, the days of the exorcist may be numbered, though the title may continue to be accorded to parapsychologists and other experts in the field who are proving more and more successful in dealing with the paranormal.

As more cases of poltergeist activity are subjected to rigorous investigation by parapsychologists, a clearer picture is emerging, not only of the possible causes of such phenomena, but also of the kinds of people

Below: an exorcism in the Italian church of St Vicinius in Sarsina. The iron ring is a relic of the saint, who wore it about his neck, with heavy weights attached, as a penance

Bottom: the Rev. Neil-Smith, of Hampstead, London, is one of the most active of Anglican exorcists. At one time he claimed to have performed over 2000 exorcisms during a four-year period

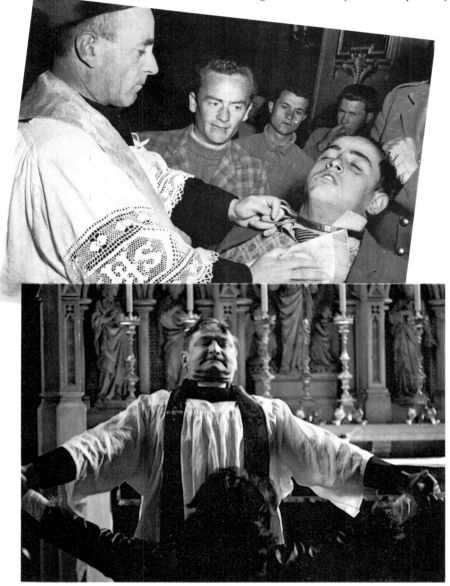

who are generally the victims.

The sexual drive, or libido, seems to be at the root of much paranormal experience. In the mid 19th century, poltergeists centring on girls stirred up a great deal of interest, and cases that were examined at that time appeared to confirm the assumption that girls on the threshold of sexual maturity were to be blamed for all mysterious incidents; only young women, it was thought, could summon up reserves of energy that could move tables, produce strange sounds and cause objects to appear and disappear.

As we have seen, many cases today involve girls at the age of puberty. But apart from this other common features have been observed in young victims of RSPK. Janet and her sister in Enfield, for example, were obsessed with Starsky and Hutch, the heroes of the television series; Shirley Hitching adored James Dean, the film star; and another girl was infatuated with Dr Who, the character in the science fiction serial. It has been suggested that this passion, this concentration of emotion on fictional characters, served to ensure that the power or force deployed by the girls was unconstrained by the influences of normal, day-to-day life.

In some cases girls are not involved at all, though a hundred years ago male victims of RSPK were often ignored or discounted, so entrenched was the view that pubescent girls were the source of poltergeist activity.

In recent years male sensitives, young boys and men alike, have received a more sympathetic hearing. One 10-year-old boy was filmed as he lay in bed, awake, while a walking-stick moved of its own accord, in erratic jerks, behind the head of his bed. Like many young epicentres, he was of an extremely nervous disposition and, again in common with other victims, he was anaemic. Then there was a fascinating case involving two boys in Glasgow between August 1974 and May 1975. The boys were 15 and 11 years old, and they lived with their parents in a tenement flat. A series of

Below: while this 10-year-old boy was being filmed, the walking-stick hanging from his bed-head jerked and jumped of its own accord

Below right: 12-year-old Alan Rhodes had his hands taped to the bedclothes to guard against trickery when his poltergeist was investigated by Harry Price in 1945. Even so, the alarm clock managed to jump onto his bed, and was later joined by a trinket case from the dressing table

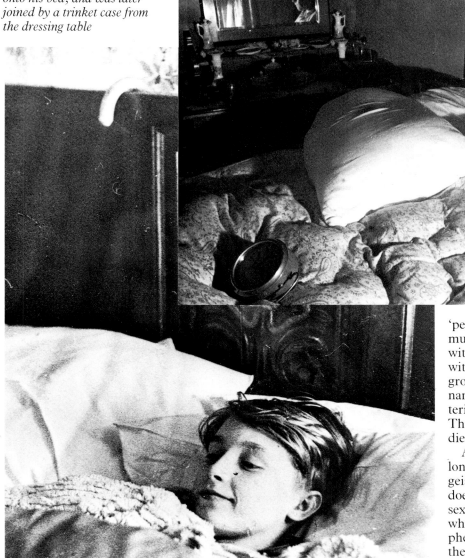

'peculiar sounds' was heard, followed by communicative raps; it turned out that the boys, without knowing it, were linked telepathically with an old man who lived in a flat on the ground floor and who was afflicted by a malignant tumour. As the old man's condition deteriorated, the raps became more frequent. They ceased, suddenly, when the old man died.

And at the other end of the age range adults long past the age of puberty experience poltergeist activity, although in many cases there does appear to be an unequivocal link between sexuality and RSPK. The majority of mediums who provoke – or claim to provoke – physical phenomena are women in their middle years, the years of the menopause, when the metabolism is disturbed, as it is at puberty.

Recent evidence has suggested that RSPK may be related to frustration and distress. A particularly strange case of this kind was documented in Rosenheim, Bavaria, in Germany, in 1967. A number of inexplicable incidents were observed by employees at the office of a lawyer named Adam, accompanied by an alarming increase in the size of the telephone bill. The electricity and telephone companies were alerted and requested to check all equipment in the building.

Engineers worked in the office for several weeks, testing wiring and equipment. Although they found no faults, they replaced the receivers and junction box – but, as this did not improve matters, they called in the post office.

Early in October, the post office installed a meter so that, as they were made, calls could be recorded visibly in the office on a counter, with a similar meter at the telephone exchange to provide an official record. At the same time, Herr Adam asked his staff, the office manager Johannes Engelhard, two office clerks and a part-time worker, to make a note of their calls.

On 5 October 1967, Adam and Engelhard were amazed to see the meter register a call although no one in the office was using the telephone. On 19 October, the same thing happened while Adam was with accountant Dr Schmidt, who produced an affidavit for Adam to show the post office. Comparing the records from his own meter, the meter at the exchange and the notes of his staff, Adam realised that these two incidents were by no means isolated. Dozens of undialled calls had been registered. The post office insisted that all the calls had been made in the normal way and, even more peculiar, they had all been made to the speaking clock.

A row broke out between the post office and Herr Adam. Adam pointed out that all his staff had watches and could hear the chimes of at least two church clocks, and could therefore keep a record of the timing of their telephone calls. Furthermore, no one was ever alone in the office, and it was ridiculous to suppose that

Top: the entrance to lawyer Herr Adam's office at Königstrasse 13 in the quiet Bavarian town of Rosenheim (inset). No 13 was to prove an unlucky address for Herr Adam as the increasing ferocity of the poltergeist there made work almost impossible

so many calls could have been made unnoticed by anyone.

Between 7.42 and 7.57 a.m. on 20 October 1967, 46 telephone calls were registered to the speaking clock. Adam further pointed out that although at least 17 seconds are needed to dial and connect with the speaking clock, even if one does not wait to hear the time, the post office claimed that as many as six calls a minute had been made, and continued to send enormous bills. Nevertheless, on 31 October, they replaced the telephones. This time, the dials were locked and only Herr Adam had a key.

This step made no difference, and on 8 November Herr Adam was extremely angry to receive another huge bill that did not correspond with the records at all. 'In five weeks,' Adam said, 'the speaking clock has been connected between 500 and 600 times. In one day, 80 times. I was very angry with the post office; I even wanted to found an association for the protection of the subscriber.' However, Adam soon had disturbances of a different nature to deal with.

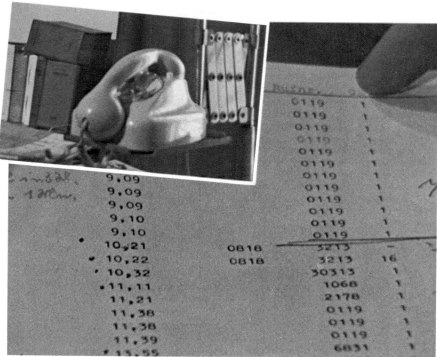

On 20 October 1967, the office lights suddenly went out with a bang. Herr Bauer, an electrician from Stern's, a local firm, was called in to repair them. He examined the lights and found that each fluorescent tube had been turned 90° in its socket and disconnected. He had finished replacing the tubes and put away his ladder when there was another bang. The tubes had twisted and disconnected themselves again. He was even more puzzled when the office staff told him that the automatic fuses in the office ejected themselves for no apparent reason, sometimes on all four circuits at once. Bauer began a full investigation of the office wiring and equipment, all of which he found in excellent order. He confessed to Adam: 'I was faced with a puzzle and called it "witchcraft".'

Since no fault could be found in the office, he concluded that something must be wrong with the electricity supply itself. The

Above: Herr Adam sits pensively in front of the painting that turned by itself, through almost a complete circle

Top: when the office's telephone records were checked it was discovered that someone – or something – had been making persistent calls to the speaking clock, using this phone (inset). The odd thing was that more calls were made than it was physically possible for anyone to dial in the time available. No electrical faults were found in the system, so what could have made them?

Elektrizitätswerk – German electricity board – was asked to take over the investigation and, accordingly, sent Paul Brunner, Auxiliary Works Manager.

The escalation of the Rosenheim phenomena can be seen when viewed chronologically. On Wednesday, 15 November 1967, extensive checks were run on the wiring and appliances at the office at 13 Königstrasse, especially in Adam's flat. Everything was found to be satisfactory and short circuits were ruled out as a possible cause of the phenomena.

On Thursday, 16 November, a Siemans Unireg – an electrical instrument that shows voltage fluctuations on a single-track pen recorder – was installed at the office. Later a Tektronix plug-in unit with a storage oscilloscope was added, giving two more pen traces that showed fluctuations in the magnetic field and the noise level. A pen recorder gave a continuous read-out of current and voltage variations at selected points in the office circuitry, and the times at which they happened. The machine was sealed to prevent tampering. Over the next few weeks, it was established that abnormal deflections on the paper record occurred, but only in office hours and never at weekends. The automatic fuses were replaced with screw-in types and, to rule out trickery, these were also sealed.

On Monday, 20 November, after a 'normal' morning of twisting tubes, inexplicable voltage variations and bangs, a fluorescent tube in Adam's private office fell to the floor and shattered. At the same moment, a huge surge in the electric current – 50 amps – was registered, yet the safety fuses did not blow. On examining the read-out, Brunner was puzzled to see loops instead of the expected straight lines. Other tubes fell as the day wore on.

On Tuesday, 21 November, as a safety measure, all the fluorescent tubes in the office were replaced by normal light bulbs. More loud bangs were heard, and the photocopier began leaking chemicals. It was plugged in but not switched on. Brunner wondered if electricity were being conducted into the building through gas and water mains. The team ran a number of tests – and this possibility, too, was ruled out.

On Wednesday, 22 November, the light bulbs began to explode. The neighbourhood was searched for freak power sources. None was found.

On Thursday, 23 November, the office apartment was disconnected from the electricity mains and was connected directly by cable to the transformer, High Tension Station K11 in Königstrasse.

On Friday, 24 November, Brunner thought

the mystery was over. He found full deflections on the paper record, some so savage that the paper had been torn by the pen. As the meter was connected directly to K11, he thought the fault had to be there in the supply itself, and that his team had been correct in pronouncing all the electrical equipment in the office satisfactory. With relief, engineers, equipment and cable were evacuated from the office and camp was set up at K11, to pinpoint the fault. But no fault was found. Camp was reinstated at the office.

The entire supply grid of Rosenheim was checked and pronounced sound.

On Monday, 27 November, a girl was cut by flying glass from an exploding light bulb. All remaining bulbs were covered by nylon bags to prevent further accidents. Four more exploded that afternoon. Between five and six o'clock, an alarming new development forced Brunner to admit that he was dealing with something outside his experience: the lights began to swing.

The next few days were spent observing

swinging lamps and trying to find an explanation for their movement: 'We leapt repeatedly up and down the floor overhead to try to make the lamps swing – without success. The traffic outside was also watched carefully, and tests were made for electrostatic charges, but none was found.'

On Thursday, 30 November, the office was severed from the mains, and power supplied instead by a 7-kilowatt generator-truck parked outside. The generator's meter showed a steady 220-volt output, yet inside the office deflections and crashes continued, lamps swung, bulbs exploded and fuses were ejected erratically.

On Thursday, 7 December, over 90 deflections were registered during the morning. Lamps swung so violently that they smashed against the ceiling, denting the plaster.

To vindicate his methods and results, and to

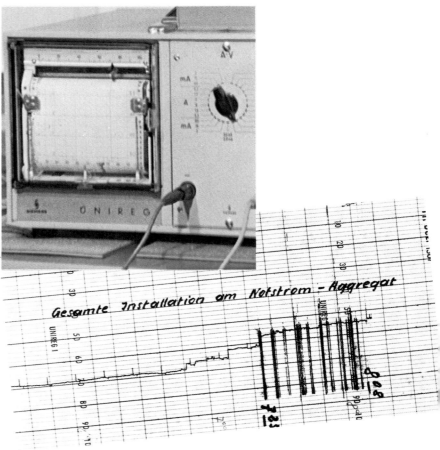

safeguard his reputation, Brunner asked the advice of Dr Karger of the Max Planck Institute of Plasma Physics, and Dr Zicha of Munich University, two of Germany's most eminent physicists. Following a suggestion from Karger, Brunner disconnected the office supply from the Unireg and placed an ordinary 1.5-volt battery across the Unireg terminals. To the astonishment of everyone, instead of registering 1.5 volts until the battery exhausted its charge, the pen began its trace at 3 volts and then zig-zagged wildly across the

Far left: Paul Brunner who, on behalf of the German electricity board, began investigations at Herr Adam's office on 15 November 1967

Below: the Unireg recorder (left) on which abnormalities in the electricity supply were detected and traced on a graph (inset). At first the investigators thought that these were caused by the local electricity substation – but they found no faults after extensive checks. The graph showed violent deflection beginning at about 7.30 a.m. – when one staff member, Annemarie Schneider, began work

be defined. It is an energy quite beyond our comprehension.

Alarmed by the thought that there was no apparent way of controlling this mysterious and often harmful energy, Brunner handed over the investigations to the physicists who had been monitoring the experiments.

Like Brunner, Dr Karger and Dr Zicha were fascinated by the scientific challenge of explaining the electrical disturbances in Adam's office, and they carried out an independent investigation using the most sophisticated equipment. They concentrated on finding the cause of the deflections on the meter, installing probes to examine voltage levels, magnetic fields and sound levels.

While measuring sound levels, they noticed that, although no sound was heard, their monitor showed a huge deflection, so they concluded that there must have been direct

Left: Herr Adam inspects one of the lamps that began to swing wildly on 27 November 1967. The lamp on the office landing moved as much as 22 inches (55 centimetres) from its normal position

Below: the desks at which the two girl clerks in Herr Adam's office, Gustel Huber and Annemarie Schneider, worked

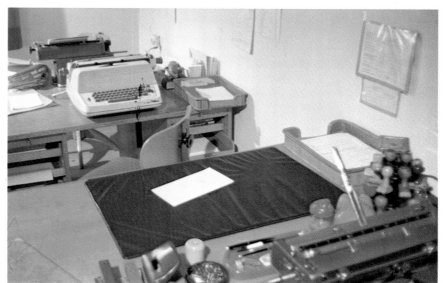

paper. The Unireg (which was in perfect working order) could not be monitoring the battery to which it was connected.

On Monday, 11 December, at 8.45 a.m., Brunner and his assistant, Mayr, were chatting together in the typists' office, when suddenly a painting twisted on its hook. Surprised, Brunner stretched out his hand to straighten the picture. Other paintings in the room started to rotate, some falling to the floor. The typists, who later said they had felt unusually tense that morning, were rooted to their desks with fear, but Mayr and Brunner stationed themselves at vantage points to observe this new phenomenon. They saw the first painting to move turn through 320°, its string wrapping itself round its hook.

At this point Brunner, realising that he was out of his depth, wound up the experiments and wrote his official report. In it he wrote:

It became necessary to postulate the existence of a power hitherto unknown to technology, of which neither the nature nor strength nor direction could

pressure on the crystal in the microphone. They speculated that a similar invisible force could be acting on the pen of the Unireg itself, causing the unnatural loops directly, independently of the electric current. They speculated further: the same force could be acting on the tiny springs inside the telephone, bypassing the dial. It was active only for short periods, its nature was complex and it was not electrodynamic. Known physics could not explain it.

Karger and Zicha also felt that the telephone anomalies suggested that an intelligent force was at work, because it had 'chosen' to focus its attention on the speaking clock. It was clear that the force resisted investigation, and this was another reason to speculate on the existence of an intelligence avoiding scrutiny. They prepared their report and left.

As the physicists left Adam's office, teams of investigators from other scientific fields were eager to take their place, including Professor Hans Bender from the Freiburg Institute, who began his experiments in mid December.

The physicists had left two important clues.

Above: this oak cabinet, which weighs over 400 pounds (180 kilograms), moved a distance of more than a foot (30 centimetres) of its own accord during one afternoon at the Adam office

Right: Hans Bender and a colleague inspect the fluorescent light fittings that spontaneously unscrewed themselves while Annemarie Schneider was present in the office

First, they had suspected that a rational being was behind the phenomena; and second, they confirmed that the 'poltergeist' was active in office hours only. Investigations were now centred on the office staff, Johannes Engelhard, Frau Bielmeier (the part-time assistant) and the two clerks, 17-year-old Gustel Huber and 18-year-old Annemarie Schneider.

As the paranormal events in Herr Adam's office continued, work became increasingly difficult. The army of investigators and reporters who were constantly present did not make things any better, and the staff, who felt they were under continuous scrutiny, became tense and nervous. It was bad enough to have to cope with the poltergeist phenomena that continually interrupted their work, but they also had to cope with mutual suspicion each time something happened.

Soon, however, suspicion began to centre on Annemarie Schneider. She appeared to be the most tense of the office staff, and she twitched strangely whenever poltergeist activity took place. The Unireg record, which had shown deflections only in office hours, was checked closely, and it was found that events began at 7.30 a.m. – the time that Annemarie reported for work. Hans Bender's team from the Freiburg Institute had discreetly centred investigations on her for some time. One day, one of Bender's assistants noticed a lamp swinging strangely as Annemarie walked along the corridor underneath it. It had already been decided that each of the office staff would take a short holiday, since things had been so trying. This would also enable the research team to check who, if anyone, was responsible for the phenomena. Annemarie was given first leave – and, sure enough, the office was peaceful again.

When Annemarie returned to work on 18 December, she seemed even more tense than before, and screamed out when a lamp began to swing. The phenomena had returned with her – and with renewed intensity. Pictures swung merrily, dropping to the floor with a force that dismantled their frames, but left their glass intact. Pages flew off the calendar, and light bulbs exploded. Drawers slid out of desks, and Frau Bielmeier had to wedge one shut with a stool weighted by a typewriter. Annemarie grew more tense every day, screaming and sobbing when phenomena occurred close to her. Fortunately, the Christmas holidays arrived.

Work at the office recommenced on 1 January 1968. When everything had been normal for over a week, Adam began to hope that he was no longer Rosenheim's principal consumer of light bulbs and fluorescent tubes – until 10.30 a.m. on 9 January, when Annemarie returned.

As before, the phenomena returned with Annemarie, and as before, they had grown still

Left: Annemarie Schneider, centre of the Rosenheim poltergeist phenomenon, photographed with her young son in April 1975. Her worst experiences behind her, she began a new life in Munich and has suffered no further paranormal happenings since

Below: Annemarie inspects a pen trace during tests conducted by Hans Bender at the Freiburg Institute in January 1968. The results of the tests, in the sympathetic surroundings of the institute, were disappointing – the strange events seemed to depend on her state of stress

more violent. The climax was reached on 17 January. With only Annemarie and Herr Adam in the office, a number of light bulbs exploded. Annemarie was so frightened that she ran upstairs to the dental surgery, where Herr Geistaller, the dentist, managed to calm her down. Later, the police came to photograph the damage. Annemarie was back at her desk, typing, when the calendar fell from the wall and desk drawers slid out. Suddenly, a metal cash box jumped out of a drawer and clattered to the floor, spilling coins and stamps everywhere.

On another afternoon in the office the girls were almost hysterical because they had been getting electric shocks in their arms and legs all day, and a 400 pound (180 kilogram) oak cabinet moved twice by itself. Chairs shifted and one table even jerked along with a horrified visitor perched on it. When Frau Bielmeier left the typing room, her chair had risen, and Annemarie and Fräulein Huber's chairs both sunk. The height of the typing chairs is adjusted with a ratchet that, to prevent accidents, cannot be altered when any weight is on the seat – yet that afternoon, Professor Büchel of the Physics Institute at Pulach, near Munich, had watched Annemarie's chair descend while she was still sitting on it. She was shocked; her face blanched, then strange red patches appeared on her skin. That day, she was given further leave of absence. As she left, she noted sadly in a diary she had been asked to keep by Hans Bender:

'18 January. As from today, I am on the sick-list. . . . I hope everything will proceed quickly so I can have my rest at last.'

Herr Adam lost no time. Annemarie was dismissed, and never returned to the Königstrasse office – and neither did the strange phenomena. During the poltergeist activity, the cost of the damage had amounted to 15,000 Deutschmarks, which the unfortunate Adam was obliged to pay.

Hans Bender took the opportunity of asking Annemarie to visit his Freiburg Institute so that he could do some laboratory tests and, after initial reluctance to leave home, she agreed to spend from 21 to 26 January 1968 there. A team of scientists duplicated the circuits and equipment of Adam's office, hoping they could

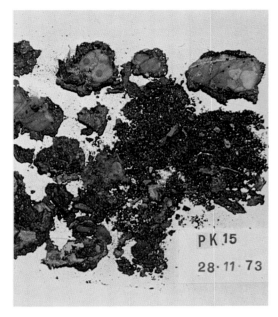

reproduce the poltergeist effects, but no deflections or other phenomena occurred. It seems that Annemarie could produce paranormal events only in certain circumstances.

Abandoning the attempt to reproduce psychokinesis, Bender tried testing Annemarie's ESP abilities. Again, nothing significant was discovered – except momentarily, when Annemarie scored highly while upset by an unpleasant memory. This seemed to confirm that stress encouraged paranormal events in her case.

Stress and frustration were seen to play a major role in Annemarie's personality. During her stay at Freiburg, she underwent extensive psychological assessment by a psychologist colleague of Bender, John Mischo. He concluded that she was unstable, irritable and suffering from frustrated rages. She was unable to tolerate denial and was aggressive, although she suppressed her aggression. He believed that her constant frustrations discharged themselves through psychokinesis, via a process yet to be explained. Her own doctor had remarked on the severity of her nervous symptoms, which included hyperaemia (an excess of blood gathering in one place) and cramps. Her cramp attacks always followed the same pattern: she would cry out, and her eyes would glaze as the cramp spread. Her hands and feet would be worst affected, fingers and toes stretched painfully rigid. Muscles in her knees and hips would also flex agonisingly.

Professor Bender looked for psychological motives for the phenomena. He felt that the speaking clock was contacted as a result of Annemarie's constant desire to know when she could leave the office. Furthermore, it seems as if the damage in the office could have been prompted by aggression towards Herr Adam, as Annemarie had felt particularly tense in his office and had disliked being in his employ-

ment. Apparently, early on in the sequence of phenomena, Adam had sarcastically said: 'All we want now is for the paintings to start moving.' Annemarie was within earshot – and, moments later, the first painting started to move.

Hans Bender has pointed out that this most remarkable of cases was observed over a period of several months by more than 40 witnesses from widely ranging walks of life – office workers, electrical engineers, lawyers, scientists, psychologists and the police. For all the documentary evidence, however, *how* Annemarie produced the phenomena remains as much a mystery to scientists as ever it was.

Scientists have, however, observed and measured several physiological reactions to psychokinesis. First, it has been noted that loss of weight is associated with the phenomenon. Laboratory trials conducted with sensitives who were concentrating on causing objects to move under controlled conditions suggested that weight loss is commonly experienced – which confirmed the claim of one

Three examples of the varied effects of poltergeist activity. A 'face' (above) formed by sulphate of ammonia, used as fertiliser at a garden centre in Bromley, Kent; this was one of several manifestations that occurred during a 1976 poltergeist case in which the epicentre was a 50-year-old man. The ash remains of clothes (above left) that were set alight by spontaneous combustion during a six-year poltergeist manifestation centred on a girl in São Paulo, Brazil. And drawers were thrown from a desk (below) by the poltergeist that focused on the Harpers of Enfield

medium, Eusapia Palladino (1854–1918), that she 'shed' 20 pounds (9 kilograms) during a seance. And experiments in Ireland with a table weighing 30 pounds (13.6 kilograms), which was wired up to equipment designed to monitor movement and weight, showed that when it was levitated (sometimes for as long as 30 minutes) it lost 15 pounds (6.8 kilograms). Unfortunately a thorough examination of weight loss among epicentres during episodes of poltergeist activity is difficult, if not impossible to arrange, as no warning is given before the levitation of objects occurs.

Second, it seems that a rapid drop in temperature is common in cases of both psychokinesis and spontaneous phenomena of other kinds. Records testify to a drop in temperature of as much as 8°F (4.4°C) in 10 seconds. This sudden loss of heat apparently releases a great deal of energy, which could account not only for the blue sparks that some witnesses claim to see but also for the malfunction of electrical equipment that is often observed. Reports of lights, cookers and televisions turning themselves on or off are not uncommon. (A frustrating consequence of this aspect of psychokinesis is that recording and monitoring apparatus is often also affected.)

The generation of highly concentrated electrical charges is another measurable byproduct of psychokinesis. During some experiments conducted in Folkestone, Kent, in 1973 it was established that a group of seven people, sitting at a table with hands joined, were able to generate a considerable electrical charge that lasted for three seconds.

The psychological causes or effects of poltergeist activity are less easy to measure, though many victims display the same symptoms and have similar experiences. For example, many victims see apparitions, some of which are replicas of living people and some thought to be hallucinatory images – although they could be apparitions of unrecognised people. At the time when the Enfield case was being investigated, the 'ghost' of Maurice Grosse, one of the researchers, was seen in the house at least twice, and dozens of other reports confirm that the experience is not uncommon, though by no means all claims have been substantiated by evidence. It seems that it is often necessary for the victim to create a visible form for the invisible agent of the disturbances to assume, in order to be able to cope with the phenomenon. In other words, the 'ghost' provides an excuse for the disturbance, and responsibility for damage can be placed on its phantom shoulders. In some instances an apparition is seen *before* a psychokinetic incident takes place, as though it were the catalyst or agent. As poltergeist activity frequently erupts when tension or trauma is experienced, the appearance of a 'ghost' may be a symptom of stress. Few adults of average intelligence are frightened by such incidents, but for children or people of a nervous disposition the shock caused by the appearance of a mysterious figure could trigger a series of inexplicable events for which the 'ghost' is

Bottom: levitation of a table during a seance by English medium Jack Webber

Right: Polish medium Stanislawa Tomczyk gives a levitation display. After her marriage in 1919 to the Hon. Francis Feilding she gave up all practices of this kind and even claimed that her act had been a fraud – but she was never able to explain how it had been done

Far right: council tenant Mrs Mary Sharman and her two sons, who were victims of poltergeist disturbance for 12 years. The trouble stopped when the family moved house

The ancient manor house at Sandford Orcas, set in an attractive part of Dorset, is the typical English haunted house – and it seems to have more than its fair share of ghosts. They include a lady in green; another in red, noted for her punctual appearances at 11.50 a.m. on the stairs; a monk; an Elizabethan lady; a local man who hanged himself in the gatehouse; and Sir Hubert Medlycott, whose family still owns the house. A ghost dog is sometimes seen, and the sound of a phantom spinet can sometimes be heard. The ghost of a footman, 7 feet (2 metres) tall, adds to the problems of the house, for it reputedly takes an improper interest in virgins. It is not, however, often seen nowadays. There are allegedly 14 ghosts in all at the manor – offering a tempting field for the energetic ghost investigator.

subsequently held responsible.

Neurosis is another psychological condition associated with psychokinesis. Professor A. R. G. Owen has suggested that 'poltergeistry' is a conversion neurosis – that in certain people acute anxiety may be converted into noise and movement of objects; but, if that is the case, why does poltergeist activity cease? 'Maybe', Professor Owen suggests, 'the activity eventually ends because it is not a disease but the cure.' And sleepwalking, another symptom of deep anxiety, is also associated with victims of poltergeist activity.

A series of laboratory tests conducted on a housewife in the Soviet Union in the 1970s revealed the extent to which physiological and psychological factors collaborate to produce psychokinetic forces. Among other things, Nina Kulagina was able to separate the yolk of an egg from the white, and then reassemble the egg, without touching the container in which it had been placed. She was also able to arrest the heartbeat of a frog by suppressing an electric current (she was not told that the wires carrying the current were connected to a living creature). In other tests small electrodes were attached to her head and recording apparatus to her heart and wrists so that electrical pulses generated during psychokinetic incidents could be monitored.

The tests proved that the electrical activity of her brain rose to a very high level, and her pulse rate increased to an incredible 240 beats a minute (a pulse rate of about 70 is considered normal). The magnetic field around Nina also increased significantly, and when all the electrical and electromagnetic forces reached their peak, they merged in a single, fluctuating rhythm. At this point she was able to move objects at some distance from her without touching them in any way. During each successful trial in which her psychokinetic power was evident Nina lost 4 pounds (1.8 kilograms).

So the generation of psychokinetic power appears to have its origins in certain psychological conditions, to which physiological symptoms bear witness. Yet the power seems, to some extent, to have an existence that is independent of those who generate it. However, it is generally acknowledged that psychokinesis is a form of 'thought force', whose origins are natural rather than supernatural. As Scott Rogo puts it in a paper in the *Journal* of the Society for Psychical Research in June 1980: 'Psychokinesis is a phenomenon of vast contradictions. It seems to be both a mental and a physical force at one and the same time.' At present an explanation for the phenomenon lies beyond the boundaries of scientific theory; general acceptance and a deeper understanding of the force will depend on strictly controlled investigation of ghostly phenomena in all their forms. Science makes progress, but ghosts and poltergeists continue to shock and mystify us.

Above: the Russian housewife Nina Kulagina, who has been able to exert considerable psychokinetic force. During one test her pulse rate was found to have increased to 240 beats per minute, and she lost 4 pounds (1.8 kilograms) in weight

CHAPTER SIX

Into Thin Air

Disappearances, Mary Celeste, Bermuda Triangle

Disappearances

People, animals and ordinary household objects that vanish into thin air or appear suddenly in unlikely places have always been part of folklore. Charles Fort coined the word *teleportation* to describe the forcible removal of a person or object from one place – or even plane of existence – to another by forces unknown and unseen. According to taste, these forces have been ascribed to God, the Devil, spirit guides, fairies and UFOs.

This notion of objects being *carried* by an invisible force accords perfectly with the spiritualists' belief that solid objects can be dematerialised and materialised through the agency of spirits. One 'spirit guide' named White Hawk described how he does it: 'I can only explain it by saying that I speed up the atomic vibrations until the stones [or other object] are disintegrated. Then they are brought here and I slow down the vibrations until they become solid again.'

Spiritualists often explain the inability of most mortals to see the 'other side' – which is said to interpenetrate our world in space and time – by pointing out that the material world is 'dense matter', which vibrates slowly; the spiritual plane is 'refined matter', vibrating too fast for our physical perceptions. A sudden change in atomic vibration removes objects – or people – from one plane to another or one place to another, rather like the 'beaming up' and 'beaming down' of the personnel of *Star Trek*'s starship *Enterprise*.

Sometimes people disappear and re-appear quite suddenly a great distance away. One unfortunate gentleman was going about his business in Goa, India, in 1665 when he found himself back in his birthplace, Portugal. This abrupt return home was witnessed by enough people to ensure it came to the ears of the Inquisition, who naturally – for them – assumed he was a practising sorcerer. He was tried and burnt at the stake.

In other instances, the disappearances are permanent.

On 29 November 1809 Benjamin Bathurst, an employee of the British Foreign Office, was about to board a coach outside an inn near Berlin. He went to look at the horses and vanished forever.

In June 1900, Sherman Church ran into a cotton mill at Augusta Mills near Lake Michigan, USA. He never came out and could not be found again.

Right: Eliza Carter, the 12-year-old schoolgirl who disappeared mysteriously in East London in January 1882. Her case was the first in a series of abductions that came to be known as the 'West Ham disappearances'

Far right: a series of sketches showing the fate of Amelia Jeffs, thought to be another victim of the West Ham disappearances. This time however, there was no mystery: police found the little girl's body

Below: fairies abducting a human child in a drawing by E. Gertrude Thomson from The fairies *by William Allingham (1886). Folklore is full of tales of children being stolen by fairies, who leave their own children – changelings – in their place*

A LITTLE GIRL OUTRAGED AND MURDERED AT WEST HAM

In 1974 pigs, sheep and heifers vanished from two farms near Manchester, England.

In some cases, the victims seem to vanish, come back, then go away again.

The 1880s saw a large number of disappearances from East London, known to this day as the 'West Ham disappearances'. One of the first victims was little Eliza Carter, who vanished from her home but later appeared in the street and spoke to some of her school friends. They tried to persuade her to go home to her family, but she said she couldn't – 'they' wouldn't let her. She was seen around West Ham for a couple of days before finally disappearing forever.

A similar case was that of Private Jerry Unwin of the US Army, who disappeared, reappeared, absented himself and appeared once more, before vanishing again on 1 August 1959.

The experience was not pleasant, and a far cry from the semi-mystical experience of the abductees portrayed in the film *Close encounters of the third kind*, but it was kin to the whole history of mysterious abductions.

But in the annals of disappearing people there is no more controversial tale nor one stranger than the alleged 'Philadelphia experiment'. In 1943 there reportedly took place a horrifying experiment into invisibility involving a ship and its crew. This was not a psychic test, but a top-secret experiment of the United States Navy. According to Charles Berlitz and William Moore in their book *The Philadelphia experiment* (1979), the surviving witnesses to the experiment still suffer harassment and have been repeatedly warned against discussing it by government agents.

A force field was created around the experimental ship – a destroyer called the *Eldridge* – as it lay in a special berth in the Philadelphia Navy Yard. The crew could see one another normally but witnesses could see only the vague outline of both ship and men through the force field. They shimmered like a heat haze before re-assuming normal shape and

density. The effect on the crewmen involved was said to be appalling. The after-effects took various horrible forms: some of the men are said to have suffered a particularly harrowing form of spontaneous human combustion, others went mad, and yet others periodically became semi-transparent or partly invisible. Some died as a direct result of their experience.

An eyewitness claimed to have seen the entire experiment take place, and even to have thrust his arm into the force field.

The US Navy deny that the experiment took place. Yet the story is too persistent and has too much inner consistency to be dismissed entirely. If 'project invisibility' did take place, then it made scientific history – but compared to 'natural' disappearances it was clumsy and very dangerous.

However, the evidence offered by Berlitz and Moore does not stand up to careful scrutiny and, as we will see with the case of the famous Bermuda Triangle, Charles Berlitz is not above embroidering the truth to spin a good story. This terrifying event may well have happened, but so far no real proof has been made available.

Below: the Philadelphia Navy Yard from where a destroyer, the USS Eldridge *(bottom), is reported to have been made to disappear, together with its crew, during a horrifying experiment in invisibility in 1943. However, as most of the evidence comes from a single witness, one Carlos Allende, whose testimony has proved impossible to corroborate, it is difficult to judge whether the experiment really took place, or the story is simply an elaborate hoax*

Mary Celeste

On 15 November 1872, a British ship called the *Dei Gratia* left New York with a cargo of petroleum bound for Gibraltar. Her skipper was a Nova Scotian named David Reed Morehouse and the first mate was Oliver Deveau. Both these men and the rest of *Dei Gratia*'s crew were highly able sailors – as later events were to prove – and no 'dirt' has ever been attached to their characters except by sensationalists.

On 5 December, shortly after 1 p.m., one of the *Dei Gratia*'s crew, John Johnson, who was at the wheel, sighted a vessel about 5 miles (8 kilometres) off the port bow. Attracted by the poor state of the ship's sails and her slight 'yawing' (listing), he called the second mate, John Wright, and together they summoned Captain Morehouse. After surveying the vessel through his telescope, Morehouse gave orders to offer assistance.

At 3 p.m., having come within about 400 yards (370 metres) of the mystery ship, Morehouse hailed her several times, but, receiving no reply from her, he decided to send some men to investigate.

Oliver Deveau, with Wright and Johnson, rowed across to the distressed craft, noting as they drew closer, its name – *Mary Celeste*. Johnson was left in the boat as the other two hauled themselves over the ship's rails. The *Mary Celeste* was deserted.

Over the next hour Deveau and Wright searched *Mary Celeste* from stem to stern. The sails and rigging were in some disarray, the wheel was spinning free and the binnacle had been knocked over and broken. The main hatch to below decks was well-battened down and secure, but certain of the hatch covers had apparently been removed and were found discarded near the hatchways. There was less than a foot (30 centimetres) of water in the galley and little of the six months' store of provisions had been spoilt. There was ample fresh water.

On a table in Captain Briggs's cabin Oliver Deveau found the temporary log. It read: 'Monday, 25th. At five o'clock made island of St Mary's bearing ESE. At eight o'clock Eastern point bore SSW six miles [3 kilometres] distant.'

In the mate's cabin Deveau found a chart showing the track of the vessel up to 24 November.

Missing from the ship were the chronometer, sextant, bill of lading, navigation book, and a small yawl, or boat, that had been lashed to the main hatch. A piece of railing running alongside had been removed to launch the boat. This at least answered the mystery of where *Mary Celeste*'s crew had gone: they had abandoned ship. But why?

The *Mary Celeste* was built in 1860 at a new shipyard in Nova Scotia. She was originally christened *Amazon* and launched in 1861, the year that saw the start of the American Civil War; her first captain died a short while later. Over the next few years, her history was one of misfortune and mishap during which she passed from one owner to another, several of whom seem to have gone bankrupt and none of whom derived any good from their contact with the ship. She eventually passed into the hands of J. H. Winchester and Co., a consortium of New York shipowners. By this time the *Amazon* was unrecognisable as the vessel that had left the shipyards of Joshua Dewis. She had been enlarged, now flew the Stars and Stripes, and on her nameboard was *Mary Celeste*.

Sometime during late September or early October in 1872 *Mary Celeste* was berthed at Pier 44 in New York's East River, preparing to take on a new cargo and a fresh crew. Her captain was a stern, puritan New Englander named Benjamin Spooner Briggs. He was born at Wareham, Massachusetts, on 24 April 1835, the second of five sons born to a seafaring family. Briggs was a man of strict beliefs and religious convictions, and although he was a teetotaller he was no monomaniac on the subject. He was described by those who knew him as always bearing 'the highest character as a Christian and as an intelligent and active

Above: J. H. Winchester, one of the owners of the hapless sailing ship that eventually became the Mary Celeste

Left: the Amazon, *built in 1860 in Nova Scotia. Until she became the* Mary Celeste *a few years later, her short career was 'unlucky' – afterwards it was disastrous*

Right: the Mary Celeste, *the Nova Scotian half-brig whose name is synonymous with the most bizarre kind of disappearance*

shipmaster'. He was also a shareholder in the *Mary Celeste*.

The first mate was Albert G. Richardson, who had served with Captain Briggs before. He seems to have been trustworthy and competent and was held in high esteem, as were the rest of the crew.

Also making the voyage were Captain Briggs's wife, Sarah Elizabeth – the daughter of the preacher of the Congregational Church in Marion, Massachusetts – and one of their two children, two-year-old Sophia Matilda. The elder child, their son Arthur Stanley, remained at home.

Late on Saturday, 2 November 1872 *Mary Celeste*'s cargo was loaded and made secure. She carried 1701 barrels of denatured alcohol being shipped by Meissner Ackerman and Co., merchants of New York, to H. Mascerenhas and Co., of Genoa, Italy.

Early on 5 November the Sandy Hook pilot ship towed *Mary Celeste* from Pier 44 to the lower bay off Staten Island, New York. The Atlantic was particularly stormy for the time of year and Briggs was forced to drop anchor for two days before he dared to venture out to sea on 7 November; he never reached his destination.

mystery would have probably faded into obscurity, but his accusations at the hearings in the Vice-Admiralty Court attracted worldwide publicity. He attempted to trump up several ridiculous charges to explain the disappearances: that the original crew had become drunk on the alcohol on board (which would have given them acute pains long before they became intoxicated) and had then murdered the captain; that the two skippers had, by previous arrangement, murdered the crew – planning to meet later to share the salvage reward (even though Briggs's share of this would have been worth less than his investment in the vessel); and that the captain and crew of the *Dei Gratia* had murdered all on board the *Mary Celeste*. Fortunately, the Vice-Admiralty Court denounced such a flag-

What possible reason could an experienced seaman like Benjamin Spooner Briggs have had for abandoning a perfectly seaworthy ship and loading his wife and two-year-old daughter and the seven members of crew into a small and comparatively unstable boat? Abandoning ship is a desperate measure, an act taken only when there is no alternative; yet as one of *Dei Gratia*'s crew said later, *Mary Celeste* was in a fit enough state to sail around the world. So why was she abandoned?

Under international maritime law anyone who salvages an abandoned vessel is entitled to a percentage of what the vessel and its cargo are worth. Generally such a vessel is a wreck, but *Mary Celeste*, a seaworthy ship, and her valuable cargo were worth a substantial sum, and the salvors could expect to make perhaps as much as $80,000. Captain Morehouse was not consumed by avarice, as many subsequent writers have implied, and was actually reluctant to lay claim to *Mary Celeste*. He could not really spare the men to form a skeleton crew without both vessels being undermanned and therefore at risk in the event of an emergency; but he was eventually persuaded by Deveau.

Deveau and two seamen, Augustus Anderson and Charles Lund, took only two days to restore *Mary Celeste* to order, and then the two ships set off for Gibraltar. *Dei Gratia* arrived on the evening of 12 December and *Mary Celeste* the following morning. Within two hours of dropping anchor *Mary Celeste* was placed under arrest by Thomas J. Vecchio, of the Vice-Admiralty Court.

The Attorney General for Gibraltar and Advocate for the Queen in Her Office of Admiralty was an excitable, arrogant and pompous bureaucrat named Frederick Solly Flood; he found the abandonment of *Mary Celeste* explicable only as a result of murder and piracy. Without Solly Flood the *Mary Celeste*

Top left: Captain Benjamin Spooner Briggs, master of the Mary Celeste. *A puritan and abstemious New Englander, his alleged religious fanaticism has been blamed for whatever disaster hit the crew. Did they mutiny, or could something have driven them mad?*

Top right: Briggs's wife, Sarah Elizabeth who, with their two-year-old daughter Sophia Matilda, also sailed on the fatal voyage

Above: the first mate, Albert G. Richardson, who had served before under Briggs and was deemed to be an excellent seaman

Above right: the ship's list giving the names of those who sailed – and vanished without trace

Reproduced from the original in the National Archives (Records of the Department of the Treasury, Bureau of Customs), Washington, D.C.

rant abuse of the law and cleared Morehouse and his crew of any suspicion. They granted them a salvage reward of £1700. In the opinion of many people the award should have been twice or three times as much.

It did not take long for the myth surrounding the disappearance of the *Mary Celeste*'s crew to be born: the story was seized upon by writers and journalists and soon caught the public imagination.

The first major piece of fiction about the ship was published in January 1884 by the prestigious *Cornhill Magazine*. It was a sensational short story called *J. Habakuk Jephson's statement* and it bore little resemblance to the actual facts. It was picked up by American newspapers however and published as fact.

Apart from its literary worth, *J. Habakuk Jephson's statement* is interesting in two ways;

it was one of the first literary efforts of a young English doctor named Arthur Conan Doyle, and in it *Mary Celeste* is called *Marie Celeste*, the name by which the ship is now most commonly known. However, Conan Doyle was not the first to make the error – this version of the name first appears in *Lloyd's List* of 25 March 1873.

Conan Doyle's story was the first of many fictional accounts that have appeared over the years; for example, a novel based on the mystery was published as recently as 1980. Some of these tales have been presented as straight fiction, others as fictionalised fact (but nevertheless proposing a serious explanation), and quite a few have been intended to be taken as fact.

While the majority of theories to explain the Triangle writers list the vessel's crew among the victims of whatever unexplained force they consider to exist in the area, imbuing that force with a singular selectivity, and in the process enlarging the Triangle so that it reaches the Azores. A superficially acceptable theory put forward by a number of rational people was that the food or drinking water was contaminated and caused the crew to hallucinate, driving them mad so that they threw themselves over the side. But Oliver Deveau and other members of the *Dei Gratia*'s crew used the food and water they found aboard *Mary Celeste* and suffered no ill effects.

No solution so far offered seems to account for all the circumstances, but it is possible to list some salient facts that might provide a few clues: *Mary Celeste* was abandoned by her

Below: the alleged suicide of the Marie Celeste's *captain – 'Tibbs' – from an illustration of Conan Doyle's story* J. Habakuk Jephson's statement. *A gripping tale, it was taken by many to be true and popularised the misnomer* 'Marie' Celeste

abandonment of *Mary Celeste* are generally a variation on the theme of murder – committed either by *Mary Celeste*'s own crew or by the men of *Dei Gratia* – other solutions are not uncommon and are frequently bizarre. The 1900s favoured 'monster from the depths' stories in which *Mary Celeste* was attacked by a huge hungry octopus that plucked the entire crew from the deck, but this theory has a number of flaws; it is highly unlikely, for example, that everyone aboard *Mary Celeste* would have been on deck at the same time or that they would have obligingly stayed there as the monster plucked them off one by one. We must also assume that for some reason the creature craved *Mary Celeste*'s yawl, chronometer, sextant, and ship's papers.

It has been suggested that *Mary Celeste*'s crew were abducted by a UFO, and Bermuda captain and crew; those who abandoned ship did so in the ship's yawl. This small vessel would have been overloaded and easily capsized, so the crew's fate is not wholly inexplicable. The ship was abandoned in a hurry: extra clothing was not taken nor – as far as is known – was any food or water, but the crew did not abandon ship in a complete panic, since they took the time to collect the sextant, chronometer, and the ship's papers (apart from the temporary log). Since there was no evidence that *Mary Celeste* had suffered any damage, whatever made the crew abandon her was

Above left: in the 1936 film version of the Mary Celeste *mystery, the bosun goes mad and kills the entire crew, including himself*

something they feared had happened or was about to happen, but clearly, whatever it was, it never came to pass.

The most likely solution was in part offered by Oliver Deveau at the salvage hearing. He said that he thought the crew had panicked, believing that the ship was sinking, a comment that needs some interpretation.

Dr James H. Kimble, once the head of the United States Weather Bureau in New York, and author Gershom Bradford have both suggested that *Mary Celeste* was struck by a waterspout, a tornado at sea; a column of whirling wind and water that can appear without warning, last for up to an hour, and then break up as quickly as it appeared.

Kimble and Bradford believe that a relatively small and harmless spout could have struck the ship without doing a great deal of damage. However, within a waterspout the barometric pressure is extremely low and, as the spout passed over the ship, the marked difference in pressure between the inside and outside of the ship could have caused the hatch covers to blow off.

In this context, the method by which *Mary Celeste* was sounded may be extremely significant. This was done by dropping a rod down the pump well to measure the water in the hold, in much the same way as a motorist checks his oil with a dipstick. The drop in barometric pressure could have driven the bilge water up the pump-well, where a valve would have prevented it from returning immediately to the hold. Although this would have been merely a temporary malfunction, the crew may not have realised it.

Suppose, then, that after the waterspout had moved on the crew were shaken and confused.

Above: Captain David Reed Morehouse, master of the Dei Gratia *(top left). Under maritime law anyone who salvages an abandoned ship is entitled to a percentage of its total worth. In the case of* Mary Celeste *this would have been considerable, but Morehouse was reluctant to lay any claim since he had no spare crew to look after the empty ship. Yet some critics still maintain that Briggs and Morehouse were conspirators who planned to split the salvage money*

Top: Oliver Deveau, first mate of the Dei Gratia *who, with only two other crewmen, brought the* Mary Celeste *into Gibraltar*

Above right: a fast, angled waterspout could have hit the Mary Celeste, *temporarily falsifying the crew's surroundings. This is a reasonable theory, but the real truth may never be discovered*

Somebody went to sound the ship to see if she had suffered any underwater damage, and to his horror found that *Mary Celeste* had leaked 6 to 8 feet (2 to 2½ metres) of water in less than a minute – or so the seaman would have thought when he removed the sounding rod. Believing *Mary Celeste* to be sinking fast, Captain Briggs gave the order to abandon ship. Perhaps this was what Oliver Deveau had meant by his cryptic statement. We shall never know, but the waterspout theory certainly seems to fit most of the reported circumstances and also explains most of the many baffling features of a case that seems destined to inspire speculation, yet remain unsolved.

Whatever happened to her captain and crew, *Mary Celeste* was returned to James H. Winchester and, under the command of Captain George W. Blatchford, she continued her voyage to Genoa and finally delivered her cargo. Winchester then sold the ship – it is rumoured at a considerable loss – and over the next 12 years the vessel changed hands no less than 17 times. None of her new owners had a good word to say about her. She lurched up and down the coast of the United States losing cargoes, sails and sailors, running aground and catching fire with depressing regularity. The superstitious would call her jinxed, and *Mary Celeste*'s story is one that would make even a hard-boiled sceptic agree that the superstitious might have a point.

Bermuda Triangle

The Bermuda Triangle, an area of the western Atlantic where scores of ships and aircraft have disappeared without trace, has been described as one of the greatest true-life mysteries of all time. The disappearances are without explanation and seem to be caused by some 'force' or phenomenon unknown to science.

Charles Berlitz, author of two best-sellers about the region, *The Bermuda Triangle* and *Without a trace*, has written:

Large and small boats have disappeared without leaving wreckage, as if they and their crews had been snatched into another dimension ... in no other area have the unexplained disappearances been so numerous, so well recorded, so sudden, and attended by such unusual circumstances, some of which push the element of coincidence to the borders of impossibility.

According to writers on the subject, the British ship *Bella* disappeared in 1854 en route from Rio de Janeiro to Jamaica. In 1866 the Triangle claimed the Swedish barque *Lotta* and two years later the Spanish merchantman *Viego* vanished. The British training ship *Atlanta* and her 290 cadets and crew sailed into oblivion in 1880. They were followed in 1884 by the Italian schooner *Miramon*.

It is said that in 1902 the German barque *Freya*, sailing from Manzanillo in Cuba to Punta Arenas, Chile, was found in the Triangle. Her crew had disappeared. The vessel itself was listing badly, was partly dismasted and showed every sign of having been caught in a particularly violent storm.

In 1918 the large collier *Cyclops* mysteriously vanished. She had carried a radio but no distress message had been received. A message *was* sent by the Japanese freighter *Raifuku Maru* in 1925 but it only intensified the mystery because the radio operator is reported as saying: 'Danger like dagger now. Come quick!' Thirteen years later, in 1938, the blue skies were cloudless and the sea was still when the steamship *Anglo-Australian* radioed an 'all's well' message before sailing into the Bermuda Triangle. She never emerged.

In January 1948 the British airliner *Star Tiger* was nearing the end of a routine flight from the Azores to Bermuda when she is said to have radioed: 'Weather and performance excellent. Expect to arrive on schedule.' But the aircraft did not arrive at all.

Another airliner, a Douglas DC-3, vanished on a flight from Puerto Rico to Florida in December 1948. The pilot allegedly radioed: 'We are approaching the field ... only fifty miles [80 kilometres] to the south. ... We can see the lights of Miami now ... all's well. Will stand by for landing instructions.' But when Miami replied a few minutes later she received no reply. Not another word was ever heard from the aircraft. The DC-3 had vanished over an area where the water was only 20 feet (6 metres) deep, yet search craft failed to locate any wreckage or survivors.

In June 1950 in calm seas and in good weather the Costa Rican freighter *Sandra* and her crew of 28 vanished. 'What could have happened to her? No one has the least idea,' says Triangle writer Adi-Kent Thomas Jeffrey.

A sinister happening is said to have been experienced by the passengers and crew of an Eastern Airlines aircraft that vanished from the radar at Miami for 10 minutes. Full emergency operations were launched but then the airliner reappeared and landed safely. Nobody on board had experienced anything odd and

Below: the island of Bermuda in the Atlantic. Is this beautiful spot at the centre of a whole series of mysterious and sinister events?

they had no explanation for the fact that every clock and watch on board was found to be 10 minutes slow.

The extent of the Triangle's range of influence startled researchers when Professor Wayne Meshejian announced that a sophisticated weather satellite operated by the National Oceanographic Administration consistently malfunctioned when over the Bermuda Triangle.

In 1945, five US Navy bombers – Flight 19 – vanished after sending a series of baffling and bizarre radio messages. A few years later the writer Vincent Gaddis called the region the Bermuda Triangle. There is little agreement among writers on its size and shape, and each region is given a different name such as Devil's Triangle and Limbo of the Lost. At its smallest, however, the Bermuda Triangle is the size of the United Kingdom and Eire, and at its largest it takes in about half the North Atlantic Ocean.

'Could magnetism or some form of magnetic phenomenon be related to the strange disappearances?' asks Richard Winer, author of *The Devil's Triangle*. Few writers have failed to mention how the compass needle usually points to the magnetic North Pole rather than to the actual North Pole – except, however, in the Bermuda Triangle.

The Bermuda Triangle is depicted as a strange place where strange things happen. Hundreds of ships and aircraft have vanished

inexplicably without trace. They hardly ever send a distress call and wreckage is rarely found.

In fact the number of disappearances is far from alarmingly high, as some writers contend. About 150,000 boats cross the Bermuda

Above: an Avenger torpedo bomber of the type that vanished in December 1945 after leaving Fort Lauderdale naval air base for a brief training flight

Triangle every year and on average about 10,000 send a distress call. However, only about 100 losses are recorded annually. While 100 losses are 100 too many it is not a significant proportion of 150,000 – 0.07 per cent.

As well as being subject to all the natural hazards of the sea – such as storms, hurricanes and waterspouts – the Triangle is the home of the Gulf Stream, a fast-moving body of water that can carry an unwary or inexperienced sailor miles off course in a matter of hours and quickly disperse wreckage.

However, when all is said and done, the backbone of the Triangle legend is that catalogue of disappearances and the claim that they defy rational explanation. Let us now examine a random sample of Triangle fatalities. The British ship *Bella* is said to have vanished in 1854 on a voyage from Rio de Janeiro to Jamaica, yet under investigation identification of the *Bella* has proved impossible. Lloyd's have a record of a ship of that name built in Liverpool in 1852, but there is no suggestion that it suffered any misfortune.

A similar case is that of the German barque

Freya. She is said to have sailed from Manzanillo, Cuba, in 1902 and to have been found in the Triangle abandoned by her crew and giving every appearance of having been caught in a particularly violent storm. Weather records apparently reveal that only light airs prevailed in the region at the time. There is evidence that submarine volcanic activity was responsible for her abandonment, but this is somewhat irrelevant since the *Freya* did not sail from Manzanillo, Cuba, but from Manzanillo, Mexico, and she was not found abandoned in the Bermuda Triangle, nor even in the Atlantic Ocean, but in the Pacific.

No hint of mystery was ever attached to either the *Bella* or the *Freya* until writers began searching for Triangle fatalities. Other ships – the *Lotta*, *Viego*, and *Miramon* – could not be traced, and it is questionable whether they ever existed.

In the 19th and early 20th centuries, ships did not carry radio equipment. We cannot be certain of where they were when disaster struck or of what form the disaster took. For example, the *Atalanta* (not *Atlanta* as many authors call her) disappeared on an intended voyage of 3000 miles (4800 kilometres), only 500 miles (800 kilometres) of which were through the Bermuda Triangle. We do not know where she was when she was overwhelmed, but we do know that she had a crew of very inexperienced cadets and that severe storms swept her route.

The first radio-carrying vessel claimed by the Bermuda Triangle was the 19,000-tonne collier *Cyclops* in March 1918. As with the *Atalanta*, her route was in the path of a severe storm, and it is quite likely that she capsized.

Above: disappearances in the Bermuda Triangle number about 100 annually. This reward poster drew attention to the mysterious fate of the yacht Saba Bank, *which vanished while sailing from Nassau to Miami in April 1974*

Left: the coast of Florida in 1563, as shown on a map by Lazaro Luis. Christopher Columbus travelled through the area, now known as the Bermuda Triangle, in the late 15th century and noted that his ship's compass acted erratically. He also recorded that 'a great flame of fire' fell into the sea

Far left: the Cyclops, *a US Navy collier, disappeared in March 1918 after leaving Barbados for the Chesapeake Bay area of the eastern USA. The vessel, 540 feet (165 metres) long, carried a crew of about 300 and was laden with manganese ore*

Above and right: the Star Tiger, *an aircraft of the Tudor IV type went missing in 1948 on a flight from London to Havana via the Azores and Bermuda, a disappearance that has been called 'truly a modern mystery of the air'. The last message received from her gave no inkling of anything untoward, but a thorough search of the seas failed to find any trace of the aircraft or its passengers*

Above, far right: storms and hurricanes provide likely reasons for some of the losses in the Bermuda Triangle. The racing yacht Revenoc *vanished between Key West and Miami in early 1958 when the Florida coast was being battered by near-hurricane-force winds*

TUDOR LOST BETWEEN AZORES AND BERMUDA

---◆---

AIR-SEA RESCUE SEARCH FOR 31 ON BOARD

FROM OUR OWN CORRESPONDENT
NEW YORK, Friday.

All aircraft and ships in the vicinity of Bermuda to-day joined in the search for the British South American Airways Tudor IV., Star Tiger, which is overdue at Bermuda from the Azores.

The search was fully maintained until darkness fell, when the United States Navy recalled all its planes. American Army Flying Fortresses and Super-Fortresses, however, continued their quest during the night, assisted by two British South American Airways machines.

The Star Tiger left London on Tuesday, but was held up by bad weather in the Azores. It was due at Kindley Field, Bermuda, at 5 a.m. G.M.T. to-day.

According to New York Coast-guard H.Q. the Star Tiger was 380 miles north-east of Bermuda when its last radio message was received at 3 a.m. The pilot reported nothing unusual.

The plane, which had a crew of

SEARCH PLANE CRASHES : NINE DEAD IN ALPS

---◆---

LOST DAKOTA SEEN

FROM OUR OWN CORRESPONDENT
PARIS, Friday.

While searching for the American Dakota which crashed in the

Her top-heavy superstructure and the nature of her cargo would have ensured that the *Cyclops* sank very quickly indeed.

The Japanese freighter *Raifuku Maru* is said to have vanished in 1925 after sending a strange radio message: 'Danger like dagger now. Come quick!' The message, picked up by the White Star liner *Homeric* but distorted by electrical interference, was in fact 'Now very danger. Come quick!' The *Homeric* sped to the freighter's assistance but encountered mountainous seas and saw the *Raifuku Maru* sink with all hands.

The Triangle writers say that the 355-foot (106-metre) freighter *Sandra* and her crew of 28 sailed into oblivion in calm seas and under blue skies in June 1950. About the only details they get correct are the freighter's name and nationality. The *Sandra* was 185 feet (55 metres) long, carried a crew of 11 and vanished in hurricane force winds in April 1950.

Hurricanes also prevailed when the freighter *Anglo-Australian* vanished in 1938.

The *Star Tiger*, a Tudor IV aircraft, mysteriously vanished towards the end of a flight from the Azores to Bermuda on 30 January 1948. Contrary to the Triangle legend, the last message from it was an acknowledgement of a radio bearing requested several minutes earlier and not 'Weather and performance excellent. Expect to arrive on schedule.' The weather, in fact, was anything but excellent. Cloud cover throughout the flight had prevented accurate navigation; and the aircraft had battled severe headwinds, forcing the pilot to revise his estimated time of arrival and reducing the safety margin of extra fuel. The airliner disappeared at the most critical stage of her flight. She had insufficient fuel to reach any airport other than Bermuda and was forced to fly at 2000 feet (600 metres) because of the headwinds. Had anything gone wrong the *Star Tiger* would undoubtedly have plummeted into the sea within seconds.

The case of the Douglas DC-3 lost on 28 December 1948 is an example of how facts have been omitted and distorted to imply a greater mystery than exists. The aircraft, carrying 27 passengers, had left San Juan, Puerto Rico, bound for Miami, Florida. The pilot, Captain Robert Linquist, is said to have radioed that he was 50 miles (80 kilometres) from Miami, could see the lights of the city, and was standing by for landing instructions. Miami replied within minutes, but the aircraft had vanished. The water over which the aircraft was flying was only 20 feet (6 metres) deep, yet search craft failed to locate any wreckage.

The DC-3 is known to have had a defective radio (though some writers have failed to mention this), so the sudden silence does not mean that the aircraft was overcome immediately after sending the message to Miami. It also removes any mystery attached to the lack of a distress call. Furthermore, the pilot did not say he could see the lights of Miami. It seems

disappearances. Many writers point out that in the Bermuda Triangle the compass needle points to the North Pole and not to the magnetic North Pole as it does everywhere else in the world. This is not strictly true. At certain places in the world the actual North Pole and the magnetic North Pole are in a straight line, the Agonic Line, and one of those places is off the coast of Florida. Accounts that mention compass needles gyrating wildly or otherwise acting strangely prove nothing either. Local magnetic variations can cause such behaviour and exist all over the world.

The cornerstone of the Triangle myth, however, is the disappearance of five US Navy bombers – Flight 19 – and a sea plane, all on 5 December 1945. According to the Triangle version of the story, the five Grumman TBM Avenger bombers left the runway at the Naval Air Station, Fort Lauderdale, Florida, at

that some writers have put these words in the pilot's mouth because he said that he was only 50 miles (80 kilometres) from Miami (from which distance the lights of the city would be visible).

However, the pilot had been compensating for a north-west wind, but the wind direction had changed during the flight and it is not known whether the pilot received notification of the fact. If not, he could have missed the Florida Peninsula and literally flown into the Gulf of Mexico. And although the depth of the sea over which the DC-3 was flying at the time of the last message is in places only 20 feet (6 metres) deep, in other areas it plunges to depths of up to 5000 feet (1520 metres). Nobody is certain where the aircraft went down.

Similarly, when we look at the claim that a weather satellite malfunctioned over the Bermuda Triangle, and only over the Triangle, we find it does not withstand investigation. In fact the satellite was not malfunctioning. It collected visual and infra-red data on cloud cover and transmitted the information to Earth. For convenience the infra-red signal was transmitted direct while the visual signal was stored on a loop of tape for later transmission. At certain times the tape became full and had to be rewound, so no visual signal was transmitted. By pure coincidence the tape was rewinding when the satellite's orbit brought it over the Triangle.

Then there was the Eastern Airlines aircraft that is said to have disappeared from the radar for 10 minutes and landed at Miami, when every clock and watch aboard was found to be 10 minutes slow. The flight number and the date and time of this event are never given and there is no record of the incident with the FAA, Miami Airport or Eastern Airlines. In short, there is not a scrap of evidence that it ever happened.

Perhaps the most popular theory is that some kind of magnetic anomaly is causing the

Top: a Douglas DC-3 of the type that vanished in December 1948. Its final position could not be located, probably because the pilot was navigating without having received notification that the wind direction had changed during the flight

Above: the British freighter Cyclops, *which went missing in the North Atlantic during the Second World War. It could have been torpedoed, but Charles Berlitz maintains that records show no German submarines to have been in the area when the ship disappeared*

2 p.m. on 5 December 1945. Charles Berlitz says that the aircraft were 'on a routine training mission . . . both pilots and crews were experienced airmen'. Berlitz says that 'pilots who had flown earlier the same day reported ideal flying weather.'

At 3.45 p.m. the flight leader, Lieutenant Charles C. Taylor, radioed the control tower. 'Calling tower. This is an emergency. We seem to be off course. We cannot see land . . . repeat . . . we cannot see land.'

'What is your position?' radioed the tower.

'We're not sure of our position. We cannot be sure just where we are. We seem to be lost.'

'Assume bearing due west.'

'We don't know which way is west. Everything is wrong . . . strange. We can't be sure of just where we are. We are not sure of any direction. Even the ocean doesn't look as it should.'

Lieutenant Robert Cox, senior flight instructor at Fort Lauderdale, had been preparing to land when he overheard these messages and he thought he knew where Flight 19 was. He radioed, 'Flight 19, what is your altitude? I'll fly south and meet you.'

Taylor should have welcomed any assistance, but for a few minutes he was silent before

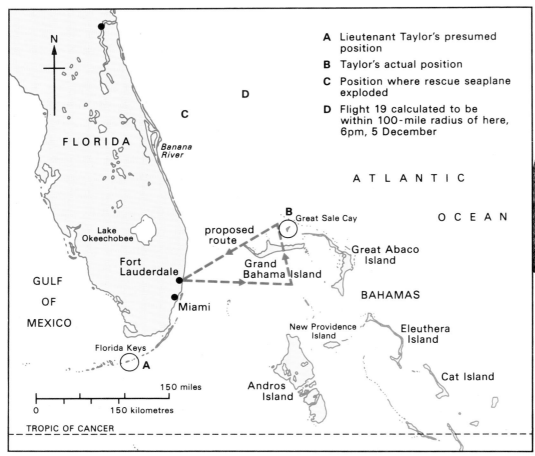

A Lieutenant Taylor's presumed position
B Taylor's actual position
C Position where rescue seaplane exploded
D Flight 19 calculated to be within 100-mile radius of here, 6pm, 5 December

Left: Lieutenant Taylor, leader of Flight 19, was familiar with the Florida Keys (A). He mistook Great Sale Cay (B), over which he was flying, for the Keys and became increasingly disorientated shortly before losing radio contact with ground control and presumably crashing

Above: Lieutenant Robert Cox, senior flight instructor at Fort Lauderdale in 1945, who received the controversial last radio message from Flight 19

Top right: Fort Lauderdale, the US Naval Air Station in Florida from where the ill-fated Flight 19 took off

Right: five US Navy bombers of the same type as Flight 19. Did it really disappear in mysterious circumstances in the Bermuda Triangle, or is there a more prosaic explanation for the tragedy?

he cried, 'Don't come after me! They look like. . . .'

Silence. The time was now 4.30 p.m. As the last message from Flight 19 was being received a huge Martin Mariner sea plane, dispatched on a rescue mission, was nearing the bombers' last estimated position. It sent one message and then followed the bombers into oblivion.

There followed one of the largest air-sea searches in history, but not a single scrap of wreckage or debris was found. There were no survivors. Investigators were baffled.

If the Bermuda Triangle version of this disappearance is correct then the case of Flight 19 must rank as the most puzzling mystery in the history of aviation. But from the official report and other reliable sources it is possible to reconstruct the events of that December day and show that the Triangle account is grossly inaccurate.

The Triangle account gives the distinct impression of cloudless skies and a group of experienced airmen flying a route they knew like the back of their hands; but although the weather was fine when the aircraft left Fort Lauderdale it rapidly deteriorated during the flight, and search craft later reported unsafe flying conditions and tremendous seas. With the exception of Lieutenant Taylor none of the crew was highly experienced. Taylor, a combat veteran with 2509 flying hours, had recently moved to Fort Lauderdale from Miami,

was unfamiliar with the area, and had never before flown the route taken by Flight 19. The flight was 'routine' only in the sense that it was an established training exercise at Fort Lauderdale. It was, in fact, an extremely complicated navigation exercise, undertaken by a largely inexperienced crew.

The first message from the aircraft was not received by the Fort Lauderdale tower but by Lieutenant Cox, who overheard an inter-aircraft communication in which somebody asked Captain Edward Powers what his compass read. 'I don't know where we are,' replied Powers. 'We must have got lost after that last turn.'

Lieutenant Cox radioed, 'What is your trouble?'

Taylor replied, 'Both my compasses are out. I'm trying to find Fort Lauderdale. I'm over land but it's broken. I'm sure I'm in the Keys, but I don't know how far down. . . .'

These initial communications provide the clue to Flight 19's ultimate fate. Lieutenant Taylor and, apparently, Captain Powers, the next most experienced man among the crew, believed that Flight 19 had taken a wrong turn and flown off course. The aircraft were over Great Sale Cay in the Bahamas, but Lieutenant Taylor, who had never flown over the area, was confused by the similarity between Great Sale Cay and the Florida Keys, with which he was very familiar. Taylor could not decide

whether he was over the Atlantic Ocean or the Gulf of Mexico.

Lieutenant Cox gave Taylor instructions for reaching Fort Lauderdale from the Keys and added, 'What is your altitude? I'll fly south and meet you.'

This is a statement that Triangle writers make much of, but the official report says that Taylor replied, 'I know where I am now. I'm at 2300 feet [700 metres]. Don't come after me.' There is no mention of anything looking remotely unusual.

Taylor did not know where he was, however, and he became increasingly disorientated. Many factors contributed to his disorientation: his compasses were not working, or he believed they weren't; he didn't have a clock or watch; his radio channel was subject to interference from Cuban radio stations, but the fear of losing contact with the flight deterred him from changing frequencies to the undisturbed emergency channel.

In the gathering dusk he led the aircraft first in one direction, then in another, and as dusk was replaced by black darkness the weather and the sea grew rough. At 6.30 p.m. Lieutenant Taylor, valiantly trying to keep his flight together, was heard to announce: 'All planes close up tight . . . we will have to ditch unless landfall . . . when the first plane drops to 10 gallons [45 litres] we all go down together.'

The last words heard from any of the aircraft were at 7.04 p.m. when one of the pilots was heard trying to contact Lieutenant Taylor. It is assumed that some time during the next hour the five bombers descended through the night to the turbulent sea below. Experts later testified that a TBM would sink in less than a minute.

An air search was launched almost immediately but was little more than a token gesture because the chances of spotting wreckage at night and in bad weather were slim. By daylight the sea would have dispersed wreckage beyond recognition.

The Triangle version of Flight 19 presents a set of wholly spurious radio messages and has the aircraft vanishing some two and a half hours earlier than was probably the case. As for the rescue aircraft that followed the bombers into oblivion it must be considered a separate incident.

Some books have the Martin Mariner sea plane vanishing some three hours before it had even taken off. In fact, the aircraft left the Banana River naval airfield (now Patrick Air Force Base) at 7.30 p.m., sent a routine departure message and is believed to have exploded in mid-air a short time later. Charles Berlitz refers to this explanation in his book *Without a trace*: 'The vanishing Martin Mariner,' he says, 'is conveniently explained by the fact that a flare in the night sky was observed by the crew of the *Gaines Mills*, a passing freighter.' What Berlitz considers to be a flare in the night sky was described somewhat differently by the captain of the *Gaines Mills* who reported seeing an aircraft catch fire, plummet into the sea and explode.

Nobody knows for sure what caused the explosion, but Mariners were labelled 'flying gas tanks' and they carried a large quantity of high-octane fuel. The fumes that gathered inside could have been ignited by a tiny spark.

The case of Flight 19 is typical of the entire Bermuda Triangle myth. Facts have been distorted, there are gross errors and distorted details. It is a manufactured mystery that has developed over 40 years as one writer has taken his information from another, elaborating bits here and there, doing little original research, and perpetuating errors – each believing that his information has already been verified by somebody else. Unscrupulous writers too have been known wilfully to ignore inconvenient facts; in *The Bermuda Triangle*, during his discussion of the disappearances of the *Star Tiger*, Berlitz says that the last message sent by the aircraft was 'Weather and performance excellent. Expect to arrive on schedule.' No such message was ever sent at any time during the flight. The facts were fully presented in the accident investigation report (published as a government White Paper) and in press reports of the public enquiry into the matter. *Great mysteries of the air* by Ralph Barker, a book Berlitz listed in his bibliography, contains a chapter about the *Star Tiger* from which it is clear that the weather was bad when the plane went missing. Lawrence David Kusche's *The Bermuda Triangle mystery – solved* gives the facts again, but although Berlitz presumably read it (because he criticised its author) he repeated the 'Weather and performance excellent' story in his later book *Without a trace*.

There is probably a great deal still to be learned about our world, and study of unexplained phenomena may one day lead to new and exciting discoveries. But extraordinary and alarming claims for unknown forces causing the loss of ships and aircraft *must* be backed by hard, incontrovertible facts. This is not the case with the Bermuda Triangle.

Below: a Martin Mariner sea plane of the type that set off to try to locate Flight 19 – and also vanished. It left the Banana River Naval Air Station (now Patrick Air Force Base) at 7.30 p.m. and is believed to have exploded in mid-air a short time afterwards. The captain of the freighter Gaines Mills *reported seeing an aircraft burst into flames and explode, and the commander of the* USS Solomons *confirmed that the Mariner disappeared from its radar screen at about the same time as the* Gaines Mills *saw the explosion. Yet strangely, Triangle writers persist in describing the Mariner's fate of a 'mysterious disappearance'*

CHAPTER SEVEN

UFOs
Fact or Figment?

The UFO paradox, Classifications, UFO tracking, Hoaxes, Identification, Crashed UFOs, Alien encounters, Abductions, UFO injuries, Vehicle interference, UFO cover-ups

In search of UFOs

'They flew like a saucer would if you skipped it across the water.' This is how, on 24 June 1947, American airman Kenneth Arnold, an experienced pilot, described some unusual flying craft he had seen over the mountains of America's west coast. Newspapermen applied his phrase to the craft themselves, and the misleading label 'flying saucer' has followed the UFO ever since, like a tin can tied to a cat's tail.

This fanciful name has deepened the reluctance of professional scientists to take the UFO seriously. Only a few have taken the trouble to investigate this bizarre phenomenon, which surely qualifies as the strangest of our time. Even that phrase, 'of our time', is a subject of controversy: many people claim that the UFO has been with mankind throughout history. But the evidence they offer is meagre and their case far from proven.

Whether or not UFOs existed in the past, there is no doubt that UFO sightings have proliferated in astonishing numbers over the past 30 years. This fact seems to be in some way linked with Man's first steps towards exploring space, and this connection is undoubtedly an important clue in trying to explain the UFO.

Estimates of the total number of UFO sightings vary so widely as to be meaningless; more helpful figures are provided by the catalogues of reported sightings prepared by individual investigative organisations. Recently a French team catalogued more than 600 encounter cases in France alone, each vouched for by responsible investigators; how many more were not reported or investigated? In the early 1970s UFO investigators made lists of all reported landing cases for particular countries: 923 were recorded in the United States, 200 in Spain.

Are UFOs real in the sense that, say, spacecraft are real? The surest proof would be actually to get hold of one, and there are persistent

Below: Kenneth Arnold's book, published in 1952, was the first full study of UFOs. Arnold began collecting accounts of UFO sightings after he saw several 'discs' in the sky in June 1947

rumours that certain governments, notably that of the United States, have indeed obtained a UFO, which is kept in total secrecy. However this remains in doubt, despite the sworn affidavits of alleged witnesses. Indeed, the whole matter of governmental involvement – or the lack of it – is a further and fascinating aspect of the UFO controversy.

In the absence of a real UFO that we can touch and examine, there is a great deal of evidence of the phenomenon in the form of a mass of photographs and a handful of movies. The majority are undoubtedly fakes. Those with good credentials are so blurred, so distant or so ambiguous that they simply add a further dimension to the problem: why, if UFOs exist, and in an age when many people carry cameras with them most of the time, have we not obtained better photographic evidence?

Perhaps the strongest evidence we have is from the effects caused by UFOs on surrounding objects, particularly machinery. In November 1967 a truck and a car approaching each other on a Hampshire road in the early

Right, below left and bottom: these three photographs typify the popular idea of UFOS. Ever since the first 'flying saucer' sighting in 1947, there has been a mass of pictures like these. All three, however, are hoaxes. Computer tests have shown those taken in New Mexico (left and right) to be crude fakes, but the one below was created by a sophisticated technique of superimposition

hours of the morning simultaneously suffered engine failure when a large egg-shaped object crossed the road between them. The police, and subsequently the Ministry of Defence, investigated the incident, but no official explanation was ever issued. Such a case may leave investigators puzzled, but it makes one thing certain: if they can cause physical effects, UFOS must be physically real.

If they are physical objects, UFOS must originate from somewhere. When the first UFOS of the current era were seen, back in the 1940s, it was assumed they came from somewhere on Earth. The Americans suspected they were a Russian secret device, perhaps developed using the expertise of German scientists captured at the end of the Second World War.

But as more reports came in it became clear that no nation on Earth could be responsible. Nor was there sufficient evidence to support other ingenious theories – that they came from the Himalayas, long a favoured source of secret wisdom, or Antarctica, where unexplored tracts of land and climatic anomalies provide a shaky foundation for speculation. Instead, ufologists began to look beyond the Earth, encouraged by the fact that our own space exploration programme was just beginning. We were starting to take an active interest in worlds beyond, and it seemed reasonable that other civilisations might have a similar interest in us. The fact that no solid evidence has been found for the extra-terrestrial hypothesis is discouraging. Although it is the best available explanation, it remains no more than speculation.

Today it is recognised that the UFO poses a problem not only for the astronomer and the engineer, but also for the behavioural scientist. The psychologist confirms that an individual's response to a sighting is conditioned by his psychological make-up, while the sociologist places such responses in a wider social context and relates them to cultural patterns. The anthropologist detects parallels with myth and traditional belief, while the parapsychologist notes how frequently sightings are accompanied by such psychic manifestations as precognition and poltergeist phenomena.

This is particularly true of 'encounter' cases in which the observer claims to have had actual meetings with UFO occupants. The entities are generally described as extra-terrestrial aliens, often ambassadors from an inter-galactic power; their purpose is to examine human beings, to warn us of misuse of resources and to bring reassuring messages from some cosmic brotherhood. With only one or two such cases on record they could be dismissed as fantasy, but there are hundreds on file.

If a single one of these cases could be shown to be based on fact, the UFO problem would be established on solid foundations and serious scientific interest assured. But in every instance it remains an open question whether the incident actually occurred or is simply a fabrication – deliberate, unconscious, or perhaps induced by some external force. Hypotheses range from brainwashing by extra-terrestrial invaders, to deliberate invention by the CIA.

Almost certainly, UFOs exist on both the physical and the psychological level. Somehow we have got to recognise that, although they are real, they are not what they seem. This is the paradox that lies at the heart of the UFO mystery and that frequently emerges in UFO case histories.

A serious study of UFOs needs to classify the extensive variation of incidents that come under that umbrella heading. In 1971, Dr J. Allen Hynek, while acting as astronomical consultant to Project Blue Book (the US Air Force investigation into UFOs), developed a classification system of UFO 'types' that has since become standard.

He divided UFO reports according to the distance, greater or less than 500 feet (150 metres), at which the UFO was observed, and subdivided each of these two sections into three, giving six categories altogether.

The commonest sightings are of the 'distant' type:

Nocturnal lights Strange lights seen at a distance in the night sky, often with unusual features such as variations in the intensity of light or colour and sudden, remarkable changes of speed and direction of movement.
Daylight discs Distant objects seen against the sky during the daytime. The shapes vary considerably: cigars, spheres, eggs, ovals and pinpoints as well as discs are often reported.
Radar-visuals Distant UFOs recorded simultaneously on radar and visually with good

Above: the nocturnal lights of a UFO? On 5 March 1979 Antonio Llopis, 26, was taking photographs of the island of Gran Canaria, Canary Islands, when suddenly he noticed a strange, swirling light in the sky over the sea. Then, a huge, dark object hurtled out of the sea straight up into the sky, surmounting a ball of fire (left). After the object had disappeared a bright trail and a golden cloud illuminated the sky for half an hour (right). Thousands of people reported the incident

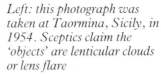

Left: this photograph was taken at Taormina, Sicily, in 1954. Sceptics claim the 'objects' are lenticular clouds or lens flare

agreement between the two reports. Dr Hynek excluded 'sightings' made solely by radar since false traces can result from a number of natural factors such as ground scatter – the signal is reflected from high ground – temperature inversions and even thick banks of cloud or flocks of birds. Radar-visual sightings are the most important category of UFO reports as they give independent instrumental evidence of the sighting; unfortunately, they are very rare.

Reports of UFOs seen at close range are the most interesting and often spectacular; these are the famous 'close encounters' of the first, second and third kinds.
Close encounters of the first kind are simple observations of phenomena where there is no physical interaction between the phenomena and the environment.

One instance was the UFO seen by Captain James Howard and the crew and passengers of BOAC airliner *Centaurus* on 29 June 1954.

The aircraft, which had left New York bound for New Foundland, was making its way steadily northeastwards when the radio crackled an order from ground control to 'hold' – a manoeuvre adopted when there is a hazard ahead. After half an hour's circling the skipper advised control that if he couldn't proceed he would have to return to New York as his fuel was low. After some delay permission was given to proceed and *Centaurus* went on automatic pilot at 19,000 feet (6000 metres), just below a broken layer of cloud and with a solid mass of cloud beneath it at 200 feet (60 metres). After some 20 minutes a glint of light suddenly caught Captain Howard's eye. On the port side of the aircraft he saw a large object of metallic appearance emerge from a gap in the clouds. Moving around this main shape were six much smaller objects, not unlike a screen of small destroyers escorting an enormous aircraft carrier.

A bizarre aspect of this remarkable apparition was that it seemed to be changing shape all the time. Captain Howard sketched on his knee pad the different forms he saw: they were a 'delta wing', a telephone handset, a pear. He has since said that, with its continual changes in shape, the object reminded him of a swarm of bees in flight. It was an estimated 4 miles (6 kilometres) from *Centaurus* and it maintained that position.

When Captain Howard turned to speak to his first officer, Lee Boyd, he found him already out of his seat, standing to watch the display. Captain Howard called up control:

'We are not alone.'

'We know.'

'What is it?'

'We don't know, but we've scrambled a Sabre from Goose Bay to investigate.'

A few minutes later the captain was in touch with the pilot of the Sabre jet fighter who, once he was in range, announced he had two images on his radar scope – one for *Centaurus* and the other, presumably, for the UFO. Then the unexpected happened: the six small objects manoeuvred into single file, bore down on the main object and appeared to merge into one end of it. Thereafter the size of the large UFO began to diminish until the Sabre's pilot announced he was overhead, at which point the object finally disappeared from the radar scope '. . . like a TV picture going off'.

Since about 1953, airline pilots have been required not to disclose to the public information about UFO sightings. In the case of *Centaurus*, however, many of the passengers had watched the display with amazement and the incident received wide press coverage. Researchers were fortunate in this, for this sighting falls into the important category of radar-visual cases. In this instance two separate radar sets were involved (at control and in the Sabre), plus visual observation by experienced pilots, air crew and some 30 or more passengers.

Close encounters of the second kind are similar to the first kind except that physical effects on both animate and inanimate matter are observed. Vegetation may be scorched or flattened, tree branches broken, animals frightened or car headlights, engines and radios doused. In cases of electrical failure the equipment usually begins to work normally again once the UFO has disappeared, as in the case of Mr Ronald Wildman, a delivery driver for the Vauxhall Motor Company. He left his home in Luton, Bedfordshire, at 3.00 a.m. on 9 February 1962 to drive a new estate car from the factory to Swansea. He had passed Dunstable, and was on the Ivinghoe road approaching a set of crossroads at Tringford, when he saw an oval-shaped object ahead of him on the road. It was white with black markings at regular intervals around the perimeter. It appeared to be 20 to 30 feet (6 to 10 metres) above the road, and was at least 40 feet (12 metres) wide.

Mr Wildman drove straight towards the object, but when he was 20 yards (18 metres) from it the power of the car's engine began to fade until he was going at just 20 mph (30 km/h). Putting his foot flat down on the accelerator did not help; neither did changing down through the gears. Mr Wildman noticed, however, that his headlights stayed on. For some 200 yards (180 metres) as he drove down the road, the UFO stayed about 20 feet (6 metres) ahead of, and above, him.

Suddenly a white haze appeared around the perimeter of the object – it was 'like a halo round the moon', said Mr Wildman – and it veered off to the right at high speed. As it went, it brushed particles of frost from the trees onto the windscreen of the Vauxhall.

In an interview, Mr Wildman recalled that his headlights were reflected from the object when it was closest to the road, and in his opinion this showed it was solid.

Below: radar blips are formed by the direct reflection of radar waves from objects. Although radar sightings of UFOS are useful, they can often be unreliable, since flocks of birds and freak weather can sometimes produce misleading images

Bottom: astronomer Dr J. Allen Hynek, Director of the Center for UFO Studies in the USA. He has spent years scientifically studying UFOS

After the UFO had disappeared, the car's engine returned to normal working and the witness, by now panic-stricken, drove as hard as he could to Aylesbury where he reported the affair to the police. They noted the distraught condition of the driver.

The credibility of sightings with only one witness rests on the trustworthiness of the person concerned. Mr Wildman's report was checked by three investigators from *Flying Saucer Review*, who were extremely impressed by Mr Wildman's obvious sincerity. They were convinced his sighting had been genuine, not a hallucination.

Interference with electrical equipment, it has been suggested, may result from electro-magnetic fields created by UFOS along their surfaces in order to minimise the effects of air resistance. Whatever the cause, this phenomenon is a disturbing aspect of such encounters.

Even more frightening are *close encounters of the third kind*, in which 'occupants' are reported in and around the UFO or in contact with a human being. Patrolman Lonnie Zamora of the police department in Socorro, New Mexico, experienced such an encounter in April 1964.

He was alone in his car, at about 5.50 p.m., giving chase to a speeding motorist who was heading out of town when suddenly he heard a roar. At the same time he saw a 'flame' in the sky, bluish and orange and strangely static as it descended some distance away. Fearful that a nearby dynamite shack might blow up, the

Above: Patrolman Lonnie Zamora whose close encounter is one of the best authenticated cases on record

Left: one of the four impressions left by the UFO that landed at Socorro, New Mexico. Later, an engineer estimated that a pressure of one ton would have been needed to make the holes

Below: an artist's impression of the UFO and aliens seen by Zamora

Below left: a visual diary of events at Socorro

patrolman gave up chasing the motorist and headed off over rough ground towards the point where the flame had come down.

After three attempts he forced his car to the top of a ridge and drove slowly westwards. He stopped when, suddenly, he saw a shiny, aluminium-like object below him, about 150–200 yards (140–185 metres) south. Zamora

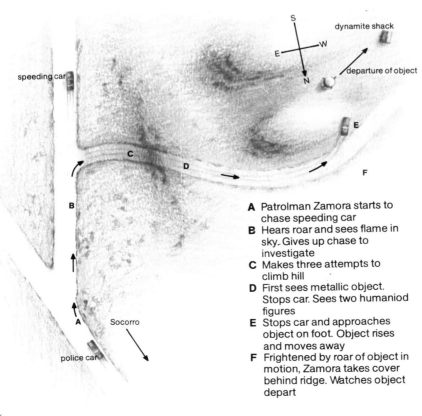

A Patrolman Zamora starts to chase speeding car
B Hears roar and sees flame in sky. Gives up chase to investigate
C Makes three attempts to climb hill
D First sees metallic object. Stops car. Sees two humaniod figures
E Stops car and approaches object on foot. Object rises and moves away
F Frightened by roar of object in motion, Zamora takes cover behind ridge. Watches object depart

said it looked like a car on end, perhaps 'turned over by some kids'. Then he saw two humanoid figures in white 'coveralls' close to the object. He estimated later that they were about 4 feet (1.2 metres) tall. One of them looked straight at him and seemed to jump. Zamora was wearing clip-on sunglasses over his prescription spectacles and couldn't distinguish any features or headgear at that distance.

The patrolman now accelerated thinking that, whoever the strangers were, they might be in need of help. The shape he'd seen was a sort of vertical oval, and looking down he could see it was supported on girder-like legs.

Bottom: two of the best authenticated UFO pictures, taken by Mr and Mrs Trent when an object appeared over their farm near McMinnville, Oregan, USA, on 11 May 1950. Ufologists found their story credible and investigated the case in detail. Computer analysis of the photographs showed the UFO was not a model, but a large object in the distance. (For further analysis [below] see page 178)

When the terrain became too rough for the car to go any further he radioed his headquarters to say that he was near the scene of a possible accident and would proceed on foot.

As Zamora left the car he heard two or three loud thumps, like someone hammering or slamming a door. These thumps were a second or two apart. When he was about 50 paces from the object there was a loud roar, which rose gradually in pitch. The humanoid figures were nowhere to be seen. At the same time he could see a blue and orange flame rise from the ground leaving a cloud of dust. Zamora beat a hasty retreat towards his car and as he reached it turned to see the oval shape, now horizontal, rising towards the level of the car. Frightened by the continuing roar, he ran on and dived for shelter over the edge of the ridge. When he realised the noise had ceased he raised his head from his hands and saw the UFO still in the air and moving away from him about 15 feet (4.5 metres) above the ground. It safely cleared the dynamite shack and continued to rise gradually, watched by the policeman, who was retracing his steps to the car. As he called up the radio officer he watched it accelerate away to clear a mountain range and disappear.

Zamora was then joined by a colleague, Sergeant Chavez, and together they noticed a bush that was still burning where the UFO had stood. When they descended to the site they found four separate burn marks and four depressions – all of similar shape – made, they assumed, by the legs of the landing gear. On three of the marks the dense soil had been pushed down about 2 inches (5 centimetres) and dirt had been squeezed up at the sides. The fourth pad mark, less well defined, was only 1 inch (2.5 centimetres) deep. When engineer W. T. Powers investigated the case he estimated that the force that produced the marks was 'equivalent to a gentle settling of at least a ton on each mark.' Four small round marks were found on the side farthest from where Patrolman Zamora had stood.

The Socorro incident was reported throughout the world's press, but despite an extensive investigation it remained a mystery. Dr Hynek was one of the baffled inquirers: 'Maybe there is a simple, natural explanation . . . but having made a complete study of the events, I do not think so.'

Traditionally, established science has tended to view the UFO phenomenon with scepticism. In his book *The UFO experience*

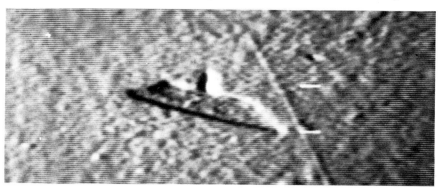

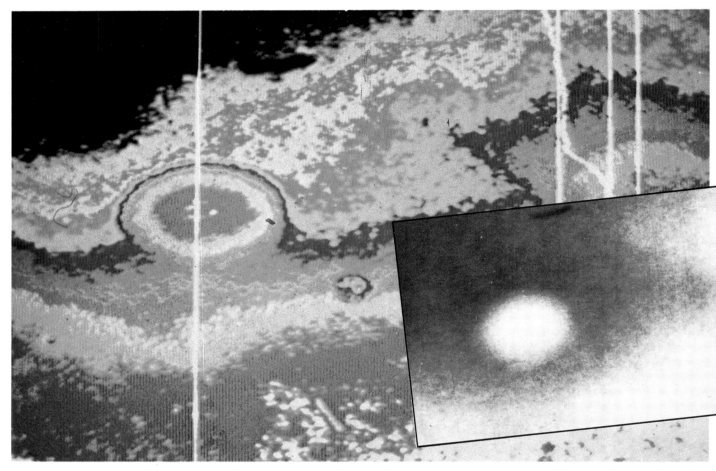

(1972) Dr Hynek, now Director of the Center for UFO Studies, tells of an event at an evening reception held in 1968 in Victoria, British Columbia, at which a number of astronomers were present. During the evening it was announced that strange lights – possibly UFOS – had been spotted outside. Dr Hynek continues: 'The news was met by casual banter and the giggling sound that often accompanies an embarrassing situation.' And, he reports, not a single astronomer went outside to look.

Even Project Blue Book – the US government's extensive investigation into UFOS –

attempted to explain away every reported sighting in terms of conventional science. It soon began to earn itself a bad name because many of its explanations were impossible to believe. In 1966 the US Air Force set up a two-year research project – to investigate, in effect, its own investigations!

The Condon Report, as it was unofficially known, was published in 1969 and stated, broadly, that since nothing valuable to science had come out of the study of UFOS, further research was not justified. After this the US Air Force relinquished responsibility for the

Top: a swirl of vivid hues is a 'computer-eye view' of a glowing disc seen over Colorado, USA (inset). The colours represent different brightness levels in the original image and clearly portray detailed structure in the UFO and surrounding sky. The lines on the coloured image are 'drawn' by the computer as it makes measurements on the picture

Left: colour-coding emphasises the form, density and focus of the Trent UFO, seen from the side. The wingless disc, with its curious off-centre tower, is unlike any known man-made craft. The computer tests also show that there are no tell-tale strings that might have been used to fake the photograph

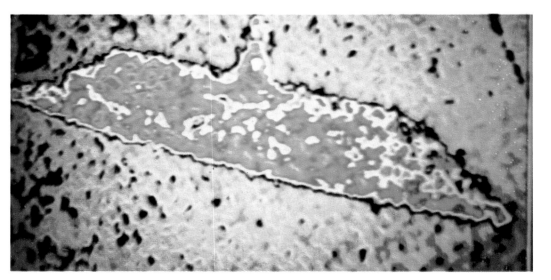

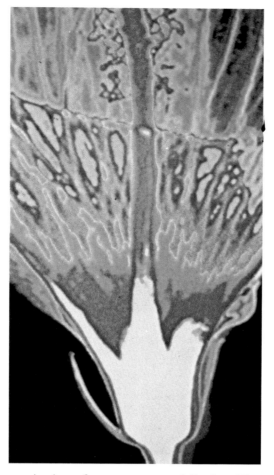

monitoring of UFO reports and Project Blue Book was disbanded in December 1969. Since 1969 research has been largely left to private organisations, such as Ground Saucer Watch and Project Starlight International in the USA, and UFOIN (UFO Investigators' Network) and BUFORA (British UFO Research Association) in Britain.

These organisations have attempted to establish the credibility of UFOs and the validity of investigating them. They approach the study of the phenomenon as scientifically as possible, trying to consider the evidence of each sighting in an objective manner.

For instance, Ground Saucer Watch, founded in Cleveland, Ohio, in 1957, brings a high level of technical expertise to the study of UFO reports. The group wanted, in the words of a statement made then, to 'see positive scientific action taken to end the elements of foul-up and cover-up in UFO research'. A network of 500 scientific and engineering consultants assists it in this task.

But most UFO research is done by amateur ufologists who have to finance their own work. It is, therefore, usually irregular and on a small scale compared with more conventional scientific study. Because of the elusiveness of UFOs, most research has to deal with second-hand evidence – investigating what people say they have seen or experienced. This gives sceptics an easy excuse to disregard all ufologists'

conclusions. What every ufologist hankers for is more direct contact with the subject of his research – something to dissect, measure or analyse. But the phenomenon always seems reluctant to oblige. So the ufologist has to lower his sights and seek confirmation of human testimony through the use of monitoring instruments – such as radar – or photographs that contain easily recognisable points of reference and other useful data.

In fact, photo analysis has recently developed into a fine science, making it now virtually impossible for anyone to contrive a fake UFO photograph. Ufologists have gained this new confidence thanks to the increasing use of computers for photo analysis.

Traditionally, UFO photo analysts have been limited to a few techniques of study. By measuring shadows they may be able to show that the picture consists of a landscape shot combined with a picture of a model taken under totally different lighting conditions. By studying the focus on the UFO they may be able to show that it is much closer to the camera than the witness claimed, and is therefore much smaller than it appears. By enlarging details they may be able to reveal the presence of a tell-tale 'Frisbee' trade mark. More frequently they can identify the shot as showing some natural object.

But all too often the label 'unidentified' has remained on the photograph because of a lack of detailed information from which to draw satisfactory conclusions. Now, at the the touch of a computer button, the photo-technician can instantly enlarge selected detail, measure distances and angles, enhance the edges of objects and, by using a colour code, can reveal the density and contours of a UFO or identify the suspicious uniform lines of a lens cap or hub cap.

Of course, ideally, ufologists would themselves like to be first-hand witnesses of UFO sightings. Not every ufologist is a reliable witness, but most will almost certainly be in a better position to judge what they see than the average man or woman in the street. In the early, optimistic days of ufology, simple sky-watching was a favourite occupation, even among the most academic ufologists. During the past 30 years it has been observed that UFO reports occur in distinct waves, often called 'flaps'. The flaps of 1954 and 1965 involved vast numbers of sightings. In fact, in the 1950s there seemed to be so many UFOs about for it to make sense for those interested in the phenomenon to gather at a favourable location with cameras and any other monitoring equipment that could be mustered – and hope for the best.

In Britain one particular location has become associated with skywatching: the hills above Warminster in Wiltshire. Over the years, thousands of casual observers have spent nights on Cradle Hill. The results, however, have been ambiguous, to say the least. If

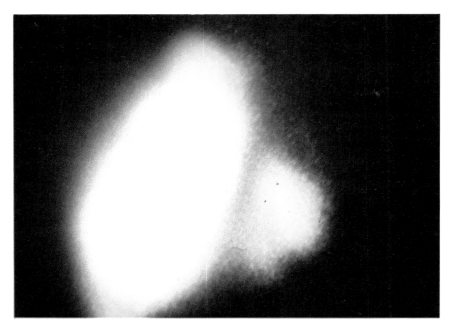

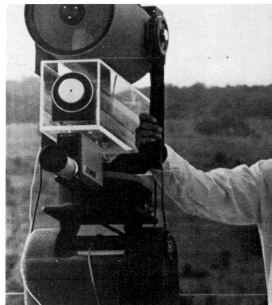

there were ever any genuine phenomena, they rapidly became overshadowed by too many reports of malobserved helicopters, car headlights, even other observers' torches or cigarette lighters – to say nothing of hoaxes.

But probably the most ambitious plan to gather some concrete, first-hand evidence of unidentified flying objects was Project Starlight International, set up by Ray Stanford in a rural area near Austin, Texas, USA.

Starting in 1973 he and his team, who comprised a research facility of the Association for the Understanding of Man, gathered an impressive array of monitoring and communications equipment. This included a radar unit, perched on a tower from which it could scan the entire valley below, and a set of recording magnetometers that monitor and automatically record a wide range of irregular events, including electrostatic effects, temperature changes, gravitational disturbances, barometric alterations, and even unusual sounds. There were also two devices for communicating with UFOs: one, the UFO Vector, employs a red laser beam that can direct a signal containing up to 2½ million units of information per second, in the form of voice or video signals, to any UFO in line of sight, and automatically records any response; the other is an array of 91 spotlights, arranged in a circle on the ground around a central light, that can be manipulated to form thousands of patterned signals. These are intended to communicate with UFOs in mathematical or other codes.

Then there is ARGUS, an acronym for 'automatic ring-up on geolocated UFO sightings', which means that when the monitors indicate that a UFO is in the area, they also alert the human observers, who then photograph the object. As the UFO moves out of the area, the monitors plot its course, alerting different observers on the ground. All the photographs are then computer-analysed to try to establish the UFO's distance, size and altitude.

Operation Starlight is a UFO observer's dream: equipment estimated as costing something like half a million dollars is clearly out of reach of most UFO organisations. But even so, what chance is there that UFOs will manifest in precisely the right place to be detected even by all this sophisticated instrumentation? Yet the project claims several impressive sightings.

For instance, on 10 December 1975 an orange-golden object was sighted, and some 42 photographs taken, before it moved away. Some of the objects monitored have been shown to be natural in origin, but even negative results are a vital part of the operation. 'This project is unique anywhere in the world,' claims Ray Stanford. 'We are trying to gain evidence so that the scientific community will take this thing [ufology] seriously.'

A totally different approach to skywatching has been adopted by Spanish ufologist Luis José Grifol of Barcelona. Since the mid 1970s Grifol has been visiting the local mountain district of Montserrat, which he believes to be particularly favoured by UFOs because of its long cultural and religious tradition. But whatever the reasons for this, between 1977 and the end of 1982 Grifol had secured some 500 photographs of anomalous aerial phenomena.

Instead of relying on sophisticated instruments, Grifol believes that UFOs communicate telepathically with him. The crew members of the UFOs he has photographed are, he claims, 'space intelligences' who come from a planet located between the stars Bellatrix and Rigel, near Mintaka in the constellation of Orion. In August 1980, in the presence of 17 witnesses, Grifol asked his alien contacts for proof of their relationship, suggesting that they move their UFOs in response to his directions. They did so, he claims, over a period of 20 seconds.

Above: Spanish ufologist Luis José Grifol on site in Montserrat. He eschews the use of sophisticated equipment and claims he has telepathic links with UFOs. Using this to track them, he has obtained hundreds of UFO pictures like this one of a coloured blob (above left) seen over Montserrat

Top: American Ray Stanford, director of Project Starlight International, with his latest gadget which he says will enable him to communicate with UFOs. The device is designed to transmit images to the spacecraft by laser beam and is just one of many specially designed, highly expensive machines he uses

Above: Arne Thomassen, one of the people involved with investigations in Hessdalen, Norway, sets up equipment preparatory to a long wait: UFOS do not always arrive on cue. One of Thomassen's colleagues on the UFO-Norge project thinks it fair to assume that 'they' are watching us watching them; perhaps this accounts for their shyness. But the long periods of waiting pay off when images like this (above right) are captured on film. Taken by Thomassen in September 1982, the photograph shows an unidentified object suspended in the skies over Hessdalen – shortly afterwards the craft disappeared from sight

But Warminster and the hills of Spain are not the only areas noted for their UFOS. Inland from Trondheim in the central region of Norway is the thinly populated district of Hessdalen. There is no obvious reason why it should be specially favoured by UFOS: yet since December 1981 there has been a continuous flow of reports from the area. This kind of concentration of 'visits' is rare enough in any case; that they were sustained over so long a period gave Norway's ufologists a unique opportunity for observation. However, it is difficult to see just why the UFOS chose Hessdalen, as Arne Thomassen comments:

Why they [UFOS] show such seemingly great interest in the unpopulated mountain valleys in central Norway is difficult to figure out. There is very little in this area to spy on, and our military capability is unlikely to be of any particular interest to such doubtless highly advanced entities. The possibility that they are visiting some selected people or programming their minds seems unlikely since Hessdalen is very thinly populated. The UFOS mostly move through valleys where no people live at all.

This eyewitness account is typical of the reports received by UFO-Norge. Bjarne Lillevold, a miner, describes what he saw on 24 September 1982:

As I was on my way home from work, I and a colleague saw a light against the mountains near Hessdalen. We drove about 5 kilometres [3 miles], and then the object began to descend towards the forest, near Ålen. When we ourselves reached Ålen, the object was hovering close to the trees. My companion, who hadn't seen the celebrated UFO of Hessdalen before, was very excited by the sight. We drove to the centre of Ålen, and then saw a second object which came from the direction of Hessdalen and halted below the other.

The objects then disappeared over a mountain.

The Norwegian investigators did manage to gather a great many photographs of UFO phenomena taken by seven different photographers. Most show vaguely shaped blobs of light of various colours. But the Norwegians hope they will at least secure sufficient evidence to convince others, who have more means at their disposal, that UFOS are worth studying.

Despite the commitment of such ufologists, their achievements are frequently undermined by countless UFO hoaxers. These tricksters exploit the elusive nature of UFOS to make money from books and newspapers, to gain publicity or simply for the purpose of a practical joke. One mysterious case was the bizarre Cergy-Pontoise affair, which swept the world's headlines in 1979.

Three Frenchmen – Jean Pierre Prévost, aged 26, Salomon N'Diaye, 25, and Franck

Fontaine, 18, who all scraped a living selling jeans in street markets – claimed that, as they were loading their car to drive to a market before dawn one November morning, they were confronted by a UFO outside the flats where Prévost and N'Diaye lived in the Paris suburb of Cergy-Pontoise.

They described the UFO as being cylindrical in shape, but otherwise unidentifiable. When it moved behind the block of flats, N'Diaye rushed upstairs to fetch a camera, thinking he might take a photograph of the object to sell to the newspapers. Prévost went in to get another load of clothing while Fontaine, hoping for another view of the mysterious object, drove up onto the main road near the flats.

Hearing the sound of the moving vehicle, his companions looked out of the windows of their respective flats. Both saw that Fontaine had stopped the car on the main road and noted that the engine was no longer running. Prévost rushed downstairs and called to N'Diaye to forget about his camera because the UFO had vanished. N'Diaye came after him saying that in any case he had no film in his camera, and adding that from his window it had looked as though the car was surrounded by a great ball of light.

Outdoors again, the two young men stopped in amazement: the rear of their car was enveloped in a sharply defined sphere of glowing mist, near which a number of smaller balls of light were moving about. While they stood watching, they saw the larger globe absorb all but but one of the smaller ones. Then a beam of light emerged, which grew in size until it

was like the cylindrical shape they had seen earlier. The large sphere seemed to enter this cylinder, which shot up into the sky and disappeared from sight.

The two hurried to the car, but found no sign of Fontaine. He was not in the car, in the road, or in the cabbage field beside the road. Prévost insisted on calling the police immediately and N'Diaye went off to do so. Prévost, remaining near the car, was the only witness to the last phase of the incident: a ball of light, like those previously moving about the car, seemed to push the car door shut. Then it too vanished.

Above: Franck Fontaine (top), who said that his 'missing' week was a blank in his mind. Salmon N'Diaye (centre) and Jean-Pierre Prévost (bottom) reported the UFO incident to the police

CONTACTS
OVNI
CERGY-PONTOISE

j.guieu
f.fontaine / j.p. prévost / s. n'diaye

1820 T 92

les carrefours de l'étrange
EDITIONS DU ROCHER

Above: Alex Birch was a 14-year-old schoolboy in 1962 when he produced this photograph (right) of five saucer-like objects flying over Sheffield, England. He was interviewed on television and by the Air Ministry. It was only 10 years later that he confessed to painting the shapes onto the window and photographing them

Left: police search a field in Cergy-Pontoise, France, for clues to Fontaine's disappearance, after it was reported he had been abducted by a UFO. In the background is the block of flats in which his friends Prévost and N'Diaye lived.
Inset: Jimmy Guieu's best-selling book Cergy-Pontoise UFO contacts

Such was the account that the two young men gave at the police station a few minutes later. They had driven to the police despite the fact that their car was uninsured, unlicensed and none of them had a driving licence. Because UFO sightings are a military matter in France, the police instructed Prévost and N'Diaye to inform the gendarmerie, which comes under the Ministry of National Defence. The two spent most of the day with the gendarmes, telling and retelling the story. The interrogators stopped for lunch, during which time the witnesses telephoned the press with their story. Later, Commandant Courcoux of the Cergy gendarmerie told the press that there were no grounds for disbelieving the young men's story, that he had no doubt 'something' had occurred, and that he could give no indication of what that 'something' might be.

The world's press had a field-day speculating about the abducted Frenchman's whereabouts; then, seven days later, Fontaine turned up, in a cabbage field next to the flats where his friends lived. Bemused, he didn't believe he had been missing for a week; he had thought it was still the morning of the UFO incident.

Ufologists and the press descended on the tight-lipped Fontaine, but the story of what happened during his abduction was kept exclusive to a well-known science-fiction writer and author of two UFO books, Jimmy Guieu. He swept them off to a secret refuge and within four months his book about the affair was in print, destined to be a best-seller. But the book – and others that followed it – shed no light on the mystery, and Fontaine's account was short on fact and long on fantasy. He claimed not to know exactly what had happened during his abduction; he could recall details only through his dreams.

In one instance that he recalled, he was in a large white room with machines that went all round the walls. They were all the same height and had opaque white glass fronts that lit up and went out almost simultaneously. He was lying on a sort of couch and two small luminous spheres were talking to him about problems on Earth and how to solve them.

Once the air had cleared after the affair, more serious ufologist groups, such as the reputable organisation Control, released critical reports about the case that uncovered a catalogue of inconsistencies. For instance, Prévost had insisted that before the encounter he had no interest in or knowledge of UFOs. The Control investigators found that his brother was a French representative of the American UFO organisation APRO. Even if Prévost did not share his brother's interest in UFOs, he could hardly have been unaware of them. Besides, in his own book about the affair, Prévost had admitted seeing several spacecraft as a child. He also denied seeing a magazine in which a UFO abduction story, very like Fontaine's, was being serialised. Yet Control established that this very magazine was in Prévost's flat at the time of the Cergy-Pontoise abduction.

Investigators also discovered that there had been two other people in the flat at the time of the sighting, one of whom had a driving licence and so could have legally driven them to the police station. Had these two people refused to be part of a hoax story and then been conveniently omitted in the accounts by the three men?

Another witness, a neighbour, cast doubt on the incident, and when a journalist discovered that Fontaine's aunt claimed he had been staying with a friend during the abduction period the possibility that the whole case was a fabrication seemed likely.

The Cergy-Pontoise case has never finally been proved a hoax – but it seems probable that there was no abduction and that the three young men put the story together for fun, for gain or for some undiscovered ideological motive.

Although there are people who deliberately fabricate UFO encounters, most sightings usually prove to be of ordinary objects in the sky that have been wrongly identified. Modern researchers have classified the causes of mistaken UFOs and turned up instances in which people have been alarmed by such objects as if they were something from an alien world.

There is the case, for example, of a woman who locked herself in her bedroom and hid under the bed for an hour, terrified by seeing an object she believed to be a UFO, but that turned out to be a star. In America, ufologist Allan Hendry has described how one man was in such a panic after seeing a well-lit aircraft, believing it to be a UFO, that he ripped his neighbour's door off its hinges, so anxious was he to escape. These examples may sound funny, but it would be wrong to assume that such people are idiots.

Jimmy Carter, for example, when Governor of Georgia, reported seeing a brilliant light in the sky in 1973. The light, which changed colour, was seen to hover silently for 10 minutes at a height of 300 feet (90 metres) before descending to roof-top level. After performing various manoeuvres, it moved on. Twelve other people witnessed the same event, and despite the 'official' explanation – that it was in fact the planet Venus – the belief still lingers that it was a UFO. Especially since Carter, a trained scientist and former naval commander used to navigation by stars, was perfectly able to recognise Venus.

A bird, a plane or a UFO?

About 45 per cent of all UFO reports involve seeing a light or a vague, shapeless phenomenon. In most cases the colour of the light is white, but there are many different coloured light sources that can be seen, and the presence of thin cloud or smoke in the atmosphere can subtly alter what is seen. If you see an unidentified light in the sky there are a number of things to look for.

First, note whether the light remains stationary or is mobile. If stationary, the chances are that it is a star or planet. Stars and planets are among the most common sources of UFO misidentification. Venus is frequently mistaken as it is the brightest object in the night sky and at certain times of the year is very close to Earth. It can be seen even in daylight, as a bright white speck, if one knows where to look. But often there are good reasons why stars are not immediately recognised for what

they are. Optical illusion, for example, and the phenomenon known as 'autokinesis', which causes a star apparently to dart about erratically in the sky, are common causes of misidentification.

If the light does appear to move, the next question is whether it follows a smooth flightpath or whether it hovers or seems to change direction dramatically. A smooth flightpath can indicate one of several things. Precisely what it is can usually be determined by the length of time the light is seen. If it is of very short duration, it could be a meteor – particles of dust or debris from space burning up as they enter the Earth's atmosphere. Meteors tend to glow for a second or two, leaving a trail of light as they streak silently through the night sky.

Occasionally, the debris is a little larger than usual and takes longer to burn up. This leads to the phenomenon known as a bolide or fireball, a brilliant light visible for up to 10 seconds and accompanied by a rumbling or whooshing sound. Fireballs have been seen in daylight too, although this is fairly rare. Usually, sightings of fireballs are so spectacular that they are witnessed by dozens of people over a wide area. They are very similar, in fact, to satellite re-entry, another common cause of UFO misidentification.

Circling the Earth are hundreds of man-made satellites. Many are too small to be seen from the ground, but others are visible at night as points of light that may take several minutes to cross the sky. As satellites re-enter the Earth's atmosphere, the pieces burn away, glowing in several colours, leaving a trail of lights through the upper atmosphere.

For instance, on 31 December 1978 two police officers in Hertfordshire, England, watched in amazement as an incredible object passed silently overhead. It had a cigar-shaped, silvery body with what looked like windows along the side. Behind trailed shimmering orange-coloured streamers. The thing moved slowly away out of sight and, alarmed by what they had seen, they radioed their headquarters.

Unknown to the policemen, hundreds of other people had reported seeing the same thing in many parts of Britain. However, it was subsequently discovered that a Russian booster-rocket re-entered the Earth's atmosphere that night. Its decay orbit took it over northern Europe and it was this that many witnesses mistook for a UFO.

Right: a guide to UFO misidentification – if you see a UFO, check the features of your sighting against the chart. This shows the three major categories of the man-made and natural objects that are most mistaken for UFOs and will enable you to eliminate them from your investigation

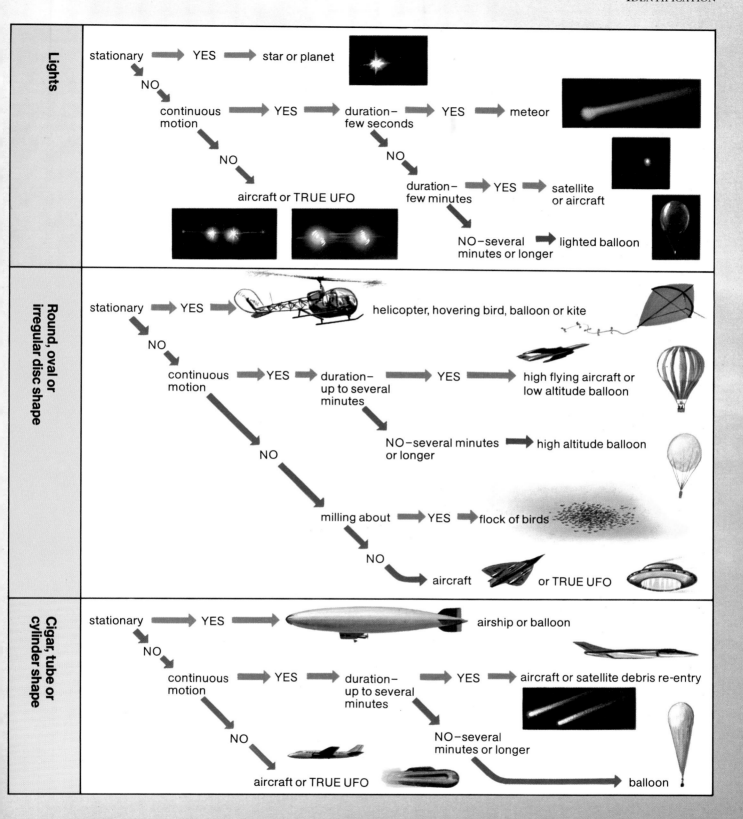

Lights

stationary → YES → star or planet

NO

continuous motion → YES → duration – few seconds → YES → meteor

NO

duration – few minutes → YES → satellite or aircraft

aircraft or TRUE UFO

NO – several minutes or longer → lighted balloon

Round, oval or irregular disc shape

stationary → YES → helicopter, hovering bird, balloon or kite

NO

continuous motion → YES → duration – up to several minutes → YES → high flying aircraft or low altitude balloon

NO – several minutes or longer → high altitude balloon

NO

milling about → YES → flock of birds

NO

aircraft or TRUE UFO

Cigar, tube or cylinder shape

stationary → YES → airship or balloon

NO

continuous motion → YES → duration – up to several minutes → YES → aircraft or satellite debris re-entry

NO

NO – several minutes or longer

aircraft or TRUE UFO

balloon

But by far the most common cause of UFO misidentification is aircraft. Since aircraft possess many different types of lighting, there are plenty of opportunities for strange effects. Bright searchlights may be used in front of the plane, visible from miles away. Seen heading towards you, such a light can appear stationary for a long time before bursting into colour as the aircraft's navigation lights come into view.

Of course aircraft are highly manoeuvrable, but helicopters are even more so. Consequently, not only might they be seen as lights on a smooth flightpath, they can also be seen to alter direction, slow down, and even stop in mid-flight.

Most of these effects would be seen only at night. But there is one object that is often seen and misidentified as a UFO during the day – the balloon. Weather centres release balloons at regular intervals, either to test wind direction or to carry instruments high into the sky from where they radio meteorological information back to Earth. At high altitude a balloon will reflect sunlight from its shiny surface while floating across the sky. From the ground, the silvery dot drifting across the sky may be seen as a round or conical shape.

Airships, under certain conditions, can be mistaken for a cigar-shaped UFO, hovering or slowly moving across the sky. Kites are another possible explanation. Seen at a distance, the controlling cord of a kite may not be visible and its irregular shape could lead people to believe they had seen a UFO. Even clouds have been mistaken for UFOs. A certain type of cloud, known as lenticular, looks like a structured disc. Though uncommon, its slow movement has fooled more than one cautious and trained observer.

Flocks of birds have also caused confusion. In daylight, the reflective underbellies of certain species can shine in sunlight and be seen as white ovals, obscuring all other detail. At night, it is even possible for street lighting to be reflected, creating different coloured oval shapes in the sky.

These are all physical explanations of real objects mistaken for UFOs because of a range of interfering circumstances. However, psychologists put forward a more complex, though more fundamental, UFO theory. Put simply, this suggests that UFOs are imaginary: not objects from outer space, but projected creations from the deepest regions of the mind.

The theory was developed by pioneering psychologist Carl Gustav Jung, who believed that mankind has had a collection of significant images or symbols firmly implanted in its subconscious since the birth of the race. One such key image was that of the disc. Jung suggested that the UFO was a modern variant of this universal shape. He made the illuminating point that 'things seen in the sky' existed throughout history, long before they took on the 20th-century guise of mysterious spacecraft out of pulp science fiction. Unnaturally mobile flying spheres, globes and discs occur prominently in annals of strange visions and inexplicable phenomena seen during troubled times of the past.

Again simplifying the theory, Jung felt modern Man is 'in search of a soul' and this search, with all its accompanying tensions, terrors and despairs, leads frequently to collective projections or hallucinations. These are most likely to occur at times of great stress or emotion, such as war; other induced effects include mass panics, visions or outlandish beliefs – hence the psychological origin of UFO sightings.

Above: the front page of the Roswell Daily Record *for Tuesday, 8 July 1947. The headline was followed by a press statement from the Army Air Force saying that the 'flying disk' had been examined at Roswell Army Air Field and was now in the hands of 'higher headquarters'. The military subsequently denied that the craft had been anything but a weather balloon*

Top left: pioneering psychologist C. G. Jung believed that UFOs were projections from Man's subconscious

Left: this American UFO sighting was clearly not a delusion, although the photograph could have been faked

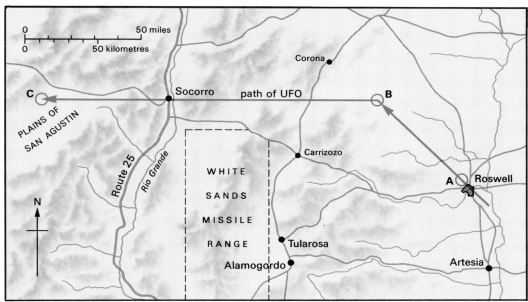

Top right: the estimated course of the 'spacecraft' first seen by Mr and Mrs Wilmot in Roswell (A) at about 9.50 p.m. on 2 July 1947. Evidence of the craft's passage in the form of some strange metallic debris was found by 'Mac' Brazel on his ranch near Corona, New Mexico (B). And on the morning of 3 July a civil engineer working at San Augustin (C) found what seemed to be a crashed UFO with dead humanoids

Right: this photograph allegedly portrays an alien corpse retrieved from a crashed UFO in New Mexico on 7 July 1948. Note the suspicious human-looking spectacles near the shoulder of the 'humanoid'

Hard evidence?

There are numerous possibilities, then, to explain away the strange sights people have seen in the skies. Set against this are 30 years of case histories that include many thoroughly documented and investigated UFO sightings. So what firm evidence is there to suggest that UFOs exist and that they come from space?

Perhaps the most striking incidents are those in which some physical manifestation of the phenomenon has been left behind for researchers to investigate. Examples include the catalogue of alleged crashed UFOs, which some say have been covered up by governments fearful of public hysteria if such discoveries were revealed. Then there are the more credible and tangible instances of people who have suffered radiation poisoning or burns, or whose vehicles have been affected after UFO encounters and the less convincing cases of UFO abductions.

The belief that a flying saucer has crashed and been confiscated by the authorities has proved very difficult either to prove or to disprove. 'Believers' point to a rich assortment of isolated facts, rumours, hints and unsupported testimonies and insist that together they make up a case that demands serious investigation. The sceptics reply that this evidence offers no solid case at all.

The first record of a UFO crash was one of a cluster of events that occurred near the town of Roswell, New Mexico, on 2 July 1947 – only days after Arnold's noted sighting that began the modern UFO epoch.

At about 9.50 that night Mr and Mrs Wilmot of Roswell were sitting out on their front porch when 'a big glowing object' zoomed out of the sky from the south-east, and headed north-east towards the smaller town of Corona. It was travelling at high speed, and was in sight for only 40 to 50 seconds; they were able, however, to describe it as oval in shape.

The following morning Barney Barnett, a civil engineer from Socorro, New Mexico, was working in a desert area, the plains of San Agustin, some 250 miles (400 kilometres) west of Roswell, and just west of Socorro. He saw sunlight reflecting off some kind of metallic object in what should have been empty desert; so, thinking it might be a crashed aircraft, he went towards it. What he found was 'some sort of metallic, disc-shaped object', 25 to 30 feet (8 to 10 metres) in diameter.

While inspecting it, he was joined by some archaeology students from the University of Pennsylvania. Together they contemplated an astonishing sight: beside the machine itself, which seemed to have been split open by explosion or impact, there were dead bodies scattered over the ground, and others still inside the machine. They were human-like, but small-eyed and hairless, and with heads over-large in proportion to their size. They were wearing grey, one-piece clothing.

Shortly after, a jeep containing an army officer drove up, and declared that the army was taking over control. The area was cordoned off: the civilians were told to leave the area, and warned that it was their patriotic duty to keep silent about what they had seen.

Though Barnett is now dead – he is one of the principal witnesses, whom investigators, of course, were unable to interview – he told

Brazel died in 1963; this account is based on an interview with his son Bill.

The previous night there had been a severe thunder storm – a not infrequent occurrence in this region – and Brazel had heard a loud explosion quite distinct from the thunder. Next morning, he rode out to check on his sheep, and found a collection of unidentifiable wreckage strewn over an area of ground some quarter of a mile (400 metres) in length, in a narrow strip running in the direction of Socorro. Having more important concerns, he didn't at the time take much interest in the wreckage; but a day or two later he thought he would go back and take another look.

What he found was fragments of a metallic, foil-like substance, very thin and pliable, but immensely tough – he could neither crease nor permanently bend it. There seemed to be some markings resembling writing, and attached to

Below: the sites of some of the alleged sightings between 1947 and 1953 of UFO wreckage in the hands of the military – and the air fields then used for weapons testing

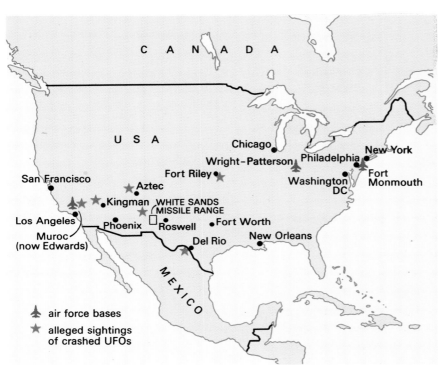

Above right: rancher 'Mac' Brazel, who discovered what was apparently UFO wreckage on his ranch near Corona, New Mexico. Two years later, his son Bill happened to mention in a tavern that he still had some of the wreckage. The very next day the military came to confiscate it; an official explanation was never given

his story to some friends. The investigators found no reason to doubt their word; nor, from what they learned of Barnett himself, did they find any reason to disbelieve what he told his friends in private. However, all attempts to check his story by tracking down the archaeological students have so far been unsuccessful.

On or close to the same date, 'Mac' Brazel, a rancher, made a strange find on his ranch near Corona, New Mexico, about 75 miles (120 kilometres) north-west of Roswell, and 150 miles (240 kilometres) east of the site of Barnett's discovery. Brazel's was a small, rough ranch in isolated country, nearly 30 miles (50 kilometres) from the nearest town. His wife and family normally lived in town so that his children could attend school, but they were with him at the time of these events.

some of the fragments was a tape-like material which, when held to the light, seemed to have a design on it, vaguely floral in appearance.

The following night he happened to visit Corona, the nearest town, and there he told friends of his find: in return he learned that several people had seen flying saucers lately in the neighbourhood – more than a dozen in all, and not apparently attributable to rocket tests from the nearby White Sands Missile Range. He wondered if his find was in some way connected with these sightings, and next day, while visiting the larger town of Roswell on farming business, he informed the sheriff. The sheriff advised him to go to the military with his story: there was an Army Air Force base just outside Roswell.

A reporter from the local radio station heard

of Brazel's discovery, and recorded an interview with him before he went to see the military. But when the local radio station started to put the story out, it was immediately silenced by the authorities, who claimed to be speaking in the national interest and threatened the station with removal of its licence. And when Brazel got to the military, he found they were very definitely interested: they held him for questioning while troops descended on his ranch and combed the area to gather every scrap of the strange material. A number of local residents had heard enough about the matter to go out to the Brazel ranch to see for themselves, but they found the road blocked by troops and the area cordoned off. It was several days before the army allowed Brazel to return home; he was discouraged and upset at the way he had been treated.

But the papers and the radio had conflicting,

Above: an aerial view of the New Mexican desert at White Sands Proving Ground, where a v-2 rocket-testing programme was in progress at the time of the Roswell incident

Left: a guided missile takes off from White Sands in a test undertaken during the 1960s. The path of the Roswell UFO passed very close to White Sands – perhaps a reason for concern on the part of the military

fragmented accounts to give their publics. Among those who had been alerted by the news to visit the Brazel ranch was reporter Johnny McBoyle, part owner of Radio KSWS of Roswell. On 7 July Radio KOAT in nearby Albuquerque, which possessed more extensive transmission facilities, received a telephone message from McBoyle, for relay: 'A flying saucer has crashed. ... No, I'm not joking ... near Roswell. I've been there and seen it. It's like a big crumpled dishpan. Some rancher has hauled it under a cattle shelter with his tractor. The army is there and they are going to pick it up. The whole area is now closed off. And get this – they're saying something about little men being on board.... Start getting this on the teletype right away.'

The operator began to comply, but the teleprinter suddenly stopped transmitting and instead printed an incoming message: 'ATTENTION ALBUQUERQUE: DO NOT TRANSMIT THIS MESSAGE. STOP COMMUNICATION IMMEDIATELY.' The caller was unidentified.

When the operator got in touch with McBoyle again, the reporter said: 'Forget about it. You never heard it. Look, you're not supposed to know.'

Discrepancies between these accounts are at once apparent. McBoyle claimed to have actually seen an object 'like a crumpled dishpan' on a ranch near Roswell, which seems to imply the Brazel ranch: yet Brazel is supposed to have found only fragments, a matter on which his surviving children today are quite clear. Curiously, too, the headlines of the *Roswell Daily Record* for 8 July read 'RAAF captures flying saucer on ranch in Roswell region'.

The story accompanying that headline was in the form of a press statement from the Public Relations Officer at Roswell Army Air Field, First Lieutenant Haut:

The many rumours regarding the flying disc became a reality yesterday when the intelligence office of the 509th Bomb Group of the Eighth Air Force, Roswell Army Air Field, was fortunate enough to gain possession of a disc through the co-operation of one of the local ranchers and the sheriff's office ...

The flying object landed on a ranch near Roswell some time last week. Not having phone facilities, the rancher stored the disc until such time as he was able to contact the sheriff's office, who in turn notified Major Jesse A. Marcel, of the 509th Bomb Group Intelligence Office. The disc was picked up at the rancher's home, inspected at the Roswell Army Air Field and subsequently loaned by Major Marcel to higher headquarters.

Was Lieutenant Haut acting under instructions from his base commander? According to his own recollections, he was: Colonel Blanchard asked him to write and distribute a news release to the effect that the Army Air Force had recovered the remains of a crashed flying saucer. Haut asked if it was possible for him to see the object, but Blanchard refused. If Haut *was* acting under instructions, his press report takes on the status of an official statement. And if so, it deserves to be taken very seriously.

Whatever the truth is, the report displeased the army at a higher level. Within hours of the press announcement, General Ramey, from Fort Worth in the adjoining state of Texas, went on the radio to tell the public that the entire affair was a case of mistaken identification. As for flying saucers, he declared, 'there is no such gadget known to the Army, at least not at this level.'

The radio disclaimer was followed by a press

conference in which the army claimed the wreckage was from a weather balloon – fragments were photographed. Brazel himself, while keeping quiet as instructed, insisted 'I am sure what I found was not any weather observation balloon.'

Brazel's son Bill collected some of the fragments, and kept them. Two years later, however, he happened to mention them in a tavern in Corona. The very next day he received a visit from the military, who told him it was important for national security and confiscated

his collection. That, two years after the event, the army should be so concerned about some stray fragments of a weather balloon is, at the very least, improbable.

We must also note as particularly strange the fact that Brazel was kept in military custody even after the authorities had identified the fragments as being from a harmless balloon. By any standards, if they were telling the truth, they seem to have over-reacted.

Later, strong evidence emerged that a large load – perhaps the wreckage of the crashed object – left Roswell under a maximum security escort. The destination of some of the material was widely alleged to be Muroc Air Force Base, California – and this was the location for one of the most incredible, yet at the same time one of the most enduring, components of the myth. It is claimed that on 20 February 1954 the President of the United States, General Eisenhower, went to Muroc to see the saucers.

In principle, it is perfectly possible. Eisenhower was at that time enjoying a golfing vacation on a friend's ranch at Palm Springs, only 90 miles (150 kilometres) away from Muroc; yet only a week previously he had returned from a quail-shooting holiday.

Main picture: the NASA *Flight Research Center at Edwards* AFB, *California. In 1947, when it was known as Muroc* AFB, *it was believed to be the secret repository of crashed* UFO *wreckage*

Left: photographs like this suggest UFOs *have landed, but most ufologists doubt their authenticity*

Would even the most sporting president, it has been asked, take two such vacations in such close succession?

The movements of the president are followed closely by the press. Yet on 20 February, for several hours, the press had no idea of his whereabouts. It was rumoured that he was dead. A press conference was hastily called to explain that he had had to have emergency dental treatment. Some years later the dentist's family was questioned; they had a vague notion of his visit – a surprisingly casual attitude to such a memorable event!

In May 1954 a certain Gerald Light, in company with some distinguished visitors, went to Muroc, and wrote a letter after his visit describing how he had seen five separate extra-terrestrial craft being studied by the air force, and confirming Eisenhower's visit.

Other cases, uncannily similar in some respects, abound. On 7 July 1948, near Del Rio, Texas, USA, unusual radar sightings led to the suspicion that an unidentified flying object had crashed some 30 miles (50 kilometres) across the Mexican border. With permission from the Mexican government, US troops went to investigate, and found a metallic disc, with the burned bodies of the crew, more or less

human-like beings about 5 feet (1.5 metres) tall. The object, which had been clocked at 2000 miles per hour (3200 km/h) by radar, had been simultaneously seen on radar by USAF Colonel Whitcomb in an F94. He landed at his home base and immediately took off for the scene in a borrowed light aircraft; he found Mexican troops in control, and the object hidden from sight. A naval intelligence officer arrived in time to see the crash area roped off and some object being loaded onto trucks.

The troops taking part were apparently warned that if they spoke of the matter they would be 'the sorriest people around'. Some photographs, allegedly of the bodies of the occupants, were circulating years later.

Sometime in 1952, at the Muroc Air Force Base in California, a USAF radar operator tracked an object descending towards Earth at great speed. After a crash had been confirmed, he was instructed 'You didn't see anything.' Later he learned that a UFO, more than 17 yards (16 metres) in diameter, had crashed in a desert area not far away. It was metallic, and badly burned: it contained bodies of beings about 5 feet (1.5 metres) tall. The debris was kept for a while at the base then allegedly shipped to the Wright-Patterson Air Force

Top left: General Ramey (left) with Colonel Dubose at an army press conference, with a weather balloon they claimed had been mistaken for the crashed UFO. Yet at an earlier press conference they displayed different wreckage. Earlier Ramey had squashed the army's admission that they were examining a 'flying disk'

Right: President Dwight D. Eisenhower – did he go to see the crashed UFOS?

Base at Dayton in the mid-western state of Ohio.

Possibly relating to the same incident is a film that was shown the following spring, apparently by the military authorities, to a select group, including a radar specialist, a Mr T. E., who was working for the army and air force, stationed at Fort Monmouth, New Jersey, and who had secret security clearance. The five-minute movie showed a silver disc-shaped object embedded in the sand in a remote desert area; it had a dome on top, and an open hatch or door. Some 10 to 15 military

191

personnel could be seen standing near the craft, and its diameter, appeared to be 6 to 8 yards (5 to 7 metres). The film also showed the bodies of three dead occupants: they were small and human-like, with over-large heads. The viewers were told to think about the film but not to tell anyone about it; two weeks later they were told it was a hoax. This would seem pointless, while the cost of setting up so elaborate a fake would have been formidable.

The most explicit item of evidence in the entire crashed UFO saga is an affidavit signed in 1973 by a certain Fritz Werner – a pseudonym, although his true identity is known – who swore that he had assisted at the investigation into a crashed unknown object. While serving as project engineer on an air force contract near Kingman, Arizona, in 1953, he was given an assignment: along with some 15 others, he was taken early one morning under strict security conditions in a blacked-out bus on a five-hour journey. They were told that a super-secret air force craft had crashed.

Werner described the object as like two deep saucers, one inverted on the other, about 11 yards (10 metres) in diameter, made of dull silver metal, with an open hatch to the interior. His particular task was to calculate the object's impact velocity from the traces. He found no landing gear, also no dents or scratches. In a tent nearby he saw a dead humanoid on a table, about 4 feet 3 inches (1.3 metres) in height.

Another incident from 1953 that may confirm the Fritz Werner report is the case of a metallurgist named Daly who worked for the air force at the Wright-Patterson AFB, Ohio. He described being taken to a location, unidentified but abounding in hot sand; for the last part of his journey he was blindfolded. For two days he was required to examine the structure of an undamaged silver metallic craft. He concluded it was not of earthly origin.

Bottom: amateur astronomer George Adamski who, in 1953, claimed to have communicated with 'beings' from alien spaceships. He wrote a best-selling book, illustrated with numerous photographs he took of the craft. Here, he is at home in California using the Newtonian reflector telescope through which he photographed his UFOS

Bottom left: a 'Venusian scout ship' photographed by George Adamski on 13 December 1952 at Palomar Gardens, California

Below: Adamski's picture of an 'interplanatary carrier' and six 'scouts'

Despite the evident discrepancies, these two reports may relate to the same incident. Relevant, too, may be the evidence given by the wife of a guard at Wright-Patterson; she alleged that, at about this time, her husband witnessed scientists examining the bodies of large-headed humanoids.

Another incident, two years later, at the Wright-Patterson base, may confirm that pilots of crashed spacecraft were taken there for examination. A woman whose duty was to catalogue all incoming material relating to UFOS stated that she saw the bodies of two dead humanoids, with large heads, being transferred from one location to another.

This evidence may confirm the suspicions of American ufologist and author Otto Binder who, as one of the most objective investigators of UFOS, wrote in 1974: 'Somewhere in the US there is a locked warehouse, guarded as no other place has ever been, accessible only to men of the highest security clearance possible in the government and the Pentagon. Because in that warehouse stronghold lies irrefutable evidence that UFOS exist.'

Close encounters

An inevitable consequence of the crashed UFO phenomenon was the flurry of accounts telling of encounters with aliens. Indeed, from 1947 to 1952, when UFOs were the centre of heated public debate, humanoids were allegedly seen in widely different parts of the world.

For instance, at Baurú, in the state of São Paulo, Brazil, on 23 July 1947 – less than a month after Kenneth Arnold's aerial encounter near Mount Rainier – a survey worker named José Higgins, and several of his fellow workers, saw a large metallic disc come to earth and settle down on curved legs.

Higgins stood his ground while his colleagues fled, and found himself face to face with three 7-foot (2.1-metre) tall beings, all wearing transparent overalls with metal boxes on their backs. One entity pointed a tube at him and moved as though to apprehend him. But Señor Higgins dodged the creature and observed that it was shy of the sunlight.

Below: this photograph of a daylight disc was taken near Saasfee in Switzerland on 25 July 1975. Experts can find no evidence of fraud

Bottom and bottom left: the aliens in the highly successful film Close encounters of the third kind *were depicted as intelligent and friendly. Is the belief in UFOs a manifestation of our need to believe that a superior, benign power is watching over us?*

The creatures had large bald heads, big round eyes, no eyebrows or beards and long legs. They leapt and gambolled, picking up and tossing huge boulders about. They also made holes in the ground, perhaps trying to indicate what could have been the positions of planets around the sun. The creatures then re-entered their craft, which took off with a great whistling noise. Three weeks later, far away in north-eastern Italy, a Professor Johannis had a similar experience with little, green-skinned aliens while walking on a mountain.

More shocking, however, are the many accounts of people who claim to have been abducted by aliens. One of the earliest reports of such an abduction was kept secret for over three years because it was deemed too 'wild' by those who first interviewed the abductee.

The actual abduction of Antônio Villas Boas, a 23-year-old farmer who lived near the small town of São Francisco de Sales in Minas Gerais, Brazil, was heralded by two unusual events. The first took place on 5 October 1957 when he and his brother were retiring to bed at about 11 p.m. after a party. From their bedroom window they saw an unidentified light in the farmyard below. It moved up onto the roof of their house, and together they watched it before it departed.

The second strange incident occurred on 14 October at about 9.30 p.m. when the Villas Boas brothers were out ploughing with their tractor. They suddenly saw a dazzling light, 'big and round', about 100 yards (90 metres) above one end of the field.

The following night, 15 October, Antônio was out in the field again, ploughing alone by the light of his headlamps. Suddenly, at about 1 a.m., he became aware off a 'large red star' that seemed to be descending towards the end of the field. As it came nearer he saw that it was in fact a luminous egg-shaped object. The

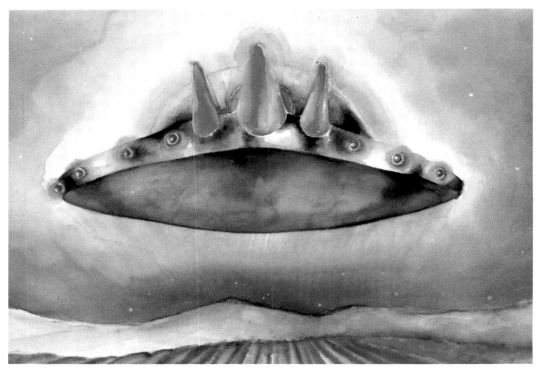

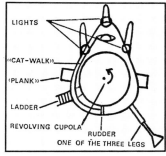

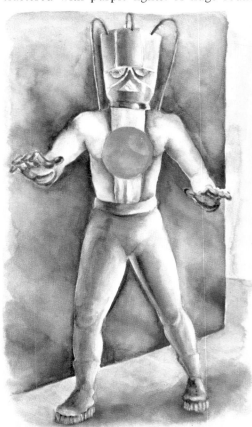

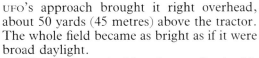

UFO's approach brought it right overhead, about 50 yards (45 metres) above the tractor. The whole field became as bright as if it were broad daylight.

Villas Boas sat in his cab transfixed with fear as the object landed about 15 yards (15 metres) in front of him. He saw a rounded object with a distinct rim that was apparently clustered with purple lights. A huge round headlamp on the side facing him seemed to be producing the 'daylight' effect. There was a revolving cupola on top, and as he watched, fascinated, he saw three shafts – or 'legs' – emerge and reach for the ground. At this the terrified farmer started to drive off but after a short distance the engine stopped.

Villas Boas found he could not restart it and in a panic he leapt from the cab and set off across the heavily ploughed field. The deep ruts proved a handicap to his escape and he had gone only a few paces when someone grabbed his arm. As he turned, he was astonished to see a strangely garbed individual whose helmeted head reached only to Villas Boas's shoulder. He hit out at his assailant, who was knocked flying, but he was quickly grabbed by three other humanoids who lifted him from the ground as he struggled and shouted. He later said:

> I noticed that as they were dragging me towards the machine my speech seemed to arouse their surprise or curiosity, for they stopped and peered attentively at my face as I spoke. . . .

He was carried to the craft. A ladder descended from a door, and his captors hoisted him up. The beings were all dressed in tight-fitting grey overalls and large, broad helmets reinforced with bands of metal at back and front. There were apertures through which Villas Boas could see light-coloured eyes.

Once inside the machine Villas Boas found himself in a square room with metallic walls, brightly lit by small, high lamps. He was set down on his feet, and became aware that there were five small beings, two of whom held him firmly. One signalled that he should be taken through to an adjoining room, which was

Above left: an artist's impression of the UFO that abducted Antonio Villas Boas (top), who had what has been called the closest encounter ever, and Villas Boas's drawings of the spacecraft (above and below)

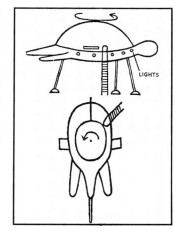

Left: Villas Boas described beings with three tubes emerging from their helmets and running into their clothing. Their sleeves ended in thick gloves, their trousers fitted tightly and their footwear had thick soles. Each alien had a kind of shield that reflected light on its chest, and was joined to a belt at the waist by a strip of laminated metal

larger, and oval in shape, with a metal column that reached from floor to ceiling.

A 'conversation' ensued between his captors, who made sounds like dog barks:

Those sounds were so totally different from anything I had heard until now. They were slow barks and yelps, neither very clear nor very hoarse, some longer, some shorter, at times containing several different sounds all at once....

This strange communication ceased abruptly, when all five set about him, stripping him of his clothing while he shouted and struggled.

The naked and shivering farmer – it was a chilly night outside, and no warmer in the craft – stood there quaking and 'worried to death'. He wondered what on earth was going to happen to him. One of the little creatures approached him with what seemed to be a sort of wet sponge, which he rubbed all over Villas Boas's skin. He said: 'The liquid was as clear as water, but quite thick, and without smell. I thought it was some sort of oil, but was wrong, for my skin did not become greasy or oily.'

He was now led to another door, which had an inscription in red over it. He tried to memorise this, although it meant nothing to him, being written in unknown characters. In yet another room one of the beings approached with a sort of chalice from which dangled two flexible tubes; one of these, with a capped end like a child's suction 'arrow', was fixed to his chin, while the other tube was pumped up and down. The alarmed Villas Boas watched the

chalice fill with what was presumably his own blood. The creatures then left him alone.

Suddenly he smelt a strange odour, which made him feel sick. He examined the walls and saw metallic tubes at just below ceiling level. Grey smoke was coming through perforations in the tubes. Villas Boas rushed to a corner of the room and vomited, and after that he felt a little less frightened. Moments later there was a noise at the door, which opened to reveal a woman standing there. As Villas Boas gaped, the woman walked towards him. Flabbergasted, he realised she was as naked as he was. The door closed, and Villas Boas found himself alone with this woman, whose slim body was the most beautiful he had ever seen.

She approached the farmer and rubbed her head against his. Her body felt as though glued to his, and she made it quite clear what she wanted. The sexual act was normal. Villas Boas recalled that she never kissed him, but once gently bit him on his chin. Although she never spoke, she grunted.

When she was called away by one of the other beings, she turned to Villas Boas, pointed to her belly, and then pointed to the sky. These gestures instilled a great fear in Antônio, for he interpreted them as meaning she would return to take him away. Later he was calmed by the suggestion that she meant: 'I am going to bear our child, on my planet.'

Then Villas Boas was told to get dressed, after which he says he was taken on a conducted tour round the craft; during this he tried to

Left: Antonio Villas Boas was examined by a doctor in February 1958, four months after the alleged abduction. The symptoms he described suggested 'radiation poisoning or exposure to radiation'

Bottom: Villas Boas's impression of the inscription above a door in the humanoids' craft

Below: the naked beauty, described in detail by Boas. She was shorter than he, her head reaching only to his shoulder – he is 5 feet 5 inches (1.6 metres). Her hair was smooth and very fair, almost white and as though bleached. Parted in the centre, it reached halfway down her neck. Her eyes were large, blue and elongated; her small nose was straight and she had high cheekbones and high, well-separated breasts. Her waist was slender, her hips wide and her thighs large, while her feet were small. The hair in her armpits, and her pubic hair, was blood red

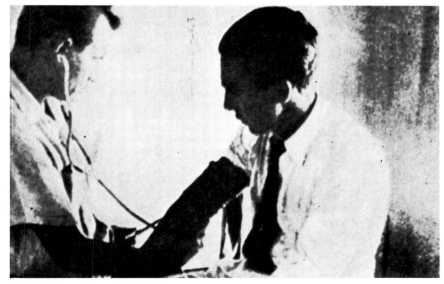

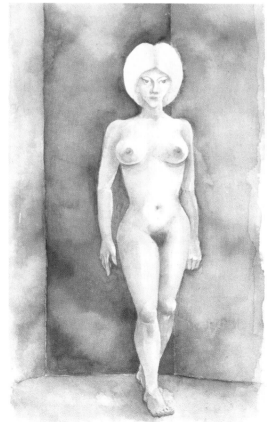

steal an instrument for a keepsake, only to be rebuffed, angrily, by one of the crew. Eventually, he was invited to go down the ladder, and back onto solid ground. The craft rose into the air, then suddenly shot off like a bullet. It was by then 5.30 a.m. and the abductee's adventure had lasted over four hours.

He returned home hungry, and weakened by his spell of vomiting. He slept through to 4.30 p.m. and awoke feeling perfectly normal. But when he fell asleep again he slept badly, and woke up shouting after dreaming of the incident. Next day he was troubled by nausea and a violent headache. When that left him his eyes began to burn. Unusual wounds, with infections, appeared on parts of his body.

Villas Boas later impressed his many interviewers with his unswerving story, and his reputation in the locality was that of an honest, serious, hard-working man.

When a doctor eventually examined Villas Boas, he observed two small patches, one on each side of the chin. He described these as 'scars of some superficial lesion with associated subcutaneous haemorrhage'. Several other mysterious scars on his body were also noted, suggesting radiation poisoning.

Physical effects

Physical injuries, such as burns or radiation poisoning, are perhaps the strongest evidence for the concrete existence of UFOs, although they do not help distinguish whether the object is from space or an unidentified military aircraft. There are numerous instances of

Above: the lonely tree-lined road in the Huffman area of east Texas where Betty Cash and Vickie and Colby Landrum saw a UFO

Landrum and her grandson Colby Landrum, had eaten at a roadside restaurant in a sparsely populated area covered by oak and pine trees and dotted with swamps. It was about 9 p.m. when the evening's terrifying events began.

As they were driving along an isolated road, Colby, an alert youngster, suddenly noticed a bright object above the tree-tops some distance away. He pointed it out excitedly to Betty and Vickie as it glowed brightly above the trees about 3 miles (5 kilometres) ahead. As they approached, it appeared to get larger and larger, rather than diminishing as an aeroplane

people suffering physical injury or even being killed after such contact. In one disturbing, well-documented case three people had the whole future of their lives changed after an encounter with a diamond-shaped UFO.

Late one chilly evening at the end of December 1980 two middle-aged women and a young boy were driving along a lonely road in the Huffman area of east Texas, USA. It was the Christmas season and they were in a festive mood. Earlier that evening the three, business woman Betty Cash, her friend Vickie

Above: heavy, double-rotor helicopters like this CH-47 were identified by several witnesses as being present in large numbers at Huffman. The witnesses were shown silhouette charts of different types of helicopter, but all agreed on the CH-47

would appear to do as it flew further away. As they realised the object was approaching the road only a short distance ahead their apprehension increased. Nevertheless they hoped to get by in time and leave it behind. But before they could do so, the object had straddled the road, blocking their way.

Vickie screamed, 'Stop the car or we shall be burned alive'.

The object, many times larger than their car, remained hovering at tree-top level and sending down an occasional large cone of fire like a rocket blast. In between these blasts it would settle downwards some 25 feet (7.5 metres) or so, only to rise again on the next cone of fire like some huge science-fiction spaceship in trouble. Vickie's vivid description of it was that it was 'like a diamond of fire'.

Scorched by a UFO

When Betty eventually brought the car to a standstill the object was less than 65 yards (60 metres) away. It looked as if it were made of dull aluminium, and it glowed so brightly that it lit up the surrounding forest like daylight. The four points of the diamond were blunted rather than sharp, and blue spots or lights ringed its centreline. Had the UFO not come to rest over the road, the cone of fire that periodically emanated from its lowest point would have set the forest on fire. In addition to the blast of the fire, the UFO emitted an intermittent beeping sound.

It is not clear whether Betty turned the car engine off, or whether it just died. Whichever it was, the three of them got out of the car to take a closer look at the thing that was blocking their way. Vickie stood by the open door on the right-hand side of the car with her left hand resting on the car roof, staring at the UFO.

Colby plucked at his grandmother's clothing and begged her to get back inside the car and hold him. Two or three minutes later, in

response to his pleading, she did so.

As Vickie held Colby to comfort him she screamed to Betty to get back into the car with them. But Betty was so fascinated by the UFO that she walked round to the front of the car and stood there gazing intently at the bright object. She seemed to be mesmerised by it. Bathed in the bright light, she remained standing there even though the heat was burning her skin. Even the skin on the finger beneath her ring was burned. Eventually, as the object began to move up and away, she responded to

Above: eighteen months after the UFO sighting Betty Cash (left) and Colby Landrum (right) were still suffering the side-effects. Betty had had intense headaches and swollen eyes; she was plagued with skin eruptions and she spent five periods in hospital. Colby had been a healthy, active boy; afterwards he was left with physical and emotional scars

Left: 'a diamond of fire' was how one witness described the huge glowing object that hovered over the road, blocking the way. Ringed with lights at the centreline, the UFO emitted a regular bleeping sound

Vickie's calls and walked back to the door. When she touched the door it was so painfully hot that she had to use her leather jacket to protect her hand while she got in the car.

As the three of them watched the departing UFO, a large number of helicopters appeared overhead. As Betty said, 'They seemed to rush in from all directions . . . it seemed like they were trying to encircle the thing.' Within a few seconds the UFO had disappeared behind the trees lining the highway. It was then that the victims became aware of how hot the interior of the car had become.

When the effects of the bright light had worn off, Betty started the engine and they sped off down the darkened highway. After a mile or so of twisting road they joined a larger highway and were able to turn in the direction of the departing UFO. This was about 5 miles (8 kilometres) and five minutes later. The object was clearly visible some distance ahead, and looked like a bright oblong cylinder of light. It was still lighting up the surrounding area and illuminating the helicopters.

By this time the helicopters were spread out over a 5-mile (8-kilometre) area. One main group was still near to the UFO, but moving in an erratic flight path. The others were clearly visible in a steady trail formation. At one point one of the large 'choppers' flew directly over

Above: a horse found dead in Colorado, its head and neck severely mutilated by radiation. Was the injury caused by UFO predators or by secret military tests?

Below left: many witnesses at Huffman identified single-rotor helicopters chasing the fiery UFO

turned away from the flight path of the UFO and drove towards Dayton, where the three of them lived. By this time they had been involved with the UFO and the helicopters for at least 20 minutes, perhaps longer.

Betty dropped Vickie and Colby at their home at 9.50 p.m. and went home herself. A friend and her children were waiting there for Betty to return, but by then Betty was feeling too ill to tell them about the incident. Over the next few hours Betty's skin turned red as if it

the car engulfing it in the roar of its engine and flap of its rotor blades. As they watched from this new vantage point the victims counted 23 helicopters. Many of the helicopters were the large double rotor type, with four wheels, and a large housing to the rear (these were later identified as CH-47 Chinooks, manufactured by the Vertol division of the Boeing company). Others were smaller, very fast, single-rotor helicopters. These were never clearly identified, but they appeared to be of the Bell Huey variety.

As soon as the UFO and the helicopters were a safe distance ahead, Betty drove on cautiously. When she reached an intersection, she

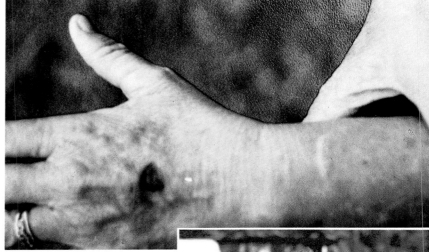

Above: the burn on the back of Vickie's hand. Eighteen months later, her face showed lasting damage around the eyes (right). Vickie, then 57, is a committed Christian who does not believe in UFOs. She thought the end of the world had come, and because she expected her Saviour to emerge from the burning craft, she gazed intently at it, thus suffering more face and eye damage than either Betty or Colby

were badly sunburned. Her neck swelled, and blisters erupted and broke on her face, scalp and eyelids. She started to vomit and continued to do so periodically throughout the night. By morning she was almost in a coma.

Some time between midnight and 2 a.m. Vickie and Colby began to experience similar symptoms, although less severe. At first they suffered the sunburn-like condition, then diarrhoea and vomiting.

Betty Cash, 51, was then running a restaurant and grocery store. She had planned to open a new restaurant the very next week. A year earlier she had completely recovered from a heart bypass operation. Her physical injuries from the encounter were to be more debilitating than any caused by cardiac surgery and were later to force her to sell the restaurant.

The morning after the encounter Betty was moved to Vickie's home, and all three were cared for there. Betty's condition continued to deteriorate, and three days later she was taken to a hospital casualty department. There, staff assumed that Betty was a classic burn victim, and treated her accordingly. They were not told about the UFO until several days later when Colby blurted out what had happened.

The burns and swelling altered Betty's appearance so radically that friends and relatives who came to visit her in hospital did not recognise her. Her hair started to fall out and she was eventually to lose more than half the hair on her head.

Since the incident Vickie has had to have three new pairs of spectacles with successively stronger prescriptions to match the deterioration in her eyesight. Her eyesight is continuing to deteriorate and she still suffers from periodic eye infections; she fears she may eventually go blind. Colby too has experienced similar problems with his eyes. Doctors suspect that the condition of all three victims could have been caused by exposure to some type of electromagnetic radiation.

The evidence of all the witnesses to the Huffman event had been consistent. All were

interrogated separately, not only about the UFO but also about the helicopters. They provided consistent descriptions and sketches that indicated they had seen a large number of CH-47s, plus helicopters of another type.

Locating the source of the helicopters proved to be a much more difficult task. According to an official of the Houston Intercontinental Airport Federation Aviation Administration, about 350 to 400 helicopters operate commercially in the Houston area. All of these are single rotor type units; there are no CH-47s. The official also said that because helicopters fly on Visual Flight Rules (VFR), they do not need to contact the airport control tower. Other information provided by Houston was that outside a 15-mile (24-kilometre) radius from the airport, helicopters must stay below an altitude of 1800 feet (550 metres), and that due to technical limitations radar is restricted to a minimum altitude of 2000 feet (600 metres) in that area.

At the US Army's Fort Hood near Killeen, Texas, press officer Major Tony Geishauser said none of their aircraft were in the Houston area on 29 December 1980. 'I don't know any other place around here that would have that number of helicopters,' he said. 'I don't know what it could be . . . unless there's a super-secret thing going on and I wouldn't necessarily know about

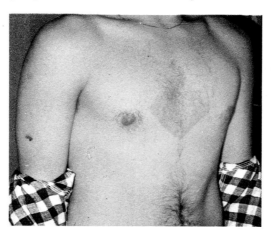

it.' Other air bases made similar denials.

In another (possibly related) incident the day before the Huffman event, helicopter activity had also been noted when UFOs were being observed. Dozens of residents of Ohio county, Kentucky, had seen strange moving lights. But when a helicopter arrived in the area, the UFOs left. Again, all military installations denied having any helicopters airborne that night.

And Betty, Vickie and Colby were not the only witnesses to the strange happenings at Huffman. An off-duty Dayton policeman and his wife were driving through the Huffman area the same night and also observed a large number of CH-47 helicopters.

Oilfield labourer Jerry McDonald was in his back garden in Dayton when he saw a huge UFO flying directly overhead. At first he

Left: in Plymouth, England, this girl was burned on the hand by the light from a UFO on 10 September 1981

Below: electromagnetic radiation consists of waves of energy of varying lengths and frequencies from radio waves to gamma rays. It is ionising radiation that is potentially most damaging to living tissue. Exposure to ionising radiation can cause skin burns, nausea, vomiting, diarrhoea, loss of hair, lowered resistance to infection and headaches. The sunburn-type injuries inflicted in the Huffman incident were typical of exposure to ultraviolet radiation. They could also have been caused by x-rays or microwaves

Below left: a Canadian man suffered these burns to his chest after encountering a cigar-like UFO in May 1967

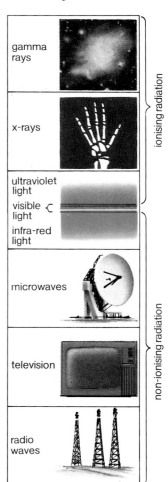

thought it was the Goodyear airship, but he quickly realised it was some unidentified object. 'It was kind of diamond-shaped and had two twin torches that were shooting brilliant blue flames out the back,' he said.

Certainly Dr J. Allen Hynek was convinced the witnesses were not mistaken. 'We are dealing with a real event,' he said, 'but we're not sure if it's a government exercise or a UFO sighting. There is a lot of top secret stuff going on that most people don't know about.'

Despite continuing investigations, a satisfactory explanation for these events has still not been found. However, members of the Houston-based Vehicle Internal Systems Investigative Team (VISIT) studied the evidence of the Huffman UFO sighting and offered, among others, the following scenarios.

Scenario 1: Betty, Vickie and Colby encountered a UFO in trouble; it was operating an emergency system (the cone of fire) to overcome the problem and get it on its way again. Two hours earlier the same craft had been tracked on radar until it dipped too low to be seen. A military team was sent to investigate.

Right: Vickie Landrum, Betty Cash and young Colby a year and a half after they saw the UFO that changed their lives

Below: all three counted over 20 helicopters in pursuit of the UFO. Some were CH-47 double-rotor models, while others were smaller, faster, single-rotor craft similar to these

The team had CH-47 heavy lift helicopters to carry troops to cordon off a crash scene, and equipment to neutralise any problem; the smaller helicopters were gunships for protection. When the UFO regained control and made for the coast, the helicopters tracked it, in case it should try to land.

Research for this scenario produced a number of other UFO sightings involving triangular or diamond-shaped objects, but only a few of these belched flames from the underside for a prolonged period. This seemed to support the idea that the Huffman UFO was in trouble. Moreover, people close to a UFO seldom suffer the dire injuries experienced in this case.

Scenario 2: This suggests the whole affair was a government classified operation and was mistaken by the witnesses for a UFO encounter. The helicopters could have been transported to the Houston area from any base in the USA or central America, and could have been taking part in anything from an annual training exercise to some special operations simulation. The 'UFO' might have been a power plant, a weapons system or an electronic countermeasures system, and it might have been slung from a helicopter or flown by remote control. The injuries could have been caused by a powerful pulsed microwave system, or by exposure to some fuel, defoliant or other unidentified liquid.

As far as this scenario is concerned, the US government categorically refuses to acknowledge ownership of the helicopters seen over Huffman on 29 December 1980. Nor were there any commercial operations involving helicopters of the heavy lift type along the Gulf coast at that time. Since six witnesses have positively identified the helicopters, and since no one will accept responsibility for them, it must be assumed that this was a secret operation and that the welfare of the victims was of secondary importance. Vickie Landrum is quite certain that this scenario is correct. The UFO was not, she says, 'from outer space with little green men, that's for sure. If the government doesn't know about it, they better find out.'

However, the story does have an intriguing tail-piece. One day in April 1981 a CH-47 helicopter flew into Dayton, Colby Landrum's home town. As the little boy watched the aircraft fly overhead, he became very upset and agitated, because it was the same type of helicopter he had seen near Huffman the previous December. To allay his fears his grandmother Vickie decided to take him to the place where the helicopter had landed, in the hope that it would seem less frightening on the ground. When they spoke to the pilot he said he had been in the area before for the purpose of checking on a UFO reported in trouble near Huffman. When Vickie told the pilot how happy she was to meet him, because she was

Above: a NASA 'lifting body' craft, launched from bombers at high altitude. Could this have been the kind of strange vehicle seen at Huffman?

Below: the parts of a car engine that are most susceptible to interference

one of the people burned by the UFO, he refused to talk to them any further and hustled them out of the aircraft.

VISIT later located the pilot and questioned him. He admitted to knowing about Vickie's and Betty's encounter with the UFO, but maintained that he had not been in the area in December, and had had nothing to do with any UFO. Unless another pilot decides to speak up, it seems that the source of the helicopters reported at Huffman will remain shrouded in mystery.

The final category of UFO evidence – which we can describe as being, at the least, proof of some physical presence – is that of mechanical or electrical interference caused by unidentified objects. Again, there are numerous examples. Consider the case of policeman A. J. Fowler who was bombarded by calls from bemused motorists on 2 November 1957.

That night Patrolman Fowler was on duty at police headquarters in the American town of Levelland, in Texas. At about 11 p.m. he received the first of several puzzling telephone calls. It was from one Pedro Saucedo, who had been driving 4 miles (6 kilometres) west of Levelland with a companion when a torpedo-shaped, brilliantly lit, yellow and white object approached the truck at high speed. As the object passed close overhead the truck's headlights went out and its engine died. The object gave off considerable heat and when Saucedo got out of the truck to look at it he had to drop to the ground. As the UFO moved into the distance the headlights came on again and the engine was easily restarted. The two men drove for some distance before telephoning the

police. However, Officer Fowler attached no importance to the call.

An hour later, a man telephoned from 4 miles (6 kilometres) east of Levelland (in the direction in which the first object had been travelling) and told Patrolman Fowler that he had come upon a brilliant egg-shaped object about 200 feet (60 metres) long, sitting in the middle of the road. As the car approached, its engine failed and the headlights went out. The witness said that the object was lit up like a large neon light and threw a bright glare over the whole area. When he got out of his car the UFO took off and rose some distance. Then its light went out. The car's engine could then be restarted.

A short time later Officer Fowler received another call. Another motorist had been stopped by a glowing object sitting in the road. His engine and lights had failed.

Soon after midnight Newell Wright was driving towards Levelland when his car ammeter began fluctuating, the engine died, and the lights went out. He got out to look at the engine, but found nothing apparently wrong with battery or wiring. He then noticed an oval object on the road ahead, similar to those of the previous sightings.

During the next hour at least four more similar reports came in. A fire marshal spoke of a red light that he saw in the sky as his vehicle lost power and its lights went out. A similar red light was reported by a sheriff and his deputy.

That November night in Levelland was exceptional. But people in all parts of the world have reported similar puzzling events. The

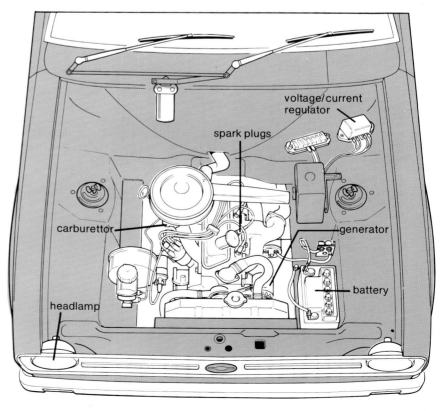

vehicle faults that have sometimes been described as occurring when a UFO has been observed have included static on the radio, rough running or complete failure of the engine, wildly fluctuating instruments, headlight failure and even severe damage to the wiring of a vehicle. In most cases the driver has been able to restart the engine when the object has left the area. In a few cases the drivers or passengers have been very shocked and have referred to strange sensations of heat or static electricity, or to unusual odours.

Aircrew have also reported disturbances to electrical systems during UFO sightings. On 4 November 1957, a Varig Airlines C-46 on a flight between Porto Alegre and São Paulo, Brazil, encountered an unusual object. The pilot and co-pilot saw a red light moving quickly towards them. Suddenly the object seemed to jump through an arc of 45° and grow larger. There was a smell of burning rubber in the aircraft and the direction finder, a

proceeding, to put some substance into these speculations.

Other causes suggested include microwaves, which could cause heating of car components, and intense ultraviolet light, which could release electrons in the metal of the car body and give rise to stray voltages and currents (and could perhaps be associated with the skin burns reported in some cases).

One of the oddest suggestions, though one

Below: a Curtiss C-46 of Brazil's Varig Airlines. An aircraft like this suffered electrical disturbance in a UFO sighting in 1957

generator and the radio transmitter burned out. The object then suddenly disappeared.

Boats have been involved, too. At about 3 p.m. on 15 December 1968 at Hawk Inlet, Alaska, two men on board the cargo boat *Teel* observed a round, white light moving slowly towards them. At 7 p.m. the object was still visible, apparently floating on the water. Then it rose and flew away over a nearby mountain.

On the following evening the same strange light was seen again. It moved slowly until it was directly above the *Teel*'s mast, at a height of about 70 feet (21 metres). There was no sound. The *Teel*'s crew contacted Elmendorf Air Force Base and the coastguard by radio. After about five minutes the boat's power and radio went dead.

Naturally, there is great uncertainty about the causes of these apparent disturbances. Ufologists speak of 'intense electromagnetic fields' as being responsible. A small amount of research has been carried out, and is still

that has been carefully worked out, is that microwave radiation could affect tungsten headlamp filaments in such a way that large amounts of current could be drained from the battery, causing the engine to stall.

However, a drained battery will not function again until it has been recharged, whereas in many cases, such as those described above, the car engine has restarted immediately upon the departure of the UFO.

Amateur UFO organisations have not the funds to research the force that might cause such mechanical disturbance, but it is probable that government bodies would be keen to investigate and harness such power. However, such research is not often revealed and only rarely do they publicly admit to such enquiries. In fact, the recent history of UFO phenomena is mined with government coverups and conspiratorial secrecy. These emerged out of the wave of public hysteria that greeted the first 'flying saucer' sightings of the 1940s.

Above: a Phantom of the former Imperial Iranian Air Force. The sophisticated electronic gun control systems of one of these supersonic fighters failed at the moment when its pilot was trying to fire on a UFO; other electronic systems were disturbed as well

Above left: an artist's impression of an unidentified floating object at Hawk Inlet, Alaska. The crew of the cargo boat Teel *observed a white light for two successive nights. It apparently affected the boat's electrical systems and diesel generator*

The UFO conspiracy

During the 1950s the government of the United States sponsored several UFO investigations. It soon became clear, however, that official research was more concerned to disprove the existence of UFOs than make an objective investigation. The official attitude – and it was common to most Western countries – was that UFOs appeared to threaten state security. After investigating them, however, the government kept its conclusions secret, providing the media and the public with contrived, often incredible, explanations.

For instance, the US government's most extensive enquiry was Project Blue Book, which began in 1952, lasted 17 years and investigated thousands of sightings. Of course many were either hoaxes or misinterpretations of known objects. Some, however, remained a mystery – yet even these were explained away by Blue Book's far-fetched theories.

It later emerged, after the release of secret files under the Freedom of Information Act of 1976, that the Central Intelligence Agency (CIA) had been influential in making the suggestion of alien UFOs appear ludicrous.

After Project Blue Book, a two-year investigation costing 500,000 dollars produced the 1000-page Condon Report in 1969. This again displayed a perverse determination to debunk even the most widely witnessed UFO sightings. And the report failed to reconcile the fact that one in three of the cases it investigated defied conventional explanation.

The Condon Report was supposed to be the US government's final official enquiry into unidentified flying objects. It was supposed to show that UFOs offered no threat and so were not worthy of government interest. But documents released under the Freedom of Information Act have shown that an official, secret investigation into UFOs has been continuing.

Among the papers are radar-visual cases, jet plane chases and a very disturbing wave of sightings between 27 October and 10 November 1975 when low-level aerial objects that were not identified repeatedly 'buzzed' sensitive missile launch facilities and military weapons stores. There is also mention of the classic 1976 radar-visual report when an Iranian jet had apparently been inspected by a 'probe' from a UFO. These accounts were often of such great interest that copies were sent to the US Secretary of State, the Pentagon, the White House and several security agencies.

Yet the cover-up remains, with ufologists fighting court-battles to gain access to other

Below: a UFO looms menacingly over the Capitol building in Washington DC, in a scene from the 1950s' movie Earth versus the flying saucers. This film was based on several magazine articles by Major Donald Keyhoe that claimed that the US Air Force had deliberately misled the public by explaining away UFO reports as misidentified mundane objects like weather balloons

documents that have been kept secret on the grounds of national security. So what do they contain, and why are governments all over the world keeping their citizens in the dark?

There are several possible answers. Perhaps many UFOs are really secret military aircraft undergoing tests. Governments preferring not to reveal such details could use the smoke-screen cover offered by the UFO explanation.

There was ironic confirmation of this in 1977, when on 20 September the inhabitants of the Soviet city of Petrozavodsk saw a 'jellyfish-like' object in the pre-dawn sky. The immediate reaction of the witnesses was that it was a UFO, and the incident aroused great interest throughout the country and even abroad. The Soviet government, like other governments round the world, denied the existence of UFOs – yet here was a sighting it could not deny. And indeed it could not – but for quite a different reason than the public supposed. For what witnesses had seen was the launching of the Kosmos-955 spy satellite from the secret base at Plesetsk – but this was, of course, an explanation the Soviet authorities could not reveal. Rather than break security, they had no choice but to allow the Russian public to go on believing they had seen a UFO; politically, it was better that it should be thought a UFO than one of their own secret devices!

Governments may also cynically perpetuate the UFO myth to distract public opinion during periods of economic or political tension. Alternatively, it could be that they maintain secrecy about UFOs because they are genuinely puzzled by the phenomenon and are investigating it without wishing to alarm the public. Or is it simply that governments already know that we have had visitations from another planet and they fear the hysteria that may result from publicising the truth?

In November 1980, the Spanish Minister of Transport said that in his opinion there was no doubt that UFOs were 'real'; while a Spanish general said publicly: 'I have for some time

held the view that UFOs are extra-terrestrial craft.' He added that many countries were collaborating on research and that the world would soon be 'told the truth'.

In June 1952 six Norwegian army jets on summer manoeuvres over the bleakly inhospitable islands of Spitzbergen spotted wreckage in a mountain area near the Hinlopen Straits. Within hours, using ski-planes, Norwegian investigators were on the site, including an expert on rocketry. No doubt a Soviet vehicle or missile was suspected, but instead they found the wreckage of a disc-shaped object, with 46 jet-like orifices on the rim that seemed to be made of an unknown metal. There was no trace of occupants.

But what is perhaps the most remarkable aspect of this incident is the comment of a high-ranking army officer, Colonel Gernod Darnbyl of the Norwegian general staff, who in 1955 said: 'The crashing of the Spitzbergen disc was highly important. Although our present scientific knowledge does not permit us to

Top: a growing public interest in UFOs in the 1950s provoked a vast collection of home-made hoaxes like this one

Left: France's ex-Defence Minister Robert Galley who, in an official radio interview, said that the information that the French Government had gathered on UFO sightings was 'pretty disturbing'

Far left: the last members of Project Blue Book, the US Air Force's full-time UFO investigation unit

solve all the riddles, I am confident that these remains from Spitzbergen will be of utmost importance. Some time ago a misunderstanding was caused by saying that this disc probably was of Soviet origin. We wish to state categorically that it was not built by any country on Earth. The materials used in its construction are completely unknown to the experts who took part in the investigation.' He added that American and British experts were being consulted. Their findings have never been published.

France, like Spain and Australia, but unlike the USA and Britain, is among the Western countries that have a more open attitude to UFOs. In a 1974 radio interview the then French Minister of Defence, M. Robert Galley,

said: 'It is irrefutable that there are things today that are inexplicable, or poorly explained. . . . I must say that if your listeners could see for themselves the mass of reports coming in from aircraft pilots, from patrol police and from those charged with the job of conducting investigations . . . then they would see that it is all pretty disturbing. . . .' Such a categorical statement is undeniably of the greatest importance. France is one of the most technologically advanced countries in the world. If its defence minister makes comments such as these then presumably they ought to be treated very seriously.

Add to this the statement from a leading member of the French government's official UFO research project, who said: 'In our opinion they [the governments of the world] do know the truth about the reality of UFOs but

have no idea how to tackle the problem.'

So what is the truth? Perhaps we are drawing closer to it. The pattern of the last decade would suggest that gradually, though perhaps reluctantly, governments are revealing more UFO information. Spain released its files to interested parties in 1976; the Blue Book documents were made accessible to the US public in 1977; France set up an official UFO study group in the late 1970s; and in 1981 Australia opened its files. In 1982 Britain announced that its UFO files would be made public, and in 1984 the Ministry of Defence officially admitted that there are UFOs. In every case, the country concerned has maintained for years that UFOs do not exist, or that no such files were kept.

Does this mean that governments are trying to discourage ufologists from further investigation, or are they gradually revealing the long-hidden truth?

One thing is certain, we have still not had access to all the secret UFO files. The fact that governments throughout the world have spent vast sums of money keeping such records is firm evidence of their concern. Their continuing secrecy serves only to maintain the tantalising mystery of unidentified flying objects.

Above: during his campaign for the presidency Jimmy Carter, who had himself filed a UFO report (above left), promised to pursue UFO cover-ups. After his election however, NASA denied Carter's request to review UFO data and he was unable to shed any light on the cover-up mysteries

Left: in 1948 Captain Thomas Mantell had a fatal encounter with a UFO above the Godman Air Force Base in Kentucky. Mantell's aircraft crashed when he climbed to chase the UFO which the USAF claimed was the planet Venus. Ufologists used the incident to persuade the public that there was an official cover-up. Years later, officials said it had been a weather balloon